Daybreak at Chavez Ravine

DAYBREAK AT CHAVEZ RAVINE

Fernandomania and the Remaking of the Los Angeles Dodgers

ERIK SHERMAN

University of Nebraska Press   Lincoln

The University of Nebraska Press is part of a land-
grant institution with campuses and programs on the
past, present, and future homelands of the Pawnee,
Ponca, Otoe-Missouria, Omaha, Dakota, Lakota, Kaw,
Cheyenne, and Arapaho Peoples, as well as those of the
relocated Ho-Chunk, Sac and Fox, and Iowa Peoples.

Library of Congress Cataloging-in-Publication Data
Names: Sherman, Erik, author.
Title: Daybreak at Chavez Ravine: Fernandomania and the
remaking of the Los Angeles Dodgers / Erik Sherman.
Description: Lincoln: University of Nebraska Press,
2023 | Includes bibliographical references.
Identifiers: LCCN 2022043572
ISBN 9781496231017 (hardback)
ISBN 9781496236364 (epub)
ISBN 9781496236371 (pdf)
Subjects: LCSH: Valenzuela, Fernando, 1960– | Los Angeles
Dodgers (Baseball team)—History—20th century. | Pitchers
(Baseball)—United States—Biography. |
Pitchers (Baseball)—Mexico—Biography.
Classification: LCC GV865.V34 S54 2023 | DDC
796.357092 [B]—dc23/eng/20221013
LC record available at https://lccn.loc.gov/2022043572

Designed and set in Lyon Text by L. Auten.

For my dear friend Jeanne Glazer
and the countless Mexican immigrants inspired by
Fernando Valenzuela to fulfill their dreams

And in memory of three iconic members of the Dodgers family
who made indelible impressions on Fernando Valenzuela
and who passed away during the creation of this project—

Vin Scully, Tommy Lasorda, and Mike Brito

CONTENTS

PREFACE

Many of my friends are writers. When I told a few of them that I planned to write a book on Fernando Valenzuela's impact on the Latino community, the idea was generally met with something along the lines of, "Wait, you mean it hasn't been done before?" I knew then that it was a story that needed to be fleshed out in book form, with a deeper dive into the transformative life of a baseball, ethnic, and cultural icon than what's been reported in the media.

I came to understand quickly why another author hadn't undertaken this task. For decades, Valenzuela has been unwilling to cooperate in the writing of a book or movie script of his life—the latter seemingly a natural for a pitcher whose star blazed brightest in the shadows of the iconic Hollywood sign. Without Fernando's help, authors and biopic producers steered clear, believing that, for as great a story as his may be, a book would truly need the input from the subject himself.

At first I was somewhat disappointed, though not entirely surprised, when my communications to Fernando's representative seeking an interview with him were met with something less than enthusiasm. But then one of those writer friends I alluded to earlier reminded me how sometimes the greatest storytelling is done by observing subjects of interest and interviewing those in and around their inner circle rather than the subjects themselves. He reminded me that Gay Talese once wrote a celebrated essay for *Esquire* entitled "Frank Sinatra Has a Cold," a profile on the legendary singer and actor despite Sinatra's refusal to cooperate with the renowned writer on the piece. It inspired me to press forward, and the result was more than I could have hoped for. Through voluminous interviews, I would capture a truth about the man that wasn't known by even his biggest fans. And I decided to press even further beyond those who knew him, expanding my reach to include prominent figures on whom he has had a profound impact.

One of the things I came to realize through my interviews, research, and even a brief interaction with the man was that while Valenzuela is a deeply private and shy individual, there has long been another side to him. While he is universally admired and respected by those around him, this often publicly stoic figure has long been playful, a prankster, and man-childish with teammates and friends. And while he is a man of measured words and an eighth-grade education acquired in Mexico, he is extremely observant and perceptive in his surroundings—whether on the pitcher's mound, his beloved golf course, or in the press room cafeteria. If his words are few and dry, and if he's maintained a poker face and made good use of the shoulder shrug in response to certain questions, it's mostly out of cautiousness, not from a lack of literacy in either his native Spanish or second language of English. He's long leaned on Ford C. Frick Award winner Jaime Jarrín, the Dodgers' Spanish-language broadcaster and very much a father figure to him, who served not just as his interpreter (even when he didn't really need one) but as a shield from beat writers. He's admittedly reserved, always thinking twice about what to say or do to achieve certain things in his life, then acts accordingly. I would hear repeatedly how his limited use of English later in his career was more by design than an unpolished or substandard understanding of it. All of this created a mystique about the man that still exists today.

He treasures his private life with Linda, his wife of more than forty years, their four grown children, and their grandchildren and has largely managed to keep them all completely out of the spotlight. When approached by promoters to appear at autograph signings, his asking price is reportedly as much as $40,000 for a couple of hours of work—an exorbitant price tag clearly designed to preclude placing himself in such very public settings. When the Dodgers celebrated the fortieth anniversary of their '81 World Series championship, Valenzuela, despite having been the brightest star of that team, was the last of the players to arrive at the ballpark; he preferred finishing up eighteen holes of golf. And after he wraps up his work on the Spanish-language broadcasts for the Dodgers' games, he regularly leaves the stadium after the seventh inning—not just to dodge the LA traffic but also to avoid being stopped every ten feet on his way out by his adoring fans. Into the night he goes, trying to stay incognito and anonymous, blending in as he enters the crowded elevator and then briskly walking to his reserved parking spot. It's not that he doesn't care about the adulation but rather that he doesn't seek the attention that these events and circumstances bring to him. He simply avoids fanfare at all costs and chooses not to fully embrace his stardom or celebrity. By contrast, he is in his greatest glory driving his silver Corvette to a country club for a leisurely round of golf with friends, joking around, and avoiding talk about himself and his halcyon playing days.

As a result, after more than four decades in the public eye and the bright lights of Los Angeles, he has never made a wrong step publicly. In all those years, he has simply never given his legion of fans a reason to be disappointed in him. As a result, he's long been one of baseball's great ambassadors—if also its least vocal one. The mere mention of his name brings a smile to anyone who knows him.

But Valenzuela's story is hardly just about a reclusive yet beloved former All-Star pitcher from four decades ago. That would sell him short. Coming from humble beginnings in the small, poor town of Etchohuaquila, Mexico, Fernando burst onto the baseball scene late in the 1980 season, dominated it the next, and instantly became a social phenomenon by being who he was and what he represented to the Mexican and Latino population in Los Angeles and around the globe. His face and likeness suddenly appeared everywhere—on murals, T-shirts, and advertisements. He was mobbed by fans everywhere he went. He was like a composite of the Beatles—only in Dodger blue. His appeal was universal. He wasn't just a baseball player, he was a healer in a time when, much like today, many Americans viewed Mexicans as second-class citizens. He was to Latinos what Jackie Robinson was to Black Americans. And their feelings for Valenzuela have only grown stronger over the years. There is still a sense of humility in the man that draws people to him. Their jaws drop when they come face to face—or even when they catch a glimpse of their hero. Yet, the sense from many who know him well is that he still doesn't recognize this reality.

The sea change Valenzuela generated on a long-embittered Chavez Ravine more than twenty years after the city's forced removal of its Mexican American residents was more impactful and profound than any no-hitter or World Series game he ever pitched. He was the driving force during this remarkable "Fernandomania" period of the early 1980s, which helped to unite a racially divided city simmering with anti-Mexican sentiment. He was an inspiration to countless Latinos who identified with him. He was like their Mexican uncle or cousin, with his everyman, unathletic-looking shape. But despite not taking on the appearance of an exemplary physical specimen, he proved he could be the very best in the world at his chosen field. He made Mexican Americans want to be not only ballplayers but doctors, lawyers, teachers, and business professionals. Whether he professed to be or not, he had become a reflection of the great Mexican American civil rights icon Cesar Chavez, a leader to a people largely doing low-paid manual labor. They had come to believe that if Fernando could succeed, so could they. He changed their lives. He was their salvation.

Valenzuela also forever changed the Dodger Stadium landscape, creating multiple generations of Mexican American fans beginning with his rookie year of 1981. Every night he pitched was like a Mexican festival, which notably included some of the very people who had been displaced by the construction of Dodger Stadium. As many as half the fans at Dodgers home games today are of Mexican descent—many of them too young to have seen Fernando pitch, yet wearing his replica jerseys nonetheless. This is a far cry from the pre-Fernando days, when the percentage of people coming to watch the home team play at the ballpark was less than 10 percent Mexican American.

But even to label Valenzuela a trailblazer for Mexican Americans and other Latinos would, once again, sell him short. He also initiated the global bridge for non-American players entering professional baseball—from Japan and South Korea and from countries across Latin America. A strong argument can be made that he introduced baseball to more people around the world than any ballplayer who has ever lived.

Valenzuela's six dominating All-Star seasons at the beginning of his career were as many as Sandy Koufax had. Fernando's mastery of his signature pitch—the screwball—baffled hitters and led him to become the first player in the history of the game to be named Rookie of the Year and Cy Young Award winner in the same year—the year he helped lead the Dodgers to a World Series championship. But his perseverance and love of the game were just as impressive. His no-hitter in his final season as a Dodger in 1990 came after he had battled back from a serious shoulder injury related to severe overuse the first seven-plus years of his career. And after being unceremoniously released by the Dodgers the following spring, with his career teetering on the brink, he spent the next several years working his way back through stops in the bedraggled Mexican League and brief back-of-the-rotation assignments with the California Angels, Baltimore Orioles, and Philadelphia Phillies before reinventing himself once more and becoming a front-line starter, leading a young San Diego Padres club to a division title in 1996.

But while much light is shed in this book on how Valenzuela's left arm captivated the baseball world at the height of Fernandomania in 1981—easily the most exciting period in Dodger Stadium history—it's ultimately a story about the emergence and lasting impact he had as a savior to both the Latino community and the Dodgers franchise itself. No other Mexican figure has come along since Fernando to assume that impactful role. Yet, in the case of the humble, mysterious, and unassuming Valenzuela, it's obvious he still doesn't fully grasp the magnitude of what he has meant to so many. Perhaps this book will show him.

Daybreak at Chavez Ravine

A Reluctant Hero

Fernando now realizes his impact, but it took a long time after he retired to think about the great things he did for the sport and for the fans.

—PEPE YÑIGUEZ, Spanish-language broadcaster for the Dodgers

The legend sits alone in the crowded Dodger Stadium press box cafeteria wearing a navy blue blazer, light blue shirt, and dark sunglasses one late August afternoon. His face is round, and his jet-black hair is cropped short. He is almost ghostlike in the sense that somehow it's easy to walk right by or sit near him without noticing the all-time Dodgers great. An icon should light up every room they enter. Instead, this one tends to blend in. He sits alone, not because he's egotistical or self-centered—in fact, quite the opposite. In a city built on larger-than-life superstars, Fernando Valenzuela is an inhibited and reclusive one.

"He's like Greta Garbo," said longtime Dodgers historian Mark Langill, referencing the actress famous for her subtle and understated nature. "I can close my eyes and think of all the times Fernando was at the Dodger Stadium front desk—just a guy in a jacket, hat, and sunglasses—very quietly and politely talking to the receptionist, and so many people would do a double-take and go, 'Wait a second, that's Fernando.'"

"Fernando always kept things from everybody since he was a ballplayer," explained Jaime Jarrín, the venerable Spanish-language broadcaster for the Dodgers who acted as Valenzuela's interpreter during the Fernandomania period and then welcomed him into the broadcasting booth for a long partnership behind the mic. "He is very tight and extremely private."

When, after a time, a reporter stops by his table, Valenzuela is reserved, soft-spoken, chooses his words wisely, and sometimes just shrugs his shoulders. Still, when something the reporter said amuses him, there is a warmness in his toothy grin and a shine to his cheeks. There is a kindness about his voice, and, despite his star quality and a certain shyness about him, he has the endearing quality of being very approachable. But no one should ever mistake his perceived detached behavior as aloofness. "He doesn't miss a thing," the insightful former Dodgers outfielder and veteran announcer Rick Monday proclaimed. "There could be twenty people walking into a room and some could be doing one thing, others doing something else, and another group doing something else as well. I firmly believe that Fernando could sit down and make a list, writing, 'Well, this guy put his wallet down over there; this guy put his phone over there; this guy made a phone call,' and so on. That's the way he was on the baseball field, and it's the same now. He takes everything in."

He doesn't always sit alone in the cafeteria. On other days he would be with his inner circle, which might include his other broadcasting partner, Pepe Yñiguez, and Jarrín, as well as the scout who signed Valenzuela—the white Panama hat–wearing, cigar-chomping Mike Brito.

There is great irony to the fact that Valenzuela, the most private of men, is a television and radio baseball analyst—a most public occupation. After two decades of that work, he continued to receive rave reviews for his understated commentary. "He picks his spots and does a very good job in not talking too much," observed José Mota, the Dodgers' Dominican-born announcer and son of former player and coach Manny Mota. "He doesn't use a plethora of meaningless information just because of who he is. I've seen his journey as a broadcaster with Jaime and Pepe and his growth and understanding of having to be objective if a call goes against the Dodgers. He only gives information when needed and does not overstep his boundaries. He respects his play-by-play people. And he sounds like Fernando—it's like he's just talking to you."

A great deal of the credit for his success as a broadcaster goes to his working with two of the best in the business—Jarrín and Yñiguez. "We helped Fernando *a lot* when he came to the booth," Yñiguez recalled. "Jaime is probably a big reason why Fernando came back to the Dodgers after finishing his career [mostly] in San Diego. Jaime was always there for Fernando from the very beginning, as his friend and translator at the press conferences. He talked with him all the time. And when Fernando joined Jaime and me in the press box, we became the Three Amigos—like in the movie."

Yñiguez was even able to get the reserved Valenzuela to display signs of his personality that only those closest to him typically see. "Fernando was so shy at the beginning," he recalled. "Even as a player, he was so shy to talk. But I told him that sometimes when the game gets slow, you can talk about any anecdote or whatever you want. So sometimes he makes some jokes on the air—and not just about baseball. I told him when Orel Hershiser came to the Dodgers booth [in 2014] that I had listened to the great job he did announcing games at ESPN and said I wanted him to be like Orel—or even better than him. I told Fernando he needed to be the best commentator in Spanish, that we're here to help him. And he's doing *great* right now."

The formula seems to be working well, as the Spanish-language broadcast team has received notable praise—even from some unlikely sources. "I spoke with Kevin Kennedy [who announced select games on the Dodgers Radio Network from 2014 through 2018] a few years ago," Yñiguez commented. "And he goes to me, 'I'm going to listen to Vin Scully the first three innings, but during the fourth, fifth, and sixth, I want to listen to you and Fernando.' I said, 'Really? But you don't know Spanish, man.' He said, 'True, but I know baseball. And I'm watching the game and listening to you guys talk about different strategies and I *learn* Spanish because of it.'"

Still, outside of calling games, Valenzuela keeps the lowest of media profiles. He has never written what would be a most sought-after auto-biography, has turned down movie deals for his life story, and almost always declines requests for interviews. He doesn't even have a Twitter account, practically a prerequisite for anyone in the broadcasting field these days. There is a mystique about Valenzuela. People want to know more, but he doesn't let his adoring public into his world. He is seen many nights leaving the broadcast booth and heading for the press box door after the seventh inning with a fast-paced walk like the one he had after retiring the side during his halcyon playing days. Still, he can't always avoid the unwanted spotlight. "People still stand by the Vin Scully press box door waiting for him to leave after he broadcasts games," former Dodgers director of publicity Steve Brener told me. "People are still in awe of Fernando."

For as much as Valenzuela might understand some of the imprint he left on the game and with the Mexican and wider Latino communities, Yñiguez believes he lacks an understanding of the full extent of it. "We walk together sometimes when we travel with the team, and kids approach him and say, 'Hey, Fernando, can you sign my ball?' And Fernando will look at them and ask, 'Do you know who I am?' But even the kids, they know who he is and what he means. I can't explain why he doesn't completely understand this. I've explained it to him many times."

One would think that if the autograph seekers of all ages weren't enough to convince him of his legendary status in the Latino community, the sea of Valenzuela jerseys worn mostly by young people at Dodger Stadium surely would. "That's when I have to remind him about the parents and grandparents talking to their kids about him," Yñiguez says. "And those Fernando jerseys aren't just seen at Dodger Stadium. Wherever we travel throughout the Western Division—San Francisco, Colorado, Arizona, San Diego—you will see people wearing them. It's *incredible*."

After finishing his pregame meal, Valenzuela puts on his COVID-era face-covering, another layer of anonymity that he likely embraces, and walks down to the first row of press tables, which give the best view of the entire stadium. Long ago he made the conscious decision to stay in the press box during batting practice to keep from being a distraction. On his way down, Dodgers radio broadcaster Charley Steiner calls out, "Hey, Lefty!" to him while another bystander extends his hand for Fernando to shake. In light of the pandemic, the ever-cautious Valenzuela shakes the man's wrist instead.

He then exchanges quick pleasantries with Venezuelan-born freelance correspondent Claudia Gestro, one of the hardest-working reporters on the Southern California sports beat and a regular presence in the Dodger Stadium press box. Gestro would later describe him to me as a nice, quiet man whom she only remotely knew. Her description of him and their relationship was consistent with other media members in the press box who knew him—friendly if somewhat detached.

And then there was this—a few private moments for Valenzuela to gaze out at the pitcher's mound, where he was a dominant presence four decades earlier with his signature eyes-to-the-sky delivery and devastating screwball. As batting practice finished up, he glances out toward left field, where two marvelous young Mexican Dodgers pitchers—Julio

Urías and Victor González—are shagging fly balls. *Would they even be in Dodgers uniforms had Valenzuela's brilliance not opened the doors for prospects from his native country?* Now looking out beyond the left-field pavilion, he drinks in the breathtaking sight of the sunset-lit San Gabriel Mountains under what Vin Scully often called cotton candy clouds—the most beautiful backdrop of any stadium in sports.

"When I think of Fernando," Nomar Garciaparra, the Los Angeles-born All-Star shortstop and current Dodgers color man, reflected that night at Dodger Stadium, "I think more about what he's meant to the Latino community than what he did on the field—which was amazing. Just look at all the Latinos in the stands here that follow and support the Dodgers. There's a generation—just like for me to be a Dodgers fan—because of what he created—from our parents and grandparents and so forth. They became Dodgers fans *because* of him."

What Fernando gave those Latino fans was someone they could relate to and be inspired by. The "everyman" Mexican with the perfect windup and the imperfect body made his fans believe that if he could reach the pinnacle of the baseball world, then they could succeed in whatever they endeavored to do in life. "He's an icon, an ambassador from Mexico and from anywhere baseball is played," Yñiguez said. "If Fernando ran for president in Mexico, he would win. He's been a great inspiration not just for people his age and older but for new generations as well."

So just what was Valenzuela—the most celebrated Mexican player in baseball history and now a grandfather in his early sixties—thinking about as he peered out from the press box to "Dodger Blue Heaven"? Was he finally allowing himself a moment to fully comprehend his career's impact on Mexicans and the countless other Latinos to whom Garciaparra and Yñiguez alluded?

To fully understand the "meaning" of Valenzuela, one must go back to the early 1950s, several years before Fernando was even born. And much of that meaning took shape where Fernando focused his gaze on this late summer evening—Chavez Ravine, in the San Gabriel Mountains—where three Mexican American neighborhoods once stood.

David versus Goliath

2

Few human beings have been as honorable as Cesar Chavez, the co-founder and first president of the United Farm Workers of America, a labor union based in Southern California. As a human rights leader and activist, he organized peaceful protests and demonstrations from the 1950s until his death in 1993, all to promote humane working and living conditions for farmworkers (most of whom were Mexican) throughout the United States. In the same vein as earlier activists such as Mahatma Gandhi and the Reverend Dr. Martin Luther King Jr., Chavez emphasized direct but nonviolent tactics, kicking out of the union those who disobeyed the peace principle—even those who fought back against aggression from others.

Chavez was the most righteous of men. He also refused to ever set foot in Dodger Stadium.

Such was the stance of many Chicanos—a term that became widely used beginning in the 1960s for natives of Mexico in the United States and their descendants to express a pride in their shared ethnic, cultural, and community identity—during the first two decades of Dodger Stadium.

Their feelings stemmed from the city's deployment of eminent domain to force more than eighteen hundred Mexican American families from three neighborhood sections of the Chavez Ravine area—La Loma, Palo Verde, and Bishop—throughout the decade of the 1950s. Though Chavez Ravine was a poor area during that period, it was still an active, joyful, and cohesive community—one its residents could call home in a place that broadly discriminated against Mexican Americans and did not allow them to live in other parts of the city. But local politicians also understood the value of land in this postwar period, when Los Angeles was in serious growth mode.

Mexican-born Teresa Romero, who in 2018 personified the American Dream by becoming the first Latina and first immigrant woman in the United States to become president of a national union—the United Farm Workers—believed Chavez's reasons for not attending Dodgers games was justified at that time. "Cesar Chavez believed in protecting people, in protecting workers," she said. "If he believed in something, he was going to stand up for it and was going to lead by example. He believed that what happened to Mexican Americans [in the 1950s] was wrong, and there is no doubt in my mind his decision of not attending a game was because he was convinced people were wronged, and he was not going to support [the Dodgers] in any way."

Marc Grossman, who served as Chavez's press secretary, speechwriter, and personal aide, felt that Chavez's outrage never waned. "Cesar literally, nearly a quarter century [after Dodger Stadium opened], still held bitterness toward it," he told me, before giving insight into Chavez's deep-rooted feelings against bigotry. "When Cesar was just an eleven-year-old boy, his father, Librado, was a migrant farmworker in the industrialized agriculture industry of California in the early '40s. His father once stopped early in the morning at a café in a little farm town in the Central Valley. Librado told his two sons, Cesar and Richard, to stay outside and not to go in with him. Well, little kids like that, they didn't pay attention. So, when they went inside, the Anglo waitress told Cesar's father, 'We don't serve Mexicans here.' Cesar told me he never forgot the expression on his father's face—pure humiliation. So, Cesar had a strong sense of what it meant to be the victim of racism. And I think that had a lot to do with his decision to refuse to go to Dodger Stadium."

Chavez would become the national director of the Los Angeles–based Latino civil rights group CSO (Community Service Organization) in 1959, the same year of the bitter episode when some of the last remaining residents of Chavez Ravine were literally dragged from their homes and saw them bulldozed before their very eyes. The visuals of the gut-wrenching scenes captured the hearts of the nation.

"The CSO was involved in the resistance as it pertained to eminent domain as a forced removal," Grossman noted. "So, if Cesar wasn't directly involved in that effort, he certainly knew about it, as his organization was involved—turning out for demonstrations and such. Cesar felt strong emotion about discrimination."

But even before the tragic events of Chavez Ravine unfolded, and well before the idea of the Dodgers building a stadium there arose, the demise of its neighborhoods was considered a foregone conclusion by some—including photographer Don Normark. He photographed life in Chavez Ravine in 1949, the year before the residents received letters from the city government directing them to sell their homes.

Decades later, after Normark published a book with his photographs, *Chavez Ravine: 1949*, Dodgers historian Mark Langill asked him why he took those photos. "He said because he didn't think Chavez Ravine was going to last," Langill said. "He saw this community by the freeway, and, in his mind, he thought with the rapidly changing landscape of the city, this probably wasn't going to last. He said he kept those photos in a drawer for about twenty years before people had a renewed interest in that area."

To be fair, the blame for the Chavez Ravine saga hardly began or should fall solely on the Dodgers. In fact, it began well before Dodgers owner Walter O'Malley had any ideas or designs on moving his club out West. It's well documented that O'Malley's original plan was to privately finance a new stadium in Brooklyn to replace the aging and small (by big league standards) Ebbets Field.

"[Walter O'Malley's] critics have claimed that he never really wanted to keep the team in Brooklyn, that he always planned to be in Los Angeles," Peter O'Malley said in defense of his father in a *Los Angeles Times* piece in 2021. "That is *not* true, and our files are very complete on this subject. It was only when he realized, after many years, he couldn't make it happen in Brooklyn that he considered alternatives. It is interesting to me that when the National League owners approved the move of the Dodgers to Los Angeles, my dad didn't have a handshake on where to play just months later or when construction could begin on the new stadium. My dad didn't shoot from the hip and believed in planning, and I have always thought the move took a lot of guts."

"Los Angeles was the ultimate 'Plan B,'" Mark Langill noted. "O'Malley was just so focused on New York. But when it came time to move to Los Angeles, he gets the territorial rights from Phil Wrigley. So, for all his planning and the genius of a businessman that he was, I just can't believe that O'Malley did not know the political climate of Chavez Ravine because, in his mind, he's just making a deal with the city. He thinks that's it. He doesn't even know there's something called a referendum. So when he gets served [a subpoena, which challenged the city's approved contract with the Dodgers] on the actual tarmac when the Dodgers' plane lands in LA and Roz Wyman, the councilwoman, asks if he knows what it was about, he was blindsided. He had no idea. He thought once [the City of Los Angeles ordinance officially asking the Brooklyn Dodgers to move to LA—binding the city by contract with the Dodgers] was approved—10-to-4—that was it. I don't think he had any notion as far as the political climate geography-wise. He knew exactly what he wanted because, from the helicopter, he could see that land being connected by the surrounding freeways.

"As far as the politics of Chavez Ravine," Langill continued, "I really think he was caught off guard. It wasn't just a question of the Dodgers and the Latino community but also the city leaders and the greater conversation as far as public use—it was supposed to be a housing project. Of course, the post–World War II [Red Scare] put an end to the project in 1953. But at that time, LA was not even on the Dodgers' radar. Regarding public use of the land, it's important that groups like Culture Clash [*Chavez Ravine: In 9 Innings*] and Eric Nusbaum's book [*Stealing Home*] discuss this because even though the team made the deal with the city, the feelings of the neighbors [weren't] in a vacuum—it's part of the city's history. I think the biggest thing was that for all of O'Malley's genius as a baseball person and all his planning, innovation, and design, this was just one of his blind spots because he honestly thought when he made the deal with the city, that was it. He was looking at it from a geographical point of view."

The fact is, the ultimate elimination of the Chavez Ravine neighborhoods resulted from a series of collective failures, starting with what many deemed a "well-intended" city housing project in 1950 that promised affordable living to thousands of Los Angelenos. That initiative would eventually be canceled amid the Red Scare hysteria brought on by McCarthyism, which was gripping the country during the early 1950s. Had the housing project come to fruition, those ravine barrios would have been replaced with apartment buildings, garden homes, and stores—the so-called "better good" phrase that city officials like to throw around in matters of eminent domain. Then, as real estate values began to soar throughout the city, shady politicians and judges refused to entertain the idea of offering the land back to the residents who had been forced to leave—many of whom had received far less than the market values of the homes they left behind.

That left the families that didn't sell their homes to the city the last remaining residents at Chavez Ravine. Once the housing project failed, they felt secure—until the City of Los Angeles designated the land for public use. With the Dodgers unable to secure a new ballpark in New York, the City of Los Angles set the bait to lure the Dodgers out West—committing millions of dollars for land improvements. Not long after, Dodgers ownership set its sights on building a fifty-six-thousand-seat stadium and parking lot on three hundred acres of city property. This seemed massively excessive when considering Los Angeles's Wrigley Field (used for Pacific Coast League baseball)—which many believed the Dodgers could revamp to accommodate their needs after O'Malley purchased it in 1957—had seating capacity for twenty-two thousand fans on just ten acres. While it was true that more and more spectators traveled via automobile at the time Dodger Stadium was being built compared to when Wrigley Field was (it opened in 1925), did the Dodgers really need *thirty times* more acreage at the cost of forcing out the remaining inhabitants of Chavez Ravine? This was one of the major issues that stuck in the craw of the residents who wanted to remain and who saw the Dodgers' move to their area as nefarious.

From an economic standpoint, the merits of building Dodger Stadium could not be denied. The new ballpark in downtown Los Angeles would create thousands of jobs, generate millions in tax revenues, and bring countless visitors to the city. Sometimes the things that people love—like having a baseball team—come at a cost. But this feeling certainly didn't resonate with the Mexican Americans who had to pay for it with their homes and neighborhoods.

"It was because the process was so tainted," opined Grossman. "The people felt that they had been deceived. It was such a David-versus-Goliath story eventually, because by the time the forest removals were happening, it was obvious what the property was going for. People felt abused by the process. There was little transparency—it was a done deal. Promises were reneged upon, and Latinos had been abused that way for decades in LA."

This all begs the question of why O'Malley didn't just cut the remaining families bigger checks for their property—considering the magnitude of the entire project—even if it was the city government that was supposed to foot the bill. "I think a lot of it is beyond the money," Grossman suggested. "It had to do with seeing the people as unimportant."

Still, there was plenty of responsibility to go around for what proved to be a very complicated and messy situation. But despite the folly of errors and insensitivity displayed by the city, what sticks in collective memory and the national conscience occurred in 1959—on the Dodgers' watch—while their stadium was being built. In the definitive book about Chavez Ravine and the forced evacuations, *Stealing Home: Los Angeles, the Dodgers, and the Lives Caught in Between*, author Eric Nusbaum gives gripping detail for one of the most heartbreaking accounts of one of the last remaining families to inhabit Chavez Ravine—the Arechigas—who refused to leave their home even after the city had sold their land to O'Malley. Family members, including homeowners Abrana and Manuel, who had lived there for four decades, and two of their adult daughters, Lola and Tolina, were *forcibly* removed from their Palo Verde house by Los Angeles County Sheriff's Department staff. According to Nusbaum's account in his book, the Arechigas family's grievance, at least financially, was that a judge had set the lot's property value at $10,050 while a city appraiser had valued it at $17,500, which was then overruled by that same judge. There was significant money at stake for the Arechigas family, not to mention the family's pride.

Nusbaum wrote poignantly of the family's violent removal by sheriff deputies:

Tolina falls to the ground crying. Her older sister Lola cries too. She is being carried down the steps by four deputies, her shoes off, her body writhing, her face contorted, her limbs splayed out, fingers pressing into her skin. This is the image that will stay with people; the thirty-eight-year-old war widow and mother of two being hauled by four men down the stairs of her childhood home. . . .

They watch as a bulldozer creeps up the road, its wide blade glinting in the midday sun, and slowly nudges their home off its foundation. It's as if the house itself is nothing: a child's toy made of leftover cardboard. One of the play forts the boys and girls used to build among the eucalyptus trees in Elysian Park. It's as if the very notion of permanence was always a joke, has been for forty years, and they are just finding out now. The front stairs fall to the ground in one piece. The bulldozer backs up, turns around. Slowly and methodically, it does its job. The roof comes down. Abrana and Manuel watch as the City of Los Angeles renders 1771 Malvina into rubble. The whole thing takes ten minutes.

It was disturbing imagery like this—with cameras rolling and newsfeeds of the event sent across the three major U.S. television networks—that would keep countless Latinos away from Dodger Stadium in the decades after it opened. "But it wasn't always Latinos watching the network news or reading the *LA Times*," Grossman notes. "There was also an incredible amount of word-of-mouth. I'll bet more people seemed to feel bitter over those forced removals because of stories they heard from other Latinos. It was a compelling episode and was seared into people's memories during that time. It would affect not just those that were of age in 1959 and witnessed those events, but also in subsequent generations, hearing it from their parents and grandparents."

Furthermore, the Dodgers came off to many as some rich and powerful New York corporation that came sweeping in—pushing poor people from their homes. "These were small, little ravines where [the Mexicans] built homes," Grossman said. "That's why they were able to afford them, because no one else wanted to live there. And the homes themselves were all very small and ramshackle. Eminent domain may have been used in other settings, but I don't think O'Malley would have considered building Dodger Stadium in Beverly Hills or Brentwood."

As difficult as some of the visuals were in connection with the Dodgers' move into Chavez Ravine, many still strongly believe it was the original sin by the housing authority that was the most devastating driver in this quagmire, because it ultimately forced out nearly four thousand mostly Mexican Americans and led to the bulldozing of more than a thousand homes. If nothing else, the city's actions gave the appearance of a classic bait-and-switch: the promise of taking the land and using it to do great things that would help businesses and provide affordable housing for the multitudes but ultimately designating the land for public use, leading to the sale to O'Malley.

"Those problems at the beginning were because people were misinformed," Jaime Jarrín indicated. "The city failed those families. They were supposed to relocate them. But some blame the Dodgers. But to be honest with you, it wasn't the Dodgers. It was city hall that made big, huge mistakes affecting those families."

While there are several sides to this complicated Chavez Ravine travesty, for all the pain it caused, a generation of Mexican Americans and Latinos in Los Angeles found themselves torn between rooting for the home team and never setting foot inside the bright new stadium on the hill nestled in Chavez Ravine.

LA Goes Dodger Blue

3

As the drama of the Chavez Ravine evictions played out in the late 1950s, there was no debate outside of that area over the excitement that was gripping California with the arrival of not just the Dodgers from Brooklyn but also their crosstown New York rival, the Giants, less than four hundred miles to the north, in San Francisco. A star-studded Dodgers team made for Hollywood included the likes of Duke Snider, Gil Hodges, Don Drysdale, Don Newcombe, Pee Wee Reese, and a young southpaw who would come to dominate the earliest days of Los Angeles baseball—twenty-two-year-old Sandy Koufax. Major League Baseball had arrived on the West Coast for the first time, striking a blow to the Pacific Coast League, a premier professional baseball league that had produced eight future Hall of Famers, including Ted Williams and Joe DiMaggio.

"I couldn't tell you what the residents that were affected by Chavez Ravine felt," historian Mark Langill said. "But, in general, there was such excitement from all corners. It just seemed like every faction was caught up in the moment and the analysis about Chavez Ravine came later."

As for the Dodgers players, the sudden shock of the cross-country move wasn't easy, especially with discussions involving it largely kept from them by Walter O'Malley. Carl Erskine, who was a star pitcher and the team's player representative at that time, told me in 2021—on the seventy-third anniversary of his first big league start—that even he was kept in the dark.

"I wasn't brought in as any part of the progression that was taking place," the ninety-four-year-old Erskine said. "So, the players were just kind of like the rest of the public. We knew what ran in the papers, but we didn't have a close up and personal exchange with Mr. O'Malley. And I was the *player representative*! Mr. O'Malley often called me in and shared some business that was taking place with the club—but not this. Now, we didn't have a union in those days, but we did have representatives sit down and talk to the owners and raise questions about conditions affecting the players. But they shared very little with us about the [move]."

Erskine spoke for many of his Dodgers teammates in expressing how they loved playing before their loyal fans at Ebbets Field. "It was such an honor to play in Brooklyn, and I really enjoyed it. The fans were great, and the period of history for both the country and baseball made it a special time. Ebbets Field may not have been a pitcher's park, but when people ask me what my favorite ballpark was, my answer is always Ebbets Field because I had so many of my best games there, including both of my no-hitters. And until Sandy Koufax came around, I had the record for most strikeouts in a World Series game [14 SOs in Game Three of the 1953 World Series]. All that happened at Ebbets Field, which is why it was my favorite park."

But the players had no say in the move out West. Erskine compared ownership's communication with ballplayers with what he experienced during his military service. "In a way, I would compare it to when I was in the Navy and you just got your orders," he said. "You didn't care what orders sounded like—you just did them. And so it was kind of the same way how the players were kept out of the loop as far as giving or receiving any input. In fact, Mr. O'Malley and his staff never brought the players into the picture, and we just kept getting rumors or things we read in the newspapers. That's how we kept informed, because they never had one meeting to say, 'Fellas, get ready, we've got a big move coming up.' We never had that experience of getting it straight from the source. We were never considered as part of the decision-making. So the players were just like the fans in that the only things we knew we read in the paper."

The Dodgers' new era in Los Angeles would begin on the bright sunny morning of April 18, 1958, hours before they would host the Giants at the Los Angeles Memorial Coliseum—their home for the next four years while their new stadium was being built. As a part of the festivities in what Los Angeles mayor Norris Poulson proclaimed as "Dodgers Week," the players assembled for a celebration that began on the steps of city hall and continued with a motorcade of convertibles that rolled past thousands of fans on a parade route from downtown to the Coliseum.

"It was kind of new territory for us," Erskine recalled. "Of course, we had been in some giant parades back in New York after winning pennants, so that part of it wasn't new. But now we were in a fresh city. They really welcomed us in a big way. We were very pleased that we had made such an impact on the very first day in LA."

As more than seventy-eight thousand fans, including Hollywood legends Bing Crosby, Jimmy Stewart, Danny Kaye, Lana Turner, Burt Lancaster, Lauren Bacall, and Groucho Marx, made their way into the Coliseum for the afternoon game, the ones who plunked down twenty-five cents to pick up a copy of the *1958 Dodgers Year Book* would see a two-page spread showing an architect's preview of their ballpark of the future, "Dodgers Home of Tomorrow . . . Chavez Ravine, Los Angeles." The envisioned park boasted unobstructed views from every seat in the four-tier stadium and views of the city and the mountains, and, the text added, "in baseball, it will stand without equal." There was no mention, not surprisingly, of the eminent domain ruling forcing thousands of Mexican American residents from their homes during that very period.

Readers of the yearbook would also spot a sort of victory-lap letter to the fans from O'Malley himself:

Dear Friends of the Dodgers:

At long last you have won your campaign for major league baseball. In 1958 and for years ahead you will be seeing the greatest stars in our National game, first, the headliners in the National League and perhaps later, the Champions of the American League, here to do battle with your Dodgers in the World Series.

We bring to Southern California a team proud of its achievements. Thanks to the organization of a minor league farm system now second to none we have won six National League pennants since World War II and twice finished in a tie for first place only to lose exciting play-off series. On another page in this Souvenir of Major League Baseball's debut on the Pacific Coast you will find an interesting standing of the clubs since 1947. These figures bring back warm memories of Dodger triumphs.

You have read in your wonderful newspapers and heard over the air our plans for Los Angeles. We recognize Southern California as the finest sports area in America. We believe it deserves the very best—in its teams, its stadia and the caliber of competition and quality of performance. We are dedicated to bringing you all of this.

For two years our games will be played in your magnificent Los Angeles Memorial Coliseum. This fine arena was built for football, track, and the Olympic Games. By 1960, if not earlier, we hope to build the country's finest and only modern ballpark at Chavez Ravine with ample parking for your cars, the latest conveniences and the finest innovations modern engineering can evolve. This park will be the first built by private baseball capital since the Yankee Stadium was opened in New York in 1923.

We are extremely grateful for the warm reception the Dodgers have received in Southern California and we look forward to many years of happy association with our new fans.

Sincerely,
Walter F. O'Malley
President
Los Angeles Dodgers

The thirty-one-year-old Erskine, by this point the dean of the Dodgers' pitching staff and possessed of the most experience pitching in big games—including eleven appearances over five World Series while in Brooklyn—got the nod from manager Walter Alston to start in the club's inaugural home game. "It meant a lot because baseball has significant dates that are pieces of the history of the game," Erskine said. "Pitching the opening game in Los Angeles was one of the highlights of my career—just such a personal accomplishment to be selected for that assignment. I remember I was very anxious the entire night before."

Despite his jitters, Erskine would come through just fine, leading the Dodgers to victory that day by striking out seven over eight innings in a 6–5 win in the first Major League game in Los Angeles. "On a personal level, ballplayers kind of have goals or hope for successes," Erskine said. "So winning that first game in LA was a very important win for me because I had already had some of my best years, and to kind of have that one left to add to the rest of my career accomplishments felt extra special. It stood out in a different way than some of the other big games. I feel honored to have gotten the first one over there."

The 1958 season would prove to be a rare down year for the Dodgers in Los Angeles, as they finished with a disappointing 71–83 record, finishing in seventh place in the National League. But one thing was certain—they had captured the hearts of their new West Coast fan base. "You might call it a culture shock coming from the raucous fans in Brooklyn to the little quieter California fans," Erskine said. "But it didn't take long for LA to embrace the Dodgers big time."

And from the Dodgers' standpoint, their community outreach to their new fan base was impressive. It was a mutual love-at-first-sight scenario. And despite the Chavez Ravine travails with Mexican American residents, the Dodgers were making attempts even then to attract a rapidly increasing Hispanic population in Southern California by airing home games in Spanish on the radio that season, with the crew of Miguel Alonzo, Milt Nava, and René Cárdenas in the booth. Momentum picked up on the airwaves the following season when future Hall of Fame broadcaster Jaime Jarrín replaced Nava to begin a remarkable run of more than a half century of calling Dodgers games.

The Dodgers' relationship with the Mexican American community was certainly a complex one with many crosscurrents—even in that very first year in Los Angeles.

The Mexican Experience
North of the Border

4

The so-called "Bloody Christmas Brawl" of 1951, dramatized in the critically acclaimed novel and film *LA Confidential*, came to epitomize the marginalization and racial profiling of Mexican Americans by the Los Angeles Police Department. On Christmas Eve that year, two LAPD officers responded to a call that seven underage males were drinking at a place called the Showboat Bar. The patrons in question, five of whom were Mexican Americans, produced identification showing that they were old enough to drink legally. The officers ordered them to leave the bar anyway. When the men refused, the officers used force—with one of the defendants later claiming to have been hit in the head with a blackjack. A fight ensued, with the two cops receiving the worst of the injuries.

Several hours later, all seven men were arrested at their homes. Six were taken to the city jail, with the seventh—according to a *Los Angeles Times* report—dragged by his hair to a squad car, driven to Elysian Park, and savagely beaten by several officers. The injuries to his face were so severe that he required two blood transfusions.

Back at the police station early the next morning, numerous officers were reveling in a department Christmas party—some having had far too much to drink—and decided to take revenge on the six inmates for injuring two of their own. According to a piece in the *Pacific Historical Review*, the prisoners were taken from their cells, lined up, and viciously beaten by as many as fifty officers over a span of an hour and a half in one of the worst incidents of police brutality ever known.

There was another problem. No one outside of the department knew about it for nearly three months, as the police-friendly media at that time focused on the fight the previous night that injured the two officers, while the LAPD covered up the jailhouse beatings. It was a defining moment for Mexican Americans as they took it upon themselves to bring about greater awareness of police brutality without cause against their own people—triggering the media to uncover numerous other complaints of unprovoked beatings.

"A lot of Latinos had a very poor relationship with authorities and the City of LA back then," Marc Grossman noted. "So it was the Latino civil rights group CSO [Community Service Organization], which was formed in 1947 in East LA and organized by a man named Fred Ross—who worked under activist Saul Alinsky of the Chicago-based Industrial Areas Foundation—that fought against police brutality. The 'Bloody Christmas' where a bunch of drunken LAPD cops beat up a number of young Latino men was a landmark event because the CSO organized itself to the point where they put pressure on the city officials to act. For the first time, those cops were indicted and convicted for beating up Latinos. Word about that spread everywhere. Cesar Chavez knew about it even as a young man in the navy at that time. So when you're talking about what happened in the early '50s when the city was promising to take this land [Chavez Ravine] and do good things with it that would help people, businesses and provide affordable housing, there was a mistrust because of the very strained relationship they had with the Latino community in those days. Latinos were probably very skeptical about the promises of altruistic use of the property. And their skepticism was borne out when it was turned over to Walter O'Malley to build Dodger Stadium."

The "Bloody Christmas Brawl" and the ensuing activism of Mexican Americans would force the hand of Los Angeles chief of police William Parker to launch an internal inquiry that would result in eight officers' indictments for assault, thirty-nine suspensions, and fifty-four transfers from the department. Although a degree of justice had been served, the mistreatment, exploitation, and prejudice against Mexican Americans in Los Angeles—and throughout the United States—would continue in the years and decades to come. Such attitudes led to the convenient displacement of Mexican Americans from Chavez Ravine.

"It saddens me," Teresa Romero lamented, "because sometimes we, as a society, do things like this to a vulnerable population that isn't documented, a population that doesn't speak English, a population that financially is struggling." She continued: "I love this country to death, and I became a U.S. citizen after coming here from Mexico, and I'm proud of it. But we have abused a certain group of people because of their color, because of their origin, and because of what they look like."

Nomar Garciaparra can relate to this injustice personally, given the plight of his own family throughout the 1950s and 1960s. "My parents are both of Mexican origin—my mother was born in California but her first language was Spanish, and my father born and raised in Mexico," he said. "They didn't grow up speaking English. They spoke Spanish and were discriminated against and looked at as not intelligent because they couldn't speak English. And it was because of that experience and everything they went through that they wanted to make sure their children spoke fluent English. They were like, 'Listen, we're here in the United States. This is where we're going to be. And we want our kids to be educated and not looked at as dumb.' That was a big priority. So we were going to learn English first because of what they experienced. So English was spoken in our household to make sure we could thrive in school."

The Garciaparra children were more fortunate in being able to learn English than many other Mexican Americans, especially those who worked on the farms in California's thriving agriculture industry.

"Cesar Chavez knew what it was like to be treated as if you were not an important human being," Grossman noted. "In 1974 there was a terrible accident near Blythe, California, when a bus carrying farm workers went off the road, crashed into an irrigation ditch, and nineteen lettuce workers died because the seats were not buckled to the floor. Everything went forward and they were all trapped—drowning to death. In the eulogy, Cesar talked about how you know that there is this farm labor system that treats people like they're agricultural implements and not important human beings. He talked about how they are important because God makes them and takes care of them in life and in death. These people were also important because the work they did was feeding America."

Chavez would also write a commentary piece for the *Los Angeles Times* a month after the bus accident. In it he lamented the tragedy and gave some of the heartbreaking details: "Among the dead, we discovered, were men, women and children. In one family, a father and his three teenage children were killed. Amid the grief there was great bitterness. The workers were—and still are—bitter because they've been through this kind of tragedy too many times before. The workers learned long ago that growers and labor contractors have too little regard for the value of any individual worker's life. The trucks and buses are old and unsafe. The fields are carelessly sprayed with poisons. The laws that do exist are not enforced. How long will it be before we take seriously the importance of the workers who harvest the food we eat?"

Chavez concluded his piece with a pledge to give meaning to the lives of those who had perished: "These terrible accidents must be stopped! It is our obligation—our duty to the memory of those who have died—to see to it that workers are not continually transported in these wheeled coffins, these carriages of death and sorrow. The burden of protecting the lives of farm workers is squarely on our shoulders. Let the whole world know that the pain that today fills our hearts with mourning also unifies our spirits and strengthens our determination to defend the rights of every worker. Let the labor contractors and the growers know that we will never stop working and struggling until there is an end to the inhuman treatment of all farm workers."

But the suffering certainly didn't stop there. A quarter century later, six years after Chavez's passing, there was yet another horrific tragedy when thirteen tomato workers died in a van crash in Fresno. The *Los Angeles Times* reprinted Chavez's 1974 commentary piece on the Blythe accident word for word because, in the editors' belief, nothing had changed.

"That's why a lot of them were bitter," Grossman said. "I think that sentiment was also behind much of the bitterness Latinos felt in the wake of the forced removal of those families from the [Chavez Ravine] barrios—that the evicted residents were not treated like they were important human beings, the way other people would have been treated. It wasn't the money so much—it was how the process was tainted. They felt they were mistreated."

It also often didn't matter how many generations Mexican Americans had lived in the United States—they were generally looked at as foreigners because they didn't fit the stereotype of Americans as being of Anglo-Saxon heritage. Grossman recalled an occasion in 1979 when he and Chavez "were flying out of San Jose Airport. . . . This was in the middle of a very bitter strike in the vegetable industry in the Salinas Valley. The growers [owners of the farms] had taken out full-page newspaper ads viciously attacking Cesar. We're at the gate and this middle-aged Anglo lady recognizes Cesar and says something like, 'Why don't you go back to Mexico?' He just ignored her because that was his way. But I kind of got angry to myself and thought how ironic it all was because Cesar's family had been in this country probably longer than hers."

From the late 1950s through the decade of the 1970s, Mexican Americans had in Chavez a leader they could trust, look up to, and be inspired by. And nobody could match the work ethic he displayed for the betterment of not just the farmworkers but for society and human rights in general. "I can't count the number of times that I'd been asked to meet up in the yard of his home at La Paz, which was on the property of our UFW headquarters near Bakersfield, at like three or four in the morning," Grossman said. "He didn't really take a vacation in thirty-one years. In leading the UFW, he often worked twelve-to-fourteen-hour days. There were times during intensive organizing and political campaigns when we were constantly on the road. Some of the most important things he taught me [were] what it means to be committed to something bigger than you are, self-sacrifice, and really what it means to be a man."

While Chavez's base was Latino farmworkers, who made up roughly 65 percent of California's agricultural workforce, he also fought for the human rights of Filipinos, Black Americans, and other groups in the late 1960s and early 1970s—thus resisting being identified as solely a Latino leader during that era. His travels took him around the United States and even into Canada, helping people from all walks of life.

Chavez was not a terribly eloquent public speaker, but his actions carried more weight than anything he could have told the masses. "He lectured by example of how he led his life," Grossman exclaimed. "He didn't talk about nonviolence. He would say, 'You know, nonviolence—you can't make a particularly strong case for it in the abstract, but it's a very powerful practice.' And so what did he do? He once stopped eating for twenty-five days to make his union recommit itself to nonviolence. But still, Cesar had to get up and talk because he needed to attract public support. He once had seventeen million American adults boycotting grapes in [1965] in support of his union. So, while he was forced to talk, he was never particularly adept at it. But while he may have shied away from the spotlight, he recognized that his celebrity opened doors for him to advance national boycott tours and to get himself into studio appearances. But speaking at such events were things that never came easy to him. He forced himself to do them."

Quite simply, Chavez became one of the most inspirational and admired civil rights leaders in an era that included such iconic contemporaries as Dr. Martin Luther King Jr., Andrew Young, Malcolm X, and Robert F. Kennedy. His avocation in life was to give people who looked like him opportunities. For a Mexican American with an eighth-grade education, he was able to accomplish more than a whole lot of people before him with greater financial resources and better education in efforts to organize farmworkers. Chavez succeeded where so many others had failed.

"He used to say that his job as an organizer was to help ordinary people do extraordinary things, to make everyone in the union believe that the job they were doing was vitally important," Grossman said. "He helped people fulfill their dreams that many of them didn't even know they had at that time. He had this unbound[ed] faith in people who looked like him, who no one thought was important. That was a big part of his motivation of why he did what he did. He wanted farmworkers to be able to sit across from their employers at the bargaining table as equals."

By the 1970s, Chavez had directly improved the lives of countless workers and galvanized multitudes of others. "People would come up to Cesar, especially Latinos," recounted Grossman, "and they would say how he inspired them to be the first in their family to go to college or become a doctor, or a lawyer, or a businessperson, or run for public office. Cesar came to understand that his work and the movement he led far transcended farmworkers—it inspired an entire people."

Grossman then recalled a young female reporter with one of the national magazines coming out to California in 1975, having been assigned to basically tail Cesar for a few days. "She went to union rallies and marches and meetings," Grossman said. "She noticed how mostly farmworkers crowded around him afterwards, talking about their troubles and complaints, and how he listened and had union staff around who could try to do something to help them. Other workers would ask him to autograph just about anything they had—leaflets, flags, T-shirts, and hats. Fathers would take photographs of their young children with Cesar using those old Instamatic cameras. So this reporter witnessed all this over two or three days. On the last day of her trip, she interviewed

Cesar and asked him what accounted for all the respect and affection the farmworkers showed him in public. Cesar kind of smiled, then paused for a moment before simply saying, 'The feeling is mutual.' He felt about them the way they felt about him."

Another gaze into Chavez's soul was revealed in a *60 Minutes* interview in the early 1980s with correspondent Ed Bradley. Chavez was pressed hard about his motivation and why he dedicated himself so profoundly to what he did over such a long period of time. Exasperated and perhaps just wanting the interview to end, he blurted out, "You know why I do what I do? It's to settle a score for what they, the growers, did to me and my family when we were migrants and what they've done to my people over the last eighty years."

Romero felt that while things were more difficult during Chavez's time at the helm than they are today, the way Mexican Americans are often viewed by the public has not improved as much as it should have. "Working for the farmworkers," she said, "you see how hard they work, how much they sacrifice, how difficult the work is for people to treat them only as labor workers when I know they are professionals that understand what needs to be done with different crops under very difficult circumstances. Today, around 85 percent of the workers are Latinos, with about 90 percent coming from Mexico. Unfortunately, in general, Mexicans are seen as troublemakers, people who do not contribute to the economy—which is wrong—but that's how we're seen. I'm very proud to say that when I look at my community, I see nothing but hardworking people. Not only in the fields, but at every level of jobs many of us would not be willing or able to do because of how physically demanding they are. But it saddens me, because whether we are documented or undocumented, we're demonized—especially during the last [presidential] administration. It's sad because we contribute a lot for this country.

"In the past," Romero continued, "the farmworkers were afraid of being deported, but it was only in the back of their heads as something that could happen—like if they got into an accident. But during the [Trump] administration, parents who had young children that were born here had to tell them what they needed to do if their parents didn't come home. Just imagine these children going to school and being worried about whether their parents would be home when they returned. It's just inhumane and it is wrong creating these second-class citizens because they are undocumented, they are immigrants, they are brown, or they are Mexican. It's wrong, but they've had to live with it."

Yet, for Romero, who arrived in the United States in the 1980s and taught herself English, being a successor to Chavez means so much. "It is a great source of pride to continue the work that Cesar started so many years ago," she said. "When I was elected to be the president of the UFW, I had all kinds of emotions. I was proud to no end. I was nervous. I was scared to death. But I had faith in the great team around me that are as dedicated as they can be in working for the farmworkers. It is the honor of my life to be able to follow the steps of Cesar Chavez."

Mexican Americans didn't realize it at the time, but just one year after Chavez became the CSO's national director in 1959—elevating him into the spotlight as a civil rights leader—another future inspirational figure for their people would be born in Etchohuaquila, Mexico. And the similarities in the two men's reserved, understated, and soft-spoken personas that would inspire so many would be unmistakable.

Uncut Diamond

5

Etchohuaquila has long been a friendly, yet poor farming town in the Mexican state of Sonora. With just a few hundred residents and harvests of primarily garbanzo beans and sunflower seeds, it lies 22 miles inland from the Gulf of California and roughly 350 miles south of the Arizona border. The nearest city is Ciudad Obregón—about 16 miles to the north—a commercial center best known for its cotton gins, granaries, and packing plants.

Life was hard in Etchohuaquila when Fernando Valenzuela—the youngest of twelve children—was delivered by a midwife in his family's mud-brick house on November 1, 1960, to Avelino and Hermenegilda Anguamea de Valenzuela. Small farms were interspersed throughout the dry, cactus-covered land, and although there was a nearby river, there was no means of irrigating the crops. Electricity to the town was still more than a decade away, and there was no running water. Telephones were rare in the area, and driving through the town meant navigating dirt roads with potholes the size of small swimming pools. Truth be told, not much went on there. Yet, the one unmistakable characteristic the town had above all others was the presence of a very modest baseball field—one with an uneven pitcher's mound and no backstop.

When young Fernando was at that golden age of eight years old, the year so many children begin watching and playing sports, he would sometimes skip school to play baseball on that field. By thirteen, Valenzuela had become such a good hitter and thrower that he was able to join his six older brothers on the town team. Originally slated to play first base, Fernando convinced the others to allow him to pitch. In his first outing, he pitched a couple of innings, striking out two, against a neighboring town's team. Despite being a boy playing among men, he was a natural.

Two years later, he gained the attention of Avelino Lucero, manager of

Los Mayos de Navojoa; he had witnessed Valenzuela striking out sixteen hitters in a game. After Lucero selected Fernando to play in a Sonora state all-star tournament in which Valenzuela would earn MVP honors, he signed the youth to his first professional baseball contract, with his Navojoa club—part of the Mexican Pacific League—and starting him out in Tepic on a farm team. At just fifteen, Valenzuela was a professional ballplayer and finished with school.

After playing sparingly at Tepic, Valenzuela signed a deal to pitch for Puebla, of the Mexican Central League. But it was only after Puebla lent Fernando to the Guanajuato team that the Dodgers started to take notice of the young prospect. According to a *New York Times* investigative report in 1981, the first scouting report card on Valenzuela was given on January 24, 1978, by a part-time Dodgers scout in Mexico by the name of Corrito Verona. Verona wrote that "Fernando was a little wild but not much; he was plump but not all over. His arms and legs are slim. He has a chance to make the Major Leagues."

Shortly thereafter, Dodgers scout Mike Brito, who would later sign Valenzuela to a Major League deal, would be dispatched by Dodgers general manager Al Campanis to see Fernando pitch for the first time. It would be the beginning of a close, lifelong friendship between the two men. The Cuban-born Brito, one of the true characters of the game, became a staple of televised broadcasts from Dodger Stadium throughout the 1980s and 1990s as the man famous for wearing white Panama hats and puffing on cigars while holding a radar gun to clock pitches at dugout level behind home plate.

"In those days, we didn't have the Lexus dugout box seats," former Dodgers publicity director Steve Brener recalled. "So Mike stood right behind home plate with the radar gun. He went to find players in Mexico. He was a real character—there's no question about that. He would go to all stretches to try and find the next player for the Dodgers from Mexico. He has two of them on the Dodgers now in Julio Urías and Victor González, so he's always been an integral part of finding players for the Dodgers in Mexico."

And about those cigars? "I started smoking cigars in Cuba when I was sixteen years old," Brito said with pride when in his late eighties. "I used to go to school smoking cigars. And I have only smoked cigars."

The legendary Dodgers scout was proud of the Mexican talent he discovered over the course of nearly half a century. He once quipped that he "feels more Mexican than tequila!" According to his recollection, "I've signed thirty-two guys that went on to the big leagues, including six just in 1992—that was crazy!" Furthermore, "when I like a guy, I don't care what anyone else thinks. I'm never afraid [to express my opinion] with anybody."

Without question, his greatest signing was Valenzuela, and he sensed the youth's star quality at the first sight of him. "Fernando was cool on the mound," he told me. "He had good first-pitch location—inside corner, outside corner. The one thing that really impressed me early about him was that after he loaded the bases twice, he retired the side both times without a run scoring. That opened my eyes. When I saw that, I told Al Campanis, 'I think he's a magical pitcher.' I really liked his poise on the mound."

At sixteen, Valenzuela was the Mexican Central League's strikeout leader despite being used primarily out of the bullpen. He would then bounce around as a relief pitcher every few months to different clubs depending on the season of the year. From Guanajuato he went to San Luis Río Colorado, where he had a 9–2 record. From there, he pitched for Ocotlán and was 3–1. In the summer of 1979, he re-signed with Puebla and was again "loaned" out—this time to Yucatán's Leones of the Mexican big leagues—where he struck out 152 hitters as a starting pitcher and was named rookie of the year. Soon thereafter, Puebla sold Valenzuela's contract to the Dodgers for $120,000, the most money the Dodgers had ever spent on a prospect. While under contract with the Dodgers, the nineteen-year-old Fernando was permitted to fulfill his lifelong dream of pitching for Navojoa in 1980 and was superbly successful—going 12–5 with a 1.65 ERA.

But now a new and even bigger dream was on the horizon—a *big league* dream with the Los Angeles Dodgers. But first, Valenzuela would be shipped to Lodi, the Dodgers' Single-A California League team, where he struggled a bit and didn't show good velocity on his fastball. It was clear to Brito and Campanis that Fernando would need a third pitch to go with his fastball and curveball, but not before Campanis read Brito the riot act for signing a pitcher with a below-average fastball in need of a third pitch. "Campanis sent me to the California League," Brito recalled. "He said to go see Fernando and find out how he's doing. So, when I came back from Lodi, I told Campanis I thought Fernando was going to need another pitch to be successful in the big leagues. Campanis got pissed off at me. He said, 'How come you didn't tell me that *before* we signed Fernando?' Then he asked me what kind of pitch I was thinking about. I said, 'Well, maybe a split-fingered fastball or a screwball.' Campanis said we didn't have anybody that threw those pitches. I told him we had 'Babo' [Bobby Castillo], who throws a screwball. So Campanis said, 'That's not a bad idea. Go talk to Babo and tell him that I want him to work with Fernando on a screwball [at the Arizona Fall Instructional League]."

Brito and Castillo had some history together. It all began in a baseball game the two played as opponents at Evergreen Park in East Los Angeles in 1975. Babo was brought into the game in relief when his club was clinging to a 2–1 lead in the eighth inning and Brito's club, the Latin Stars, was threatening with the bases loaded and just one out. Brito came to the plate looking to give his team the lead. Castillo's first four pitches were all fastballs, bringing the count to 2–2. Brito was looking fastball all the way. "[Castillo] throws me a pitch that I missed by a lot to strike me out," Brito said. "After the game, I asked him what pitch he threw me. He said it was a screwball. So, I asked him if he wanted to play baseball in the Mexican League and he said yes. So I signed him."

At the time, Brito was a scout for the Reynosa team of the Mexican League. His signing of Castillo—for $1,500 a month—proved to be a bargain, as Babo would win fifteen games for Reynosa. The signing and positive results had an impact on both men. It induced a beleaguered Campanis, miffed that the Dodgers didn't have Castillo—a native of Los Angeles, no less!—on their radar, to hire Brito as a Dodgers scout in Mexico. One of his first duties was, not surprisingly, to sign Babo to a Dodgers contract during the 1977 season.

If Brito's initial connection to Castillo, which had already led to one of the most prolific and high-profile Major League scouting gigs, wasn't enough, now their link would go up a notch with Castillo's task of teaching Brito's biggest signing how to throw a screwball—arguably the toughest pitch to throw in baseball. Many have tried to throw the screwball, but few have truly mastered it. The pitch is basically a curveball in reverse—a very difficult pitch to learn. It also puts massive stress on the arm. If added to a pitcher's repertoire, however, it's a highly effective pitch.

The list of screwball pitchers in baseball history is small but includes the likes of Hall of Famers Christy Mathewson, Warren Spahn, and Carl Hubbell, as well as the charismatic Mets and Phillies reliever Tug McGraw. Hubbell, who famously struck out Hall of Famers Babe Ruth, Lou Gehrig, Jimmie Foxx, Al Simmons, and Joe Cronin in succession during the 1934 All-Star Game—all on screwballs—is widely credited with inventing the pitch.

Castillo proved to be a proficient teacher and Valenzuela a gifted student as the left-hander quickly adopted the new pitch for his arsenal. "In one week," Brito said, "Fernando learned the screwball and was like a different pitcher than before."

Word started to spread around the Arizona Fall Instructional League over the course of its sixty-day season that a Dodgers prospect had developed the rare screwball. One person who heard about it was the "Godfather of the Screwball" himself, Carl Hubbell, then a seventy-six-year-old part-time scout for the San Francisco Giants. Hubbell would attend a game that Fernando pitched and later say, "Valenzuela's screwball is the best since mine. He's a natural." High praise, indeed.

After those two months at the Arizona Fall Instructional League, the lives of Valenzuela, Castillo, and Brito would never be the same. For Valenzuela, he was on the cusp of greatness—embracing the screwball to the point where he ended up throwing it at different speeds and with three variations of it—one that dropped straight down in the strike zone; another with a side-to-side sweep; and, finally, one that hung in the strike zone. All of them kept hitters off balance and made his fastball and curveball more deceiving and tougher to hit when mixed in with the screwballs. For Castillo, a serviceable yet unspectacular pitcher while with Los Angeles, teaching Valenzuela the screwball during the winter of 1979 forever cemented his place in Dodgers lore. He would join a select few who assisted pitchers to greatness, like Roger Craig teaching Jack Morris and Mike Scott the split-fingered fastball (the so-called "pitch of the 1980s") and Sparky Lyle tutoring a young Ron Guidry on the slider. Babo Castillo and Fernando Valenzuela would remain friends until the former's passing in 2014. The headline for his obituary in the *Los Angeles Times* read, "Bobby Castillo Dies at 59; Former Dodger Pitcher Taught Valenzuela Screwball." As for Brito, at the time of our interview for this book he had been a Dodgers scout for forty-four years, and he remained one of the most recognizable, endearing faces in all of baseball until his death in July 2022.

*

Throughout spring training of 1980, some of the players in Dodgers camp took notice of the reserved Minor League invitee with the sharp-moving screwball, though Fernando largely remained anonymous to most everyone else. So quiet was Fernando—often answering with one-word answers even in his native Spanish—that some of his teammates began referring to him as "Señor Silent."

However, Manny Mota, the team's Dominican former outfielder and pinch-hitting specialist-turned-coach, knew what the Dodgers had in Valenzuela. "My father [Manny] was immersed in the culture of prospects coming up and being recognized," Dodgers announcer José Mota told me. "He had known Fernando for a long time before that because he and Mike Brito were *compadres*—very good friends for a long time. So my dad always kind of looked out for Fernando because he was a protégé of Brito's. I got to go to spring training in Vero Beach in 1980—a fifteenth-birthday gift from my dad—and met Fernando for the first time in person. He was a young, extra-shy, humble kid—but cheerful. You could see all the traces of his background in Mexico—like the native inhabitant of his land in his face. He had a real pudgy big face, big hair, and very reflective, expressive eyes. In my mind, I was thinking, *Well, Mike Brito signs good players*. But still, when this kid flourished later like he did, I was like, *Is this the same guy? That's Fernando?!*"

After the team's more than two decades in Los Angeles, had the Mexican savior the Dodgers always craved finally arrived? The club was hopeful. "Walter O'Malley always would ask me when I was going to find him a 'Mexican Sandy Koufax,'" Jaime Jarrín said. "It was so important to him. Cultivating the Latino market started with him. He found out quickly that there were so many Mexicans, so many Mexican Americans, and so many Latinos in Southern California. He saw this and said that he wanted to give bilingual coverage of Dodger games so [everyone] could enjoy and understand fully the game. He was the one with that vision that no other Major League organization had. We were the first ones to cover every single game [in two languages]. Our Latino audience is made up of mostly hardworking people. They work from early in the morning to late at night. We give them entertainment and baseball in their own language. I think that in [announcing] a baseball game, I am not only describing what's going on on the field, but I am also doing a public service because I'm giving something special to our audience."

Not only did the Dodgers desperately want to tap into the vibrant and growing Mexican community around Los Angeles, but they wanted to try to rid themselves of the black mark left on the franchise because of the forced removals at Chavez Ravine while Dodger Stadium was being built. "Walter O'Malley and Peter O'Malley knew exactly what had happened in the past," José Mota averred. "So they felt like they owed something [to Latinos]. The Dodgers had Spanish radio broadcasts knowing that it was a way of saying, 'We respect you. We want you. We want to give you, that [Latino] blue-collar worker a chance to listen to our games and, maybe, forgive us, maybe forget the past a little bit, but this is a terrific sport that we want to bring to you.' And the Dodgers did it. The Dodgers were not broadcasting games in Spanish because they were making money. Jaime himself had to do other jobs in the winter and at other radio stations. But the Dodgers had this vision, and they carried it on without saying, 'Let's look at dollars and cents.' They did it right. Just imagine not having Spanish radio and then, suddenly, they're saying, 'Hey, we have this guy Fernando Valenzuela—how are you going to promote him [with the Latino audience]?' They set things up well with their vision. They would be able to tell [the Latino audience], 'Come join the party—Fernando's pitching today!'"

Despite Fernando showing signs that spring of being able to crack the big league roster, the Dodgers' rotation of Jerry Reuss, Bob Welch, Don Sutton, Burt Hooton, and newly acquired big-money free agent Dave Goltz proved too daunting for a nineteen-year-old to break into. Fernando would start the season at the club's Double-A San Antonio club in the Texas League.

The big stage of Dodger Stadium would have to wait.

Prelude to Greatness

6

In an era before relief pitchers played the prominent role they do in today's game, Ron Perranoski stood out as a rarity. Relieving for the Dodgers from 1961 through 1967 for a staff that included Sandy Koufax and Don Drysdale in their prime would seem to be a lonely job. Yet, three times over that span he led the National League in pitching appearances. And in 1963 for the World Series champion Dodgers, his 16–3 record earned him the highest winning percentage (.842) in all of Major League Baseball. He would finish fourth in the National League MVP voting that season.

For a later generation of Dodgers fans, Perranoski is remembered as a pitching coach from 1981 through 1994. Unlike so many of today's coaches and managers, Perranoski, despite a celebrated thirteen-year playing career, first had to pay his dues as the Dodgers' Minor League pitching coordinator for eight seasons before being promoted to the big leagues. And it was in his final season roaming the Minors that he made his biggest impact.

Following spring training in 1980, Valenzuela spent the first half of the season at San Antonio using his newfound screwball as his changeup. As the season got closer to the midway point, Perranoski noticed that Fernando had worked to perfect throwing the pitch at different speeds. Still, Valenzuela was hardly realizing his potential with a record of 6–9.

It was at this point that Perranoski began working more closely with Valenzuela, teaching him the cerebral part of pitching by using his fastball more as a weapon to set up a hitter for his devastating array of screwballs. The results were remarkable. Fernando would go 7–0 with a 0.87 ERA over his next eight starts—including a couple of two-hitters, a pair of three-hitters, and a duo of four-hitters. In his final thirty-five innings in San Antonio, he didn't allow a single earned run.

Señor Silent had become "Señor the Man," a now dominant pitcher with a quiet confidence that was ready to take on the world. And on September 10, he got the call to "the show." As it turned out, his greatest challenge would be entering the United States. Valenzuela didn't have a birth certificate, much less a passport. But in the name of a pennant race, the Dodgers were able to cut through some red tape and get him into the country.

"Most people looked at [Fernando] when he came up and saw, oh, a kind of roly-poly guy that they didn't know a lot about," the great Dodgers first baseman Steve Garvey said. "Previously, especially with the O'Malley family, they always educated the fans on who was coming up from the Minors. They would put up a 'How are things out on the farm?' posting on the message board. So there was some visibility about Fernando, but people still didn't know much about him."

Some of that lack of visibility from the Minors no doubt had a lot to do with the dynamics of the Dodgers' Major League club. "We were in this dominating period of strong personalities," Garvey added. "Lots of success. We had been to the World Series in '74, '77, '78, with some second-place finishes."

At the time of Fernando's promotion to the Major Leagues, the Dodgers were a star-studded club, though they still found themselves locked in a first-place tie atop the National League West with the Houston Astros—their new chief rival in a division that for so many years saw Los Angeles battling it out against the great Reds teams of the 1970s. But this Houston team in no way resembled either of those power-hitting Dodgers or Reds clubs.

"We played in the Astrodome," Houston's All-Star reliever Joe Sambito recalled, referencing the team's former home, a cavernous domed stadium. "And because of that, our team was built a little differently than most teams. At the Astrodome, the fences were deep—especially in the power alleys and center field. So our team was built on pitching, speed, and defense, and that's how we were able to win in Houston. The Astrodome was very difficult for visiting players, especially for outfielders in tracking the ball off the roof there. Also, the big bats didn't give visiting teams the advantage they may have had in their own stadium. The Dodgers were a good example. We hit just 75 home runs as a team in 1980 [compared to 148 by the Dodgers] but were able to manufacture runs. We scored many times in the first inning to give our pitchers a little breathing room. And our pitching was outstanding with Joe Niekro, Nolan Ryan, Ken Forsch, Vern Ruhle, and the dominant J. R. Richard before he suffered that stroke, just after the All-Star break, that ended his career."

When Fernando arrived, there were just twenty-three regular-season games remaining on the 1980 schedule. The eventual Rookie of the Year—Steve Howe, the Dodgers' fireballing left-handed reliever—was struggling a bit with a late-season swoon, so Valenzuela's role was simply to complement Howe until he got back on track. But Fernando would end up doing so much more than that. First, however, he had to bide his time before making it into a game.

"I was anxious to see what the situation was, to have the experience of being in a Major League stadium and face hitters at that level," Valenzuela told MLB.com in a 2012 interview. "At times, you didn't have that opportunity because starting pitchers pitched eight innings and then you had the closer. I waited a week, more or less, and the opportunity arose. It wasn't nerves, but anticipation and adrenaline of being there on the mound in a Major League stadium."

In his first Major League appearance, on September 15, he pitched an impressive two innings of relief despite some shoddy Dodgers defense (a couple of errors), yielding a duo of "unearned" runs in Atlanta. Four nights later, pitching in Dodger Stadium for the first time, he breezed through three innings of scoreless ball against the Big Red Machine, striking out four, including the great Johnny Bench. Two days later, again versus the Reds, he would pitch a scoreless ninth inning.

People were starting to take notice of the young phenom, but because he was appearing in relief of games in which the Dodgers mostly trailed, he had yet to captivate the fans and media. "Although he pitched so well after he was called up in 1980," Steve Brener said, "he was still generally under the radar. Although Mike Brito was always talking him up, saying all along he would soon be in Los Angeles, it wouldn't be until 1981 when he broke with the club that everybody would be in awe of what he would do at the beginning of the season."

Brito was not just Valenzuela's greatest advocate; he also played the role of father figure to him. Prior to Fernando being called up to Los Angeles, Brito had accompanied Valenzuela to his first Minor League stop in Lodi before paying frequent visits to his ensuing stops with Phoenix and San Antonio to offer his support. And upon Valenzuela's arrival in Los Angeles, Brito arranged to have him move into a guest house behind his own—inviting him over to have regular meals with his family.

While on the road, Fernando often hung out with another young and up-and-coming Latino superstar, teammate Pedro Guerrero. Valenzuela "didn't speak *any* English, and he didn't give a shit," Guerrero recalled with a grin. "He was quiet then, and he's quiet now. When we went out to dinner, we would be sitting at a table, and he would eat and drink a beer or two and didn't say a word. That was Fernando."

Next up, on September 24, in a game against the San Francisco Giants, Valenzuela came in to relieve Reuss with one out and runners on first and second base in the seventh inning. He would get out of that jam and then proceed to pitch a perfect eighth inning, helping the Dodgers to an eventual twelve-inning victory to move them back into a first-place tie.

Fernando's multimonth scoreless streak across the Minor and Major Leagues continued with his first Major League victory, on September 30 in San Francisco, as he struck out four without giving up a hit over the final two innings of the game. A Guerrero home run in the tenth turned out to be the game winner.

But for all of Valenzuela's exploits, the Dodgers found themselves three games out with three games to play on the morning of October 3. With the final three games of the season to be played at Dodger Stadium against the Astros, the Boys in Blue held their fate in their own hands. If they could sweep the series, it would force a winner-take-all playoff game at Dodger Stadium. And the prospect of a Dodgers sweep of the Astros was very real to Sambito and his teammates. "We didn't play too well in LA," Sambito recalled. "There was something about that place—it wasn't good for us—despite the games generally being low-scoring, tight affairs."

Just a month earlier, Fernando was pitching before no more than three thousand fans in San Antonio. Now he would be thrust into a pressure-packed, playoff-like atmosphere at Dodger Stadium in front of crowds of better than fifty thousand. But he continued to meet every challenge set before him—remaining cool and unflappable with the adrenaline rush of the big moments.

"Fernando handled it so well," Rick Monday said. "If he had the jitters, or if he had doubts, a poker player should be able to hide it as well as he did. Think about it—he's in a stadium that has more people than the portion of the country he's from. It's the largest gathering of people he'd ever seen before. It's the loudest he's ever heard people be. It's deafening [in Dodger Stadium] with fifty-seven thousand fans—*deafening*. It's like standing behind a 747 at the airport."

"He may have been nervous on the inside," Garvey told LasMayores. com in 2021, "but exceptional players are able to mask that nervousness. It's almost a confidence game. You're trying to portray that at all times. He just had that at a young age. Was it fully developed? No. But was it good enough to get the job done as a rookie? Absolutely."

In the first game, he pitched the ninth and tenth innings of a tie game before a dramatic Joe Ferguson home run won it in the bottom of the tenth, 3–2. The Dodgers would take the second game of the series without the services of Valenzuela, as Reuss outlasted Nolan Ryan in a classic 2–1 pitcher's duel of aces. But in the season's 162nd game, Fernando would toss two no-hit innings over the sixth and seventh before Dodgers third baseman Ron Cey's two-run home run in the eighth provided the margin of victory in a 4–3 Los Angeles win. After six months of regular-season baseball, the Astros and Dodgers had identical 92–70 records—tied for first place.

Mark Langill, then a teenager, witnessed the Dodgers' win in game 162. "I was in the left-field pavilion, and the Cey home run off of Frank LaCorte actually landed in the row behind me," he recalled. "I was lucky I wasn't killed by that thing because I couldn't judge a fly ball to save my life! I'm like, *Oh my God, that thing landed six inches from me!* Nobody realized at the time when the Dodgers won that game, 4–3, that Cey was playing hurt. So when you flipped on the television the next day [for the one-game playoff], nobody knew why Cey wasn't playing or that he had been up all night icing his foot.

"The other amazing thing about that Sunday [game 162] was that Sandy Koufax saw [Don] Sutton in the clubhouse around the fifth inning after his workout, and Sutton's pouring himself a glass of wine. Sandy says, 'You better get down to the bullpen in case they need you.' And of course Steve Howe gets in trouble in the ninth inning with a 4–3 lead and Sutton actually had to come in to save the game. There was like a ten-minute delay while he took his sweet time walking in from the bullpen."

The charismatic Dodgers left-fielder Dusty Baker saw the evolution of their three-game sweep of the Astros coincide with pressure building on Houston with each passing defeat. "Before the first game, I was by the batting cage with 'Penguin' [Ron Cey] and Joe Ferguson," Baker recalled. "We watched as the Astros were over there playing pepper without hats on and stuff. And I said, 'We're going to beat them, man.' So, boom! We beat them on the first night. Now the second night, about 30 percent of them were feeling a little nervous—you could tell. They had their hats on, not playing pepper, and not laughing as much. I heard they had champagne on ice. Second night, bam! We beat them again. On the third day, there was *nobody* playing pepper, nobody was smiling, nobody doing anything. And I thought, *Those Astros, we're going to beat them. We've got them on the run.* So, bam! We beat them again. Now we're tied!"

While Cey's home run in that final game of the series made all the headlines, Valenzuela had become the Dodgers' secret weapon in keeping them in games down the stretch run of the season. "To me, Fernandomania didn't start in 1981," Jaime Jarrín said. "To me, it started in 1980, when we had that last series against the Astros. That's when people *found* Fernando, when people *discovered* Fernando. That's when we saw his character and his guts. He did a fantastic job."

"Up until that Astros series," Langill recalled, "Fernando was still under the radar. He was still coming out of the bullpen. But don't forget, he was not the type to blow people away. It wasn't like he was a strikeout artist like an Eric Gagné—a *pump-your-fist-oh-my-God-you-can't-touch-him* kind of guy. Fernando was effective, but he was *quietly* effective. It's not like he was striking out six in a row at any time—like a Dwight Gooden or somebody like that. He was effective and just part of that surge in September when the Dodgers were chasing the Astros."

It would not be an exaggeration to say that Dodgers manager Tommy Lasorda would now have to make the most difficult decision of his long and illustrious managerial career. Should he start Dave Goltz, the high-priced veteran pitcher who had struggled for much of the season with a 7-10 record and an ERA of more than four runs a game? Or does he go with the nineteen-year-old Valenzuela, with less than a month of big league service time but the owner of a fifteen and two-thirds innings scoreless streak? Goltz was clearly the "safe" move, as going with a green rookie and having it blow up in Lasorda's face would be the kind of decision that gets a manager in hot water—or worse.

But at the time, the sentiment in the clubhouse and up in the press box leaned toward giving the "flawless one" the ball that day. "Many people thought Fernando should have started," Jarrín confirmed. "But Tommy decided to pitch Dave Goltz instead." Garvey backed up Jarrín's view, adding, "Late that season, I'm not sure that Goltz wasn't struggling, somewhat, with his control. I think the feeling on the team was, 'Let's go with Fernando—he's really starting to master this screwball. Let's go with him.'"

Baker, a true clubhouse leader by then, was another one of those players who wanted to see Valenzuela start his first big league game with the season on the line. "We *begged* Lasorda to pitch Fernando," Baker said emphatically. "Nothing against Goltz, but we wanted to go with ability versus the veteran. And it was one of the only times I disagreed with Tommy. Going with Goltz against Joe Niekro was a non–second-guess situation where you go with the veteran, and, if we lose, then you don't have to answer for it. But if you go with the kid, then you open yourself up for second-guessing."

Still, while many of the Dodgers might have questioned the decision, the overriding sense was that they didn't dwell on it when taking the field that day. "We had a ball game to win," Monday said. "In that moment, you don't really have a lot of time to analyze." Garvey was on the same page. "I learned early on that life is vertically integrated," he said. "Whether it's at home when we answer to our wives or if it's in baseball when you answer to the manager who then answers to the general manager and so on. My job was to play my position, to be a leader on the team, to do all the little things I could to get everybody pulling the same end."

That being said, most of the Astros players were miffed and relieved by the move to start Goltz over Valenzuela, though Sambito was more pragmatic about Lasorda's decision. "We felt we had a better chance against Goltz than the hotshot rookie," he said. "Fernando was amazing at that time—unhittable. But you know, if I'm the Dodgers, looking back at it now, I wouldn't have a problem going with Goltz. It's a tricky decision in my eyes if I had to make that decision. A lot of things probably went into it. Fernando was inexperienced in playoff games and had much less pitching at the Major League level. He was just nineteen, and, even though he was a cool customer who showed poise and had a mound presence that was outstanding for someone that young, there were reasons why he wouldn't be the choice. There are a lot of things that go into choosing a pitcher in a big game, so I'm sure [Lasorda] had his reasons."

"The Dodgers called up young Fernando and he was really good," added Bruce Bochy, who was the Astros' backup catcher and a future three-time world champion manager. "But Goltz was good, too, and the guy just got a big contract. But looking back, you realize who they had as an option and how the game went. I mean, hindsight is 20/20, but they had a pretty good one in Fernando, who was fresh and could have started."

Unfortunately for the Dodgers, Goltz would get in trouble early, giving up four runs—two earned—on eight hits in just three innings of work. Rick Sutcliffe, the first reliever out of the bullpen, was even worse, as he battled wildness to load the bases before Joe Beckwith came in and allowed all three inherited runs to score. After just four innings, the Astros led 7–0. The game was over before it was even half over. "At some point, when you get behind like that, and when the other guy is throwing really well, things move quickly and all of a sudden you run out of time," Garvey lamented.

On the Astros' side, Niekro was superb, going the distance in notching his twentieth win of the season. It would end as a crushing 7–1 defeat for a Dodgers team that had valiantly won their previous three games—all nail-biting, one-run affairs—to get one step away from a division title. But it wasn't to be.

The move by Lasorda not to start Fernando would haunt Baker for many years. In 1993 he tried to exorcise those demons at the end of his first season as a Major League manager with the Giants. "We got the last game of the regular season, and we're tied with Atlanta for first place [in the National League West]," Baker recalled. "Colorado hadn't beaten the Braves all year long. They ended up 13–0 over the Rockies that season. So I take [twenty-one-year-old rookie] Salomón Torres out the night before to get a read of his barometer, his feelings, and stuff. And I decided to start Salomón Torres. People asked me, 'Why did you start Salomón Torres?' It was because I went with the ability over the veteran because the other choices I had were [thirty-three-year-old] Jim Deshaies and [thirty-six-year-old] Scott Sanderson. I went with the 'stuff' over the veterans because of that decision by Tommy Lasorda to pitch Goltz over Fernando. I swear to God, that was the reason I did it. It didn't work, but neither did Goltz work out over Fernando."

If there was any solace for Dodgers fans that day, it was the sight of Valenzuela entering the game in the sixth inning to try to extend a nearly monthlong scoreless streak out of the bullpen. The kid wouldn't disappoint, shutting down the Astros over two more frames to finish his 1980 campaign with seventeen and two-thirds innings of scoreless pitching across ten relief appearances. If you add his scoreless streak at the end of his Minor League stint at San Antonio, Valenzuela closed out the year with a staggering fifty-two and two-thirds consecutive innings without yielding an earned run.

Still, it was bittersweet for the Dodgers and their fans as they pondered what could have been had Valenzuela started the final game. "I seem to recall some grumblings afterwards—all off the record, of course," sportswriter Lyle Spencer said of the Dodgers players in the clubhouse. "Nobody really wanted to piss off management. Even though free agency had opened things up by then, management still had a lot of control."

But Langill actually saw a silver lining to an otherwise agonizing afternoon at Dodger Stadium. "I think the best thing that could have happened was [the Dodgers] losing that playoff game," he theorized. "Think about this. If Fernando starts that playoff game, then there's no Fernandomania [the next season] because the cat's out of the bag. Whether he wins or loses, he's already big enough to start that game. Everybody would have known who he was. So, the Dodgers losing that game actually preserved Fernando's freshness, his anonymity. By not starting, he's still in the 'witness protection program' with no hype going into the off-season and into 1981. It also kept the Dodgers hungry."

And it would set things up for a mesmerizing and historically significant 1981 season for both Fernando and the Dodgers.

The Fable That Came to Life 7

Major League Baseball was riding a sugar high in the spring of 1981. The previous year had featured a magnificent season-long quest for the Kansas City Royals' George Brett to become the first big leaguer to bat .400 in nearly four decades. It was also the greatest season for the Philadelphia Phillies' Mike Schmidt, as he belted 48 home runs. Their respective ball clubs, after losing league championship series from 1976 through 1978, would at last make it to the Fall Classic. The Phillies would prevail over the Royals in six games, winning their first title since the World Series began in 1903. According to Nielsen Media Company, the 1980 World Series remains the highest-rated and most watched of all time.

As a result, revenue was flooding into the game in the form of television and advertising revenue, ticket sales, and merchandising. The Yankees, with four postseason appearances in five years, sent shockwaves through the baseball world with the signing of free agent Dave Winfield to an unheard of ten-year, $23 million deal—easily the richest in sports history at that time. The Bronx Bombers' former manager, the fiery Billy Martin, brought his "Billy-Ball" style of aggressive and opportunistic play to a young Oakland A's team and instantly turned them from an American League doormat into contenders after flamboyant longtime owner Charlie Finley sold the team.

Baseball was celebrated in song—most notably by Terry Cashman's "Talkin' Baseball (Willie, Mickey, and The Duke)," which poetically described baseball from the game's golden age of the 1950s through 1980. The song was so popular that Cashman soon thereafter began recording versions of the medley using the history of various teams.

These were the glory days of baseball.

Still, despite all the good vibrations, on the baseball labor front there was unrest between the players and the owners looming over the season before it had even begun. A potential strike would threaten to take down the game following a celebrated 1980 season that had elevated the popularity of professional baseball to new heights. From a public relations standpoint, it would be devastating for baseball—especially as the United States was suffering economically through a double-dip recession at the time while Major League salaries were climbing at a staggering pace since the advent of the free agency era five years earlier.

Meanwhile, over in Vero Beach, Florida, the spring training home of the Dodgers, the club was at a crossroad. The old guard of veterans that had produced so many big moments over the last decade was nearing the end of its tenure in Los Angeles, slowly to be replaced by what was sometimes called "Lasorda's Kiddie Corps"—a promising collection of emerging talent, all twenty-five years old or younger, that included such players as Steve Sax, Alejandro Peña, Steve Howe, Dave Stewart, Mike Scioscia, Bob Welch, Pedro Guerrero, and of course Fernando Valenzuela. Aside from veteran outfielders Dusty Baker, Rick Monday, and Reggie Smith, and pitchers Burt Hooton and Jerry Reuss, the legendary infield of Steve Garvey, Davey Lopes, Bill Russell, and Ron Cey—a unit now together for a record-setting ninth season—constituted the core behind three pennant-winning seasons to that point. The big question in camp was whether they had one more run at an elusive World Series championship in them before the inevitable team turnover.

"Having been a batboy for the Brooklyn Dodgers in spring training [as a youngster] and knowing the history of the club," Garvey said, "I knew it was always their philosophy that it was better to move a player a year too early than a year too late. And I did know that the contracts were running out. I figured we probably had one full year in terms of all the guys together and then, after that, we might lose Lopes, which would break up the infield. So there was an anticipation for '81 to finally win the big one. It's like in football; you can look at Buffalo, you can look at Denver for so many years, and even Minnesota teams—teams that came close several times but didn't win it all. We were starting to run out of time, too."

"We didn't have any so-called middle-aged baseball players for the most part," added Tom Niedenfuer, a Dodgers rookie relief pitcher in 1981. "We had lots of twenty-two- and twenty-three-year-olds, but we also had plenty of thirty-three- and thirty-four-year-old guys, too. Nothing really in between. So we were hopeful our new guys would pan out, because we knew as the years went by we were going to lose the great older leaders on the team."

Rick Monday felt added pressure that spring to win it all—"from *day one*," Monday said definitively. "You could look around the locker room and think, *This team is not going to be together much longer*. Because of the influx of some very talented young players, it was time to pass the baton; roles were going to change. That's because there's a constant evolution of the game and the players anyway. There's been nearly twenty thousand players in Major League Baseball history. Even the '27 Yankees team eventually weren't playing together. For us that spring, it was about time that some of these younger guys were going to be flourishing. They were going to be on the stage. So this was the last hurrah for the older guys—you could see it."

Others veterans, like Baker, believed that as long as the team kept playing serious October baseball, it would make replacing the veterans more difficult—and slow down the process. "We learned from the Yankees that if you win, they can't get rid of all of us," he explained. "Instead, they can only get rid of one or two at a time. By winning, we could back up our Minor League system. That's what happened with the Yankees back then because they had [future stars] like Fred McGriff and Willie McGee, and we had Greg Brock, Jeff Leonard, and Mike Marshall. It seemed like many teams in baseball ended up with some top prospects from either the Dodgers or the Yankees because that's what winning did—it backs your Minor Leagues up. Why do you think the Dodgers had Rookies of the Year five, six years in a row? Because they were inserting a top Minor Leaguer in and [replacing] one veteran. They had Davey Lopes coming out, and here comes Steve Sax. Then later, here comes Mike Marshall in for Garvey. I learned from the Dodgers that you don't have to do a total refill."

It would be understandable, if individualistic, to see veterans who are holding on to their twilight playing years distance themselves from their younger, upstart teammates who would eventually take their jobs. But this Dodgers team wasn't at all like that, and it was a credit to their manager and team leadership. "When I got called up," Niedenfuer recalled, "Tommy called me into his office and said, 'You're here to help us win and we're *expecting* you to help us win. It's not like you're playing for the Seattle Mariners and you're just going to get your feet wet. We're expecting you to be a part of the team.' So instead of just being happy to be in the big leagues, all of us young guys expected to help contribute to the winning atmosphere the Dodgers had. And I think you have to give our veterans a lot of credit. They didn't talk down to us like rookies. I mean Rick Monday, at spring training, if he thought you were going to be on the team as a youngster, he'd want to take you out to dinner or say, 'Hey, we're going to go play golf at this time.' The veterans knew they were going to need us at some point in the year down the line."

For Fernando, that veteran mentorship began in earnest during spring training from the bilingual Dusty Baker, who helped Valenzuela with his English. "Dusty was like a big brother to every Latino player that came into that clubhouse," sports journalist Lyle Spencer recalled. "He took guys under his wing. I called Dusty 'the unifier.' My experience with him dates to [his early playing days] in Atlanta. I got to know him a little bit then. . . . He took all the young players under his wing and taught them the ropes and let them know they had certain rights. Dusty has a way about him that is pretty unique in my experience in his ability to reach *anybody*—any nationality, any color. He has the ability to bring people together like few athletes I've ever been around. So having him there at that time was *perfect* for Fernando because he could lean on him. And Dusty was such a force because I've always said he's not only the smartest guy in whatever room he's in, he's also the toughest guy. Nobody's ever messed with Dusty if they have any idea who he is. They're going to give him some distance if he gets upset or has something to say. So he was a very positive force for Fernando in terms of helping him maneuver his way through everything that was coming his way."

It would be the beginning of a beautiful friendship between Valenzuela and Baker, one that still exists today. And while they were able to communicate in two languages with one another, their closeness blossomed quickly out of a strong mutual admiration for one another. "Fernando was very respectful right from the beginning," said Baker, who learned Spanish in school, as well as from his mother, who taught it, and from his sister, who was a missionary in Colombia. "So I helped him out as much as I could. I would do things like bring him food to eat. I bought him his first suit. And if he was breaking curfew, which he rarely did, I wouldn't tell on him. That was between me and him, because he was young. I remembered when I was in that position. What helped me with Fernando was remembering how I was treated by Hank Aaron, Clete Boyer, and Bob Uecker. Those guys did a lot for me. All I was doing for Fernando was passing on what was already given to me by those guys. That's what we did for respectful rookies. If he would have been disrespectful, I wouldn't have given him the time of day. But Fernando was *very* respectful—and he would handle stardom better than any [standout] rookie I ever saw. I would call him 'Estrella,' which is Spanish for 'star,' but he would tell me, 'Tu estrella,' which means 'You are the star.'"

Spencer recalled vividly how Valenzuela's talent was complemented by humbleness—and how positively that resonated in the Dodgers clubhouse. "There was tremendous admiration for him from teammates and rivals during that period," Spencer said. "I know Dusty loved playing behind guys he really liked, like Bobby Welch—and Fernando was certainly in that category. He would never attempt to separate himself and put himself on higher ground."

It was clear almost right from the start that Valenzuela would be treated better than most players entering the first full season of their Major League career. "It's because Fernando acted like a veteran in the clubhouse in terms of being a professional," Mark Langill suggested. "Normally we'll hear about rookie hazing and everything like that. But once the spotlight hit Fernando, all those older players were kind of like mother hens and wanted to protect him and make him feel like he was part of the team. They realized he was a special player, but his disposition and the way he went about his business was honestly what they liked just as much. Fernando just wanted to be a part of the team, and I think that was the key. There were no high-profile pranks on him because there came a point after the second or third week of the season when things got crazy that they realized to be a good teammate they needed to sort of form a cocoon and make him feel comfortable."

For Spencer's part, the sportswriter also lent a hand in trying to teach Valenzuela some English. "Someone in the PR department asked me to help Fernando with his English while we were in Vero Beach in the spring of '81," he recalled. "I didn't have many dealings with Fernando in September of '80 because the Dodgers were in a tight race with Houston and there was too much going on to have cultivated a relationship with a young player then. But in the spring, there were nights when we would walk around the Dodgertown campus, and I would work with him on his English. That was when I got to know him and understood what a sweetheart of a guy he was even though it didn't pan out that well with teaching him English. He really struggled with grasping it, and I think after the third or fourth time, he decided to stop. But it was great for me because it opened me up to really know who he was and what a deep and down-to-earth and humble guy he was and remains to this day."

There was a warmth and camaraderie around Dodgertown that enabled Fernando to be himself. While he was known to be a reserved young man, he was also quickly identified as a practical joker with a great sense of humor. "While there was a shyness about him, there was also a playfulness," Monday said. "On days he wasn't pitching, Fernando was always like a kitten playing with a ball of yarn. If he needed to smack it this way, he could do it. If he needed to smack it in a different direction, he could do it. If he needed to wind up the ball of string again, he could do it. And he had this little thin rope lariat that he was always twirling. A guy walked by and Fernando lassoed his shoe. He was always doing that. There was one day when I was sitting with Manny Mota in the dugout and I go to him, 'Well, Fernando's 10-for-10—he hasn't missed a shoe yet walking by. Well, I don't know if I should walk by him or not.' And Manny goes, 'No, he won't do it to you.' I said, 'Really?' And Manny explained why, saying, 'No, he respects you. He won't do it to you.'"

Other Dodgers would sometimes feel a tap on their shoulder, only to turn around and find no one there. Invariably, the culprit was Fernando. "Fernando was a kid," Baker told LasMayores.com in 2021. "Other than when he was on the mound, he acted like a kid. He used to crack us up."

Valenzuela had quickly integrated himself into the clubhouse culture—a trait that typically takes at least a season or two. "He had a great sense of humor," Spencer said. "He was a prankster in his own sort of subtle way. He was just one of the guys. And the players responded to that."

What the players also responded to was, most importantly, his performance on the mound. "He comes up to us in 1980 and pitches very well in the playoff game, especially for an emerging talent," Garvey said. "And then in '81 he comes in and starts to be very solid in spring training."

A passage in Jason Turbow's wonderful book on the 1981 Dodgers,

They Bled Blue, offers a telling story of just how impressive Valenzuela was that spring to his teammates during a batting practice session: "Lasorda . . . gathered three of his top-line guys—Reggie Smith, Dusty Baker, and Pedro Guerrero—to do their damnedest in the batting cage, then ordered Valenzuela to let loose. Three pitches and Smith was done. Three more pitches, and so was Baker. Likewise, Guerrero."

Monday is familiar with the tale. "It has become a living legend," he said. "Fernando was motivated by Tommy Lasorda to get the guys out and challenged him to do it."

Baker didn't recall—and had some doubts—about the episode. "Number one, we were never striking out [in batting practice]. Number two, *all three of us on nine pitches?* There's a good chance he pitched wonderfully and his timing and everything was more together than ours. So Fernando might have [struck us all out], but we didn't keep track of that stuff because we know the pitchers are ahead of us at [spring training]."

The question became whether the pitching-rich Dodgers would have a spot in the rotation for Valenzuela. But the exit of Don Sutton via free agency opened that door for him, and, after continuing to perform well that spring, Fernando was slated to pitch the third game of the season—a low-key assignment in early April after all the hoopla and majesty of Opening Day and well before more meaningful games further on in the season.

Outside of Dodgers camp, Valenzuela remained a relatively unknown asset. "Fernando wasn't even hyped in spring training," Langill recalled. "The thinking on the Dodgers wasn't like this guy can replace [a star like] Sutton."

"I wasn't thinking he would be the ace of the staff—that's for sure," said Fred Claire, who was then the Dodgers' vice president of public relations. "Because when you look at our pitching staff at that time, it was very talented. But certainly this was a pitcher, by what had been shown to us by the reports and the handful of games he pitched for us in 1980, [who would] be a very talented and promising pitcher—someone who could help our club. And he was one that, certainly in the front office, [stirred] a lot of excitement in terms of his appeal to the Hispanic population. But, keep in mind, that was a staff that included people like Bobby Welch, Burt Hooton, Jerry Reuss, Rick Sutcliffe, and Dave Goltz. We knew Fernando was a pitcher who could really be significant, but to say, well, did we think he would be the ace of that staff? No. We couldn't envision how great he would be, but we knew there was potential. I can recall in my early years with the Dodgers when [owner] Walter O'Malley, a true visionary, was always interested in and saw the potential of what a pitcher from Mexico might mean to the Dodgers."

What was the hope and dream of O'Malley and his front office a quarter century earlier still held true in 1981—the emergence of a "Mexican Sandy Koufax." Everyone in the Dodgers organization was hopeful Fernando Valenzuela would, at last, fit that bill.

A Star Is Born

8

And a little child shall lead them.

—VIN SCULLY after Fernando Valenzuela's 1981 Opening Day victory

The stunning news came out of the blue. Less than twenty-four hours before the first pitch of Opening Day before a sellout crowd at Dodger Stadium, the Dodgers' deep rotation suddenly needed a starting pitcher. Jerry Reuss, the 1980 National League Cy Young Award runner-up and the ace of the Dodgers' pitching staff, was slated to start the big game but was a late scratch due to a calf muscle injury he sustained during a workout the day before. Their number-two starter, Burt Hooton, was not an option, as he was nursing the painful aftereffects of a procedure to remove an ingrown toenail. The club's third option in the rotation, Bob Welch, was recovering from a bone spur in his elbow. The fourth and fifth options, Dave Goltz and Rick Sutcliffe, were healthy enough, though unavailable—each having just pitched in an exhibition series against the California Angels.

This left Valenzuela—the last man standing—as Lasorda's only recourse.

"It's a memory I always have of saying, '[Lasorda] gave me this opportunity; I have to take advantage of it," Valenzuela told the *Los Angeles Times* in 2021. "He asked me if I could pitch that day and I said, 'That was the chance I was waiting for.'"

The twenty-year-old Fernando, who had thrown batting practice at Dodger Stadium that day, had *never* started a Major League game. The assignment would make him the first Dodgers rookie to ever start an Opening Day in the club's history. He would be opposed by Joe Niekro, the pitcher who had not only ended the Dodgers' season in the one-game playoff the previous October but who, together with his brother Phil, would eventually become half of a record-setting duo to combine for the most wins—539—by any pair of brothers in baseball history. To say that Valenzuela and the Dodgers faced a tall task on Opening Day would be an understatement.

Upon receiving the news from Lasorda, Valenzuela returned to Mike Brito's guest house and told the scout who had signed him that he would be the Dodgers' starting pitcher the next day. Brito recalled how Fernando didn't seem nervous about it at all. "He was relaxed—like he was going to pitch a game in Mexico," Brito said.

Going into the game, the Dodgers players didn't know what to expect of their young southpaw. "It wasn't because we didn't think he was capable of doing the job, we just hadn't seen enough of him," Rick Monday recalled. "He was interesting, very interesting. But what that meant, we didn't know. Well, Fernando was thrust into having to carry the show in the first game of the 1981 season—was literally pushed onto the stage— and he didn't shy away from the bright lights."

For the Astros, there was at least initially a great deal of relief when they heard the news of the Reuss scratch. "Reuss was always really tough on us," Sambito recalled. "He was a power guy and didn't back down to anybody. Everything I feel is important to pitching he did well. We never seemed to do well against Reuss. So when we heard that Reuss wasn't going to start and that we were going up against a rookie, we felt we had a much better chance against [Valenzuela] than the veteran all-star."

But Fernando was clearly up for the challenge. So, on a typically sun-splashed Southern California Thursday afternoon, on April 9, 1981, true to form, Valenzuela was remarkably relaxed and confident from the time he arrived at Dodger Stadium. After the Dodgers took batting practice, he adjourned to the trainer's room, lay down on one of the tables, and took—*wait for it*—a nap! After catching some sleep, he made his way to the bullpen to warm up before walking through the tunnel in the bowels of the stadium to the dugout to take part in the preliminary Opening Day festivities.

Valenzuela's cool demeanor left an impression on longtime Dodgers executive Fred Claire that remained distinct decades later. "I was the vice president of public relations at the time," Claire told me. "So I was very much involved with the team and game preparations and so forth. Having been involved in the pregame stuff, I was standing there in the dugout when Fernando came in. I'll never forget standing near him. I've been around a lot of players in the big leagues, but I've never seen someone about to make their first start in a Major League game that was so calm. The contrast to other players [in that position] and his calmness was overwhelming. I've really thought about this, and it occurred to me that he was prepared in this life for the stage—and the stage was set for Opening Day—and he knew what he could do. In a way, it would be like a talented young pianist who could be twelve or thirteen years old—a genius who goes on stage at Carnegie Hall—and delivers the performance that shocks everyone but themselves. And that's exactly what it was. It was almost like he said to himself, *I've prepared all my life to do this—and now I'm about to do it.*"

The Dodgers' shiny, brand-new pitcher whom nobody knew much about took the mound. Portly but very well coordinated, the Mexican southpaw would begin his trademark windup with his hands clasped at waist level, then lift them high above his head while glancing toward the heavens—*perhaps for divine inspiration*—before bringing them down to meet his right leg and following through with his pitch. The deceptive delivery was poetry in motion and, soon after this game, would begin to be mimicked by countless young fans on Little League fields and in Wiffle Ball games throughout the baseball world. One of those youngsters would be Nomar Garciaparra. "I would at least try to look up to the sky like Fernando did when throwing in the backyard," he said. "That was one of the great things about him—people mimicking everything about his windup. That's the greatest form of flattery, right?"

Appropriately enough, the first pitch of the season Valenzuela delivered was a perfect screwball on the outside corner; the Astros' Terry Puhl flailed at it for a strike. Puhl would hardly be the only Astros hitter that afternoon to miss badly on a pitch. In fact, Houston would barely touch Fernando through the first five innings, collecting just two singles—one of them never even leaving the infield. Valenzuela was cruising, and the fans took notice—growing louder and louder with each passing shutout inning.

One of the 50,511 Dodgers faithful in the stands that day was future Hollywood voice actor David Marc Bronow, a college student at Cal State Northridge at the time. With no classes that afternoon, Bronow and his roommate, itching to go to Opening Day, took a chance they could score tickets and succeeded with a pair of field-level boxes on the first base side. Bronow could hardly believe what he was witnessing.

"While I did recall a couple of Fernando's relief appearances the previous September, they weren't super memorable to me at that time," Bronow recounted. "So when we get to the park and see this kid starting for the Dodgers—on *Opening Day!*—I thought, *Boy, I wonder how many pitchers are on the disabled list or are down.* But by the fourth inning, this kid is just throwing 'magic' out there. I turned to my roommate and said, 'Take a look at this crowd. Listen to the excitement. There's something special that's building up.' Numerous people sitting around us had their transistor radios blaring, so you could hear Vin Scully and his broadcast partner of many years, Jerry Doggett, calling the game. As the strikeouts and scoreless innings started piling up, Scully was getting more and more excited. Fernando just seemed *unhittable*."

Meanwhile, the Dodgers put up a run in the bottom of the fourth when Steve Garvey tripled, and Ron Cey brought him home with a sacrifice fly to make it a 1-0 game. It would prove to be the only offense that Fernando would need that afternoon.

Valenzuela's *only* trouble came in the sixth inning, when, with one out, Craig Reynolds singled and César Cedeño doubled to put runners on second and third. But Fernando would retire the Astros' cleanup hitter José Cruz on a soft liner to short and Art Howe on a come-backer to the mound. After that threat, Valenzuela was nearly flawless the rest of the way—retiring the next eight Astros in a row until Howe singled with two outs in the ninth. Then, with the crowd cheering and on its feet, Fernando ended the game like he started it—with a screwball—to strike out Dave Roberts on his 106th pitch of the afternoon. The twenty-year-old Fernando had pitched a dominating five-hit shutout (two of those hits off broken bats and one an infield single) in his first big league starting assignment, and the wild celebratory scene on the field and in the stands at Dodger Stadium appeared as if the Dodgers had just won the pennant.

"I was like everyone—just watching the ball game and hoping that we'd have a chance to win," Reuss said. "But Fernando recorded out after out with a series of mixing his pitches all out of the same arm slot. He had Astros hitters flailing at his pitches, as they couldn't quite figure him out. And before you know it, the Dodgers put a couple of runs on the board and Fernando throws a complete game shutout. Everyone was saying that it was the most amazing thing they've ever seen. I couldn't run out on the field like [my teammates], because I couldn't run anywhere, so I had to wait in the dugout to congratulate Fernando and everybody else. I remember saying, 'You know, I guess the right guy was pitching today because he pitched a shutout and the Dodgers won.' I was as happy as I can be. But at that time, I didn't know that a legend was beginning."

"I was completely shocked," exclaimed Lyle Spencer. "I don't think anybody was prepared for that. I would guess Lasorda was hoping to get five or six innings out of him—maybe. I don't think he was that stretched out in spring training, so that performance was stunning. And he made it look so easy, so effortless—like it was routine for him."

"The one thing I noticed, and even from the players I talked to about Valenzuela," sportswriter Ken Gurnick said, "was the ease and confidence with which Fernando *always* played. . . . And I think that it's the confidence and knowledge he just always seemed to have that made him feel like he knew what he was doing at all times. It gave him composure. It's hard to learn composure, but when you come into a setting, whether you're an athlete, a young lawyer, or a teenager playing among men, like Fernando did, and you're exceptional at what you do, you're going to be composed. It's rare that people are like that, but I think that's the common thread with Fernando and other great players I covered."

As for Lasorda, he was less surprised, at least publicly, by Valenzuela's extraordinary Opening Day performance than most. "You judge a guy by what he does in battle, not basic training," Lasorda told reporters after the game. "We brought him up in the heat of last year's race, and our scouts said he could be used in any situation. Just *look* what he did."

Valenzuela's catcher that day was a kid himself, twenty-two-year-old Mike Scioscia, playing in just his second season. Steve Yeager had been the Dodgers' primary catcher for years, but Scioscia, who would go on to catch nearly three-quarters of Valenzuela's starts with the Dodgers, knew some Spanish from his time playing winter ball in the Dominican Republic—a skill that came in handy when working with Fernando at the start of his career. From that very first Valenzuela start, he knew that the pitcher's makeup would contribute to his stardom. "He had a very slow heartbeat," Scioscia told LasMayores.com in 2021. "He could slow the game down and make a pitch. And that's what made him such a great finisher of games, because as the game got deeper, and hitters would bear down more, he was able to rise to that challenge and continue to make pitches, continue to compete."

And as for Valenzuela's secret weapon that day, his nasty screwball, what Scioscia remembered most was the sound it made as it crossed the plate into his catcher's mitt. "When you can hear the spin of the ball, you know that there's a high spin rate [and] that pitch is going to break a lot," Scioscia told LasMayores.com. "You could hear it occasionally on pitchers' curveballs, sliders. With Fernando's screwball, it was so tight, and you could hear it come in. That's how he was able to make it look like a fastball that would just break out on its own last second."

While an Opening Day victory in April may not have held anywhere near the significance of a pennant-winning game in October or avenged Houston's one-game playoff victory the previous fall, Valenzuela's masterpiece was noteworthy in far more important ways. It would mark the beginning of the single most dominating run of victories to start a pitcher's career in the history of baseball. And it would also spark a phenomenon in which this remarkable young Mexican pitcher would begin to heal a long-fragmented relationship between the Dodgers, the city of Los Angeles, and a largely marginalized Latino community.

Fernando Valenzuela had come out of the blue and was about to change everything at Chavez Ravine.

The Kiss That Sparked a Movement   9

When Fernando pitched, it wasn't just a sporting event, it was a
social event. People wanted to learn Spanish and about Mexico.
It was a wonderful way to bring two countries together.

—JAIME JARRÍN, Hall of Fame Spanish-language broadcaster

The young woman of Mexican descent, with dark brown hair flowing
over the "Valenzuela 34" lettering on the back of a three-quarters-sleeve
Dodgers T-shirt, dashed onto the field at Dodger Stadium. She made a
beeline toward the pitcher, who by that evening of April 27, had captured
the imagination of the baseball world. It was the ninth inning of a game
against the Giants, and Valenzuela, working to close out a 5-0 shutout,
was taking a short breather on the infield grass behind the pitcher's
mound. Concerned for Fernando's safety, second base umpire Paul
Pryor rushed over to within a yard of Valenzuela before yielding, as
the exuberant fan extended her arms, grasped the pitcher's shoulders,
pulled herself in close, and planted a kiss on Fernando's right cheek.
Mission accomplished, she then raised her arms victoriously into the
air, jumping up and down several times on the pitcher's mound before
being escorted off the field by stadium security. The crowd went crazy.

Norma Echevarra didn't realize it at that very moment, but her act of
affection would soon become a lasting image and symbol of the love and
adoration being bestowed by millions of Mexican and other Latino fans
on their new hero—Fernando Valenzuela. Her kiss might as well have
been from each and every one of them. With his everyman physique
and looks, he reminded them of a Mexican uncle or cousin. But he was
an everyman who was doing incredible things. And he *belonged* to them.

"It was like a festival of Latino pride," Lyle Spencer recalled of the days

Valenzuela pitched. "The energy was just distinctly different. The ballpark was just crackling. It was like a playoff game whenever he pitched. It was an *event*."

Echevarra's "Valenzuela 34" shirt, like so many others in the ballpark that night, was homemade. "This was an era before the Dodgers had personalized jerseys or bobbleheads or anything like that," Mark Langill noted. "So people were scrambling to try to find Fernando souvenirs. There was no eBay! But back then, the Fernando T-shirts, the bumper stickers, and all the rest of his merchandise was being generated [by individuals] because people wanted to own something—anything—related to Fernando. There was no 'official' Fernando souvenir except for maybe a postcard. If the Dodgers could have sold Fernando jerseys, I can't imagine how many they would have sold, but back then the mechanics weren't there to sell individual player merchandise. So everybody took it upon themselves to make homemade T-shirts and everything else that had 'Fernando' on it."

According to the 1980 U.S. Census, there were 2,065,724 people of Spanish origin in Los Angeles County—and that figure was growing quickly. But the Dodgers had drawn exceedingly poorly from the Latino demographic up to then.

"I started covering Dodger home games in '71," Spencer said. "The crowds pre-Fernando, if I had to break it down, would be 80 percent white, 15 percent African American, and 5 percent Latino. It was a white crowd, although the Dodgers did draw Black fans because—and this gets overlooked in baseball history—in the early '60s they were breaking ground. They had lineups that had a majority of Black players, with Willie and Tommy Davis, Maury Wills, and John Roseboro, so the big part of their core was Black on those great '60s teams. They were breaking ground even after Jackie Robinson, and they deserve a lot of credit for that."

But now, for the first time ever at Dodger Stadium, mariachi bands were playing, "Viva Valenzuela" banners were all the rage in the bleachers, and Mexican flags were draped on railings and waving throughout the park. The entire city of Los Angeles, with its booming Latino population, was embracing him as much if not more than any other Dodger since their move out West more than two decades earlier.

"I don't think you can always see the full extent of how impactful

Fernando was in that [Latino] community," Spencer theorized. "And I think it persists to this day. When you go to Dodger Stadium now, there are times when it seems like half the crowd is Latino. So that has endured. I don't think you can put any kind of number on what that means, but I know it means a lot. It means a lot to the [Latino] people and a lot to the game."

Another part of the social significance of Valenzuela was how he became a bridge between Los Angeles's traditionally white culture and the rise of Latinos in a city that was wrestling with anti-Mexican sentiment. Now Los Angelenos of all different backgrounds had something in common—their admiration for Valenzuela. "I think he was the best ambassador of Mexico in the United States," Jaime Jarrín averred. "People *adored* him."

Perhaps most remarkable about the fervor over Fernando was how it spread like wildfire in the first month of the 1981 season. Following his previous win, a 1–0 shutout over Don Sutton and the Astros on April 22, this game against the Giants became the hottest ticket in a city known for red carpet events. "Within twenty-four hours after he beat the Astros on Wednesday, we sold out the reserved seats for his next scheduled start," Fred Claire said at the time. "That's unprecedented."

"He was initiating a Hispanic, almost phenomenal, fanatical, commitment to the game," was how Garvey described it to the *Los Angeles Times* in 2021.

"I'm not certain there's anyone who can explain it," reflected Rick Monday. "But to see the way people reacted, to see Mexican Americans so proud of this young man and his pitching to the point where they were brought to tears when they saw him—that was something to behold. I think it took us a while to understand how important he became to his culture and how important he became to the culture of baseball. He captured everyone's attention—not right away, but when he did, he owned it."

Whether Valenzuela was loved by the Mexican fans for his savior-like presence or for his everyman image at that time is up for debate. Vin Scully, referred to by some as the "Voice of God" for his sixty-seven seasons of eloquence calling Dodgers games, believed the spectacular emergence of Valenzuela was more on the spiritual side.

"Fernandomania, to me, looked like an almost religious experience,"

Scully told the *Los Angeles Times* for its *Fernandomania @ 40* documentary series. "We would see Hispanic families that had little teeny children with them. I could hear the mothers and fathers saying to their children, 'You see that man out there? He's from nowhere.' And you knew the parents were giving their children 'hope'—'There's nothing that can stop you. You can be as good as that man.' It was a remarkable atmosphere."

After hearing Scully's remark, Marc Grossman had a different take. "With all due respect to Scully," Grossman began, "I think, among Latinos, Valenzuela reminded them that they are not all that different from him. And if he can do it, they can do it. For a lot of Latinos, they're constantly reminded of being treated as second-class citizens. It was and is still pretty pervasive [from the time] when a young child gets into public elementary school. The odds are stacked against them, and they're not given the same assumptions that their Anglo counterparts get to see. But while they're capable and intelligent, they [often] don't get into the AP [advanced placement] classes. So, when someone like Fernando came around and they saw him shooting to the top so quickly just by sheer talent, I don't think it was a religious experience but rather an affirmation of what they always believed [about] themselves—that they were as good as anybody else if given the opportunity."

To Grossman, the similarities in how Mexican Americans looked at Valenzuela and how they viewed another of their icons, Cesar Chavez, were largely the same. "Cesar was not a terribly impressive speaker," Grossman recalled. "He never raised his voice, and when he would tell stories, he would be very anecdotal. And when people would first see him, they were sometimes taken aback—not disappointed, but surprised. He was about 5 foot 6 with jet-black hair, dark Indian features, and he would wear work clothes. He would look and talk and act and dress pretty much like the people that he was committed to help. And so when farmworkers and other Latinos would see him for the first time, they would be looking for someone who was 6 feet tall, regal looking, and a great orator. Instead, they'd see this short little guy who was like them. They would say to themselves or to each other, *You know, he looks like my father, my son, my uncle, my brother. And if he can do these great things, maybe I can, too.*

"Sometimes we keep our heroes too high and far removed. Cesar was not that far removed from people. And I think that was the source of his appeal. I theorize whether that may have been the source of a lot of Latinos' appeal and convention with Valenzuela. Like Chavez, Valenzuela came from very humble origins. He also was not formally educated [neither attended high school]. He was also very humble. And yet, he had such amazing talent and discipline and performance, and people thought, *Well, man, maybe I can do that, too.* So, I understand Scully's analogy, but it may be an observation from someone outside that [Mexican] community."

Others, like Spencer, believed there was room for both points of view about Valenzuela as "savior" to some and an "everyman" to others. "I really think it was a little bit of both," the esteemed sportswriter said. "It was very clear that, even though he didn't speak English and was speaking through [interpreter] Jaime Jarrín, he was a very modest guy. And he was also just a kid. There was all this speculation that he was older. It was legitimate speculation. But there were so many things [to embrace], like the way he pitched with that delivery no one had ever seen, with his eyes to the sky, and his build. He looked like a guy that could be cutting your grass—just that average guy. And I think that had to impact particularly the Latinos who were always trying to find their place in society. I think the enthusiasm around Fernando had a profound effect in that way. It was a spirit that was created. Latinos could say, 'This is one of our own. He's not just good, but he's the *best* in the game!'"

"People were just in *awe* of what he was doing," Steve Brener added. "It was phenomenal and once he got rolling, people wanted to see him pitch."

The quiet and polite Valenzuela was not political then and still isn't. He never publicly made any effort to assuage with rhetoric the pain induced by the forced evictions at Chavez Ravine more than two decades earlier. He had instead made the conscious choice from the beginning of his career to allow his fabled image on the field and his humble nature off it to flow over the top of the long-festering controversy that took place before he was born. "He basically let his performance on the field speak for him," was how longtime Dodgers beat writer Ken Gurnick saw it. "He provided the [Latino] community with someone to rally around and turn baseball into a sport that the Latinos could connect with. It was something that the O'Malleys had always hoped for. They had a large Dominican presence in the Caribbean players, but as far as [a] Mexican superstar, there hadn't been one. Fernando filled that bill, as if he had been created to do it."

What Fernando's performance on the field was ultimately, and most importantly, beginning to do during this period was to unify the city of Los Angeles and its Dodgers with a younger generation of Mexican Americans while trying to make amends for past sins committed against the previous one. To be sure, some of those families displaced and marginalized by the construction of Dodger Stadium—Fernando or no Fernando—refused to ever attend an event there. "It's hard to separate the history of the building of Dodger Stadium and the individuals and families impacted," Claire explained. "The Dodgers had, in '81, been accepted in Los Angeles, went on to win the World Series championship, and had a great following on the Spanish-speaking stations. It can all be examined, looked at, and researched, but what was certain was a firestorm of publicity and attention on Fernando."

Aside from bringing Mexican Americans into Dodger Stadium in droves, Fernando was also drawing female fans to his games in numbers the Major Leagues had never seen before. This made someone like Echevarra—who was a part of both demographics—"Exhibit A" for this new type of fan coming out to Dodgers games. "So many of the new fans were ladies," Jarrín confirmed. "It was unbelievable. Some of the ladies—especially mothers—were seen *praying* for him on the days that he was pitching. They had rosaries with them at the games. Of the Latinos coming to the ballpark, which made up nearly half the crowd, 80 to 90 percent of them were Mexicans and Mexican Americans. And the thing is, it's still like that today. When you walk around Dodger Stadium during a game, you can hear probably as much Spanish as English, even in the different levels of the ballpark. He really did something unique in baseball. He created, more than any other baseball player, *new* baseball fans, because the people of Mexico, Central America, and South America didn't care much about baseball. But thanks to this kid from Mexico, they started to learn the game. It really was amazing."

While Jarrín's bold statement that Valenzuela created more new fans than anyone—more than even Babe Ruth and Jackie Robinson had—might be correct, what's positively provable was Fernando's impact on attendance figures. The proof was in the staggering difference in attendance at games he pitched for the Dodgers versus the ones he didn't. In

Valenzuela's twenty-five starts in 1981—all pitched in different series—his games sold more tickets than the others in twenty-two of them (two of the ones that didn't pull as many spectators were in April, before fans became truly aware of the phenomenon). And the differentials in attendance numbers, particularly on the road, were often double or triple the mean of those teams, with an overall boost of a dramatic 71 percent. No National League pitcher has even come close to that percentage in at least the last half century.

But of all those hundreds of thousands of exuberant new fans coming to see Valenzuela pitch, none of them displayed their fervor more than Echevarra with her sprint to the pitcher's mound that night. To be sure, the sight of fans running on the field during this period was generally nothing extraordinary, as it happened with more regularity and certainly with more tolerance from security in the pre-9/11 world than it does today. "Oddly enough, I wasn't that surprised by seeing [Echevarra] run on the field," Spencer remembered. "Going back to that time, we had streaking and Morganna the Kissing Bandit. There [was] all kinds of crazy stuff going on. I remember I was an official scorer one day in '79 or '80 and this woman right below the press box—a beautiful woman—out of nowhere, turns toward us and flashes her boobs. We're all stunned. After a couple of plays, I got on the microphone in the press box and said, 'If anyone noticed what happened over the last five minutes of the game, I would appreciate it if you would come let me know because I missed it!' Then another time, a streaker ran the bases and slid into home—*nude*. So, a woman running on the field to hug a player—it was unusual, but it wasn't *that* unusual."

But Echevarra's act was different. *Much* different. "That was *a moment*," said Spencer, still moved by it all these years later.

To that point in the game, Valenzuela had been Babe Ruth–esque, allowing just six hits while collecting three singles of his own at the plate to raise his batting average to a ridiculous .438. He was proving that he could do everything on the field with excellence—except run. When Fernando was scheduled to bat in the seventh inning with a chance to go 4-for-4, Lasorda thought he would have a little fun with his veterans on the bench that night. Lasorda first turned to Reggie Smith and told him that Fernando's arm was stiffening up and that he wanted him to pinch-hit for him. "No way!" Smith shouted, predicting bedlam from the fans if Valenzuela were removed from the game. "I'm not getting myself killed!" Rick Monday and Joe Ferguson also wanted no part of pinch-hitting for Fernando, instead offering up Pepe Frías as a "sacrificial lamb." But Lasorda, as he often did with his players, was just having a little fun; he never intended to pull Valenzuela from the game. Fernando would fly out to left field before resuming his mastery on the mound.

Following Echevarra's kiss, Valenzuela would finish off the Giants— ending the game with a strikeout of Jim Wohlford with the crowd of 49,478 (on a *Monday* night in April) on their feet and cheering wildly for the pitcher who already had a nickname. "El Toro" was the result of a *Los Angeles Herald Examiner* contest, and that moniker would stick through the rest of his seventeen-year Major League career. Dodgers second baseman Davey Lopes was in awe. "That's the fourth time in five games he's struck out the last batter," Lopes told reporters that night. "He's a star now. He owns the city. We want to do everything we can to help him maintain that, because he's a super kid. He's doing things nobody's ever done before. He's entitled to everything he's getting."

"He seems to think there's a better league somewhere else," an incredulous Lasorda told the Dodgers beat writers in his office after the game. "And he's trying to pitch himself out of here."

In between his stunning Opening Day outing and this latest victory to go 5-0 with a microscopic 0.20 ERA were three other gems. In his second game at a frigid Candlestick Park against the Giants on April 14, Fernando breezed to a 7-1 win, giving up just four hits while striking out ten. However, Fernando's Major League scoreless streak of thirty-four and a third innings came to an end in the eighth inning of that game, when Larry Herndon doubled to left-center field and Enos Cabell singled him home. Combined with the thirty-five scoreless frames Valenzuela threw to end his time in San Antonio, it was the first run he had given up in sixty-nine and a third innings—a remarkable feat.

In his third game of the season, this one in San Diego on April 18, pitching on just three days' rest, he fired a five-hit shutout with ten more strikeouts and no walks to run his record to 3-0. "By that point," recalled Monday, "he had made the transition from being a guy that was interesting to being a guy that was riveting. He would pitch a good ball game. Then he pitched another really good ball game. And he pitched yet another great ball game. You got to the point that you began to expect it every time Fernando went out there. When you saw the reaction of the [opposing] hitters, and their frustration, and how Fernando worked on the mound and competed, it was incredible."

In his fourth game of the year, in the Astrodome on April 22—a true test for Valenzuela, as he would again be pitching on three days' rest and against a team that had just seen him two weeks earlier—he continued to baffle and dominate Houston, this time hurling yet another complete game shutout, by the score of 1-0. The only run the Dodgers would muster that night was an RBI single, by none other than Valenzuela himself—one of two hits he would get in the game. The opposing losing pitcher was the man Fernando had replaced in the Dodgers rotation, Don Sutton, who would drop to 0-3 with a 5.71 ERA with his new club. "I hope he comes back to earth, or they find a higher league for him," Sutton told a group of writers after the game.

After his fifth win of the season, the "kiss game" over the Giants, the Dodgers were 14-3 and led the NL West by four and a half games despite an anemic offensive output to that point in the campaign. Valenzuela had led the way with four shutouts in five games and was well into a new scoreless streak—having run it to twenty-eight and a third innings. To this point in his career as a Dodger, he now had an unprecedented 0.14 ERA. The poise and command of this merely twenty-year-old pitcher was just as impressive. He seemingly was performing in an impenetrable zone.

"Usually, you might help a kid get adjusted coming up to the big leagues," Jerry Reuss told me. "But I don't recall doing anything. For a kid, he had a lot of poise. In fact, he had poise that veterans of ten years don't have. It appeared that he just wasn't concerned about anything. Of course, there was the language barrier—and maybe that was to his advantage—but as far as us helping him, well, I think it was the other way around. He was helping *us*."

Fernando was also unwittingly helping the newspaper business. "On a personal level, they put [the Valenzuela columns] on the front page of the [*Los Angeles Herald Examiner*] all during that winning streak," Spencer recalled of his work in 1981. "It was the main story in our newspaper. I had never experienced that before, and the only other time it would happen was when the Lakers would win a championship. It was such a phenomenon that his games during that run were the lead story in the newspaper."

Valenzuela's success was bringing a fresh infusion of companies—many of them Mexican or Latino—to spend advertising dollars to promote things like Mexican-brewed beer and tortillas during Dodgers games for the first time. And it was all because Latinos—suddenly a huge part of the Dodgers' television audience—had a player they could identify with in Valenzuela. For Fernando's part, his agent, Antonio De Marco, had already reportedly turned down hundreds of thousands of dollars in endorsement money on behalf of his client so he could continue focusing on his stellar pitching. The two believed the money would come later, so for the time being Valenzuela would have to get by on just his $42,500 salary.

"I can recall an *enormous* number of calls and mail coming in—people wanting to connect with Fernando," recalled Claire. "Obviously, we didn't have the internet, but we had just a tremendous amount of inquiries from advertisers or sponsors of the Dodgers or from people who wanted to be connected to Fernando. I had not seen anything like it in my previous years with the Dodgers. It was huge."

In Valenzuela's sixth game, on May 3 at Olympic Stadium in Montreal, he would run his latest scoreless streak to thirty-six innings when, with a 1–0 lead, he gave up an RBI single to Chris Speier with two outs in the eighth to end the string and tie the contest up at 1–1. Before that, Valenzuela had been nothing short of overwhelming, as the Expos were unable to even hit a ball out of the infield until the seventh inning. After Fernando tossed a scoreless ninth, the Dodgers offense came to life, scoring five runs in the top of the tenth to give Los Angeles a commanding 6–1 edge. Steve Howe would come in to pitch a scoreless bottom of the tenth to preserve Valenzuela's sixth victory of the season against no losses. It was the first game Fernando had pitched that season that he didn't finish. But even pulling him for a pinch hitter worked out, as Reggie Smith singled in the go-ahead run to get the Dodgers' rally rolling.

Based on the evidence of a tremendous Montreal crowd of 46,405 and his continued dominance on the mound, Valenzuela had easily become the biggest draw in all of baseball. Everyone wanted to know when Fernando was going to pitch again. And if you couldn't get a ticket, a Fernando start had become "must-watch" TV. "Here was this young man that really came out of nowhere and very humble beginnings," Monday reflected. "We had seen him in '80 in the bullpen toward the end of the season, and then it built into this crescendo—a crescendo of not just baseball but a crescendo of emotion. And I think, with the Mexican culture, also a great deal of pride. Because here's a young man that came along, very unassumingly, maybe not high expectations to begin with, who was thrust into Opening Day and throws a shutout. Then he begins winning all those games in a row and the crescendo kept building and building because he came from anonymity. And it went all the way to fiesta. And then, when we went on the road, when people started to understand what was going on, it was like little satellite fiestas in the other ballparks that were taking place.

"To see him pitching in front of bigger crowds than you had populations within how many square miles was unbelievable," Monday continued. "But when he got on the mound, there were times I'd hear people ask, and we'd ask it ourselves, too, 'Has he lived this before? Has he experienced this inning before?' It was uncanny, because he's not reacting like a kid from, *where*? There were other times that we'd say, 'He's out there like he's got eyes in the back of his head.' He was never flustered. He was never caught by surprise by things that took place on the field. Again, it was like he'd lived it before. One time, Fernando walked a guy, which he didn't do very often. The guy went to first base, and Reggie [Smith] was on the bench and, like he was talking to the runner, says, 'Okay, you drew a walk. Now you're in trouble.' And it was like ninety seconds later the guy was picked off at first. The same would happen with a runner on second trying to steal third. It's like he had a sense about him. Somebody once asked me who was the greatest player I ever saw. I said that Willie Mays had ability above and beyond everyone else. But as for instincts and command, not just for the game but also for the moment, that's what Fernando had [above others]. I mean, we were in awe at times."

The hysteria around Valenzuela now had a name—Fernandomania—and his baseball magic act was about to make its way to the media capital of the world—New York City.

Fernandomania!   10

Fernandomania was a very spontaneous, organic thing because it wasn't a creation of image makers. It just happened pretty much overnight.

—LYLE SPENCER, former *Los Angeles Herald Examiner* sports columnist

Valenzuela's next opponent, the New York Mets, wasn't just an awful team; they were boring, too. Attendance at Shea Stadium was abysmal, and there was no electric excitement evident in the stands. There was simply not a good reason to see a ball game there in 1981 unless one came to see stars from *other* clubs. They were regularly drawing far fewer than ten thousand fans a game, and the three contests before this upcoming Dodgers series averaged fewer than six thousand tickets sold.

However, for one night, on May 8, that sad situation would change. Thanks to Fernandomania, Shea Stadium would become the center of the baseball world.

"The only decent players the Mets had in those days were Craig Swan and Lee Mazzilli," recalled Art Shamsky, the Mets' color analyst from that time. "The Shea Stadium crowd for Fernando's game [39,848 fans] was by far the biggest of the season for us to that point."

"There was a lot of excitement that night," said Jay Horwitz, the Mets' director of public relations. "We sold *a lot* of extra tickets. There was always a buzz when the Dodgers came to town, as you still had fans from their Brooklyn days coming in. But this game was even more so—it was close to a sellout."

The Mets would have to erect two extra ticket booths near the subway entrances to accommodate the massive number of additional fans. By this point, Valenzuela was becoming accustomed to pitching before big crowds, but what would be substantially different would be the tremendous media presence from around the world before this start. This was New York, with far more reporters and photographers covering his outing than there had been in Houston, San Francisco, San Diego, or even Los Angeles.

"Fernando had already started to capture the headlines and interest from around the country during our first road trip," recalled Steve Garvey. "But when we came to New York, that became his real national coming-out party. The press in New York, with the *Post*, the *Times*, and the *Daily News*, and all the others, and the iconic writers back then like Dick Young, made it different from the other cities."

"We had a pretty big press box, but there was a ton of media demand, so we had to open up the auxiliary press box, too," Horwitz said. "We had a lot of requests from Mexico. I had an initial meeting with the Dodgers' Steve Brener just prior to that series, and we laid out a plan for the press box to take care of the people we needed to take care of. We even had to use the old Jets locker room for Fernando's postgame press conference because we needed the extra space. In all my years with the Mets, the only comparisons I can make to the media presence that Fernando had in '81 [were] the games Doc [Dwight Gooden] pitched in his rookie season of '84 and when Hideki Matsui of the Yankees had all the Japanese press following him around [from 2003 to 2009]."

The Dodgers had already put into place special media guidelines to handle Fernandomania, with one press conference for Valenzuela's first day in each city and another after he pitched—*no exceptions*. And while the team entertained requests for Fernando to appear (with an interpreter) on New York–based programs like the *Today Show* and *Good Morning America*, they never pressed Valenzuela to appear on them, even with all the positive publicity they would have brought to him and the team.

"I think the Dodgers' PR staff deserves a lot of credit," Mark Langill said. "They had seen what happened with George Brett [in his quest to hit .400] the previous year as far as the craziness it created with the press. Fred Claire and Steve Brener also were aware of what Roger Maris went through." Maris, in his quest for the single-season home run record in 1961, faced 24/7 demands for interviews, and reporters were not subject to any rules about interviewing him. Langill recalled that "it was nice that the Dodgers [protected Fernando] like they did because while you would think it would be something done normally, many times it's not thought of. The very fact that they put up those parameters helped Valenzuela stay focused on his pitching. The Dodgers would do the same thing with Hideo Nomo [during his own Nomomania experience] years later. And then you had Fernando's teammates sort of taking him under their wing to make him feel more comfortable."

One of those notable teammates was Rick Monday. "We respected Fernando," he recalled. "And quite frankly, he became our little brother. We didn't want anybody to mess with him. And for Jaime Jarrín to be there and to be able to interpret and let him know not just the words but to make sense of it all was extremely helpful. Fernando had to come out of his comfort level day after day. This was all new to him. It was new to many of us, too, but for him it was really fresh."

Monday noted how Dusty Baker, who spoke both English and Spanish, played important roles as big brother and advocate for Fernando, as well as with other young Latino Dodgers players. "Dusty could really break the ice and talk to someone in their comfort level instead of them having to come to him," Monday recalled about his fellow Dodgers outfielder. "For most of us, we could speak enough Spanish to either not starve, maybe get directions, maybe get slapped, and maybe get arrested! But finding out how a guy's doing and how he's feeling and things like that, that was something else. Dusty could go over and maneuver through a language and be able to reach out and touch someone like that. Fernando learned English very rapidly. I don't know how much he understood beforehand, but if you start looking and listening to the other interviews that he would do, after a while he was beginning to answer the question before it was actually finished being asked or not waiting for the interpretation by Jarrín."

The day before Fernando's Shea Stadium start, more than a hundred reporters crammed into the stadium's Diamond Club for a press conference that seemed more like one for a foreign dignitary than a baseball player. "It was *packed* in there," Brener recalled. "It was incredible. Fernando's popularity was second to none. There were all types of media—English, Hispanic. He didn't seek the limelight, but it found him."

For some other reporters on the "Fernando beat," they had descended on his hometown of Etchohuaquila to find out more about this mysterious pitching phenomenon. "This was before cable television, so you would have these newspaper reporters make pilgrimages to Mexico to file reports," Langill noted. "It was really the first time that a player's background had become relevant. He comes to the Dodgers and suddenly everybody wanted to know where he came from. So, in a role reversal, Fernando comes up to Los Angeles and every other journalist goes down to Mexico just to find out more about his hometown, his family, and anything else about his life story. Some people even wondered if he was really twenty years old. There was such a curiosity about him. Mexico is so close to Los Angeles, yet it seems so far away because something like this had never happened before. There had never been a star that came up from Mexico. The amazing thing was that nobody wanted to wait until the next game Fernando pitched to know more about him."

"I remember the late Stu Nahan at KNBC-TV going to Etchohuaquila because there was so much intrigue on Fernando," recalled Steve Brener. "Tommy Lasorda always joked that Fernando didn't have an actual alarm clock in Etchohuaquila—that his alarm was a *rooster*. But everybody was clamoring for Valenzuela stories, and the attention he was getting was just unbelievable. I can't recall another player who captured the [imagination] of the fans and the media the way he did."

The efforts of the media to find out anything at all on this relative unknown from nowhere anyone had heard of was eerily like the fictional Roy Hobbs character from the book-turned-movie *The Natural*, in which Robert Redford played the protagonist. In Valenzuela's case, because of all the doubts raised over how a twenty-year-old could have so much poise and command on the mound, the discovery of his elusive birth certificate prompted newspapers to reprint it, with one of them giving this caption: "Proof: Valenzuela Isn't 40."

"There was so much interest in Fernando in the beginning that I started getting media requests from everywhere—the phones would just light up at Dodger Stadium," said Brener. "Everyone wanted to know when Fernando would be pitching next. And this didn't just come from people in Southern California; this came from all the places on the road we would visit during the season. The interest in Fernando was rather rapid."

Earlier in the season, the shy and English-challenged Valenzuela had Dodgers coach Manny Mota and Dominican infielder Pepe Frías alternate in interpreting for him. But Claire was concerned that the job was taking time away from Mota's and Frías's on-field responsibilities, so he turned to the team's Spanish-language broadcast announcer Jaime Jarrín to assume the added duty of interpreting the English questions for Valenzuela in Spanish and then repeating Fernando's answers back to the media in English. "When Fernando came to the Dodgers, he couldn't speak *any* English," Jarrín remembered. "So one day Fred [Claire] came to me and said, 'Jaime, it's not right for us to be bothering the older players or the coaches to translate for Fernando. Since you work for the Dodgers and you go with the team everywhere, would you help us translate for Fernando?' I said, 'Of course, no problem. It would be my pleasure.' So that's how I started interpreting for him. I was the first interpreter in the history of the game. Before me, nobody ever interpreted for any player."

"It was clear that we needed somebody with Fernando at all times to handle [the media]," Claire explained. "And for me, Jaime was definitely the guy. Jaime was young and energetic, and it was a natural pairing of the two. Jaime played such a key role in making Fernando feel comfortable. So, having Jaime in that role took a lot of pressure off everybody else, because it really became a matter of meeting the media's high demands. The significant amount of coverage the Dodgers had at Dodger Stadium and elsewhere had just become something even more because of the phenomenon that was Fernando."

Jarrín, a future Ford C. Frick Award winner who would eventually be recognized as one of the game's legendary broadcasters, had already enjoyed remarkable success to that point in his career. An Ecuadorian who had moved to the United States on June 24, 1955 (ironically, the same day as Sandy Koufax's Major League debut) and who began calling Dodgers games four years later, he had already covered President John F. Kennedy's funeral and the Watts riots; filed dispatches from the Olympics; and reported on world championship boxing matches (including the "Thrilla in Manila" between Muhammad Ali and Joe Frazier), visits of foreign leaders with Presidents Lyndon Johnson and Richard Nixon, and Pope John Paul II's trip to the United States in 1979.

But despite more than two decades as a much-respected broadcaster and prominent journalist, it wasn't until the exposure he received as Valenzuela's interpreter during his press conferences in 1981 that he truly became a major media celebrity. "I have to recognize that Fernando helped me a lot because up until [Fernandomania], I may have been well known, but you would only hear something about my years of service with the Dodgers, and the Dodgers have always been a very popular team," Jarrín said. "People in Southern California knew exactly who I was not only because I did the games, but because I did a lot of public service work at the station, special events, as well as news events. But in New York, Atlanta, St. Louis, and other cities, they didn't know who Jaime Jarrín was. But when I started to interpret for Fernando, and we had press conferences everywhere we went, they slowly started knowing who I was, and that really helped me a lot in my career."

For those who knew Jarrín and his stellar work in the Dodgers' broadcasting wing of the press box, they were thrilled that his time in the spotlight had finally arrived. "Jaime worked in the same town as Vin Scully, and Vin was so universally known," Langill noted. "You might have appreciated Jaime's presence, but if you didn't speak Spanish, you didn't truly understand the magnitude of what he meant because you weren't able to enjoy his work. Now suddenly, Jaime becomes famous as an interpreter even though this is a guy that not only was a great baseball play-by-play announcer but was a qualified and distinguished award-winning news reporter who in 1958 was asked by the Spanish station [KFWB] to learn baseball and be able to announce it with one year's notice. It's a remarkable story."

Claire, like Jarrín and Langill, saw Fernando's emergence as a harmonic convergence of events for the broadcaster's career. "The Dodgers early on [after their move to LA], to the credit of Walter O'Malley, saw the need and potential of the [Spanish-speaking] market," Claire said. "This was something that just grew in such a quick and huge fashion with Fernando that things really propelled for Jaime and, without question, brought the Dodgers station KFWB to a totally different level. Jaime was perfect for that role. The words I would use to describe Jaime would be honesty, integrity, and professionalism. He is all those things. He's just a professional at the highest level and as far as one can be from self-promotion. He's someone with great skill. And all those reasons are why Jaime and Vin Scully have such a close association. We knew we needed someone there who understood the game, who understood Fernando, and who understood the needs of the media. And Jaime was the perfect person."

"I would describe him in the exact same mold as I would describe

Vin Scully in terms of being a gentleman, a thoroughly prepared professional, and someone who is eloquent and knows how to describe the moment," Langill added about Jarrín. "He also knows his huge impact with Dodger fans. . . . Jaime and Vin are both Hall of Famers, and any compliment I would have about Vin would be the same I would give to Jaime. There would be no difference in terms of the magnitude of who they are and their talent level."

Even many of the players themselves understand what Jarrín has meant in the annals of Dodgers broadcasting history. "Jaime Jarrín is the Vin Scully of Spanish broadcasting, and Vin Scully is the Jaime Jarrín of English broadcasting," is how Garvey glowingly described the two iconic Dodgers announcers. "They're that comparable."

As a result of the efforts from the Dodgers' publicity department and Jarrín, what could have been hectic and stressful press conferences for Valenzuela were for the most part smooth events. "They were pretty well organized and structured," recalled Lyle Spencer. "I thought Jaime handled everything beautifully. I don't think you can give him enough credit for helping Fernando along. He's a very calm and composed guy. You can never overlook his impact on Fernando. He was just another example of the right guy being there at the right time. The press conferences weren't bedlam—they were made up of just a lot of people who were curious. Fernando wasn't fancy with his answers because it wasn't his nature. He was willing to do it, but I don't think it was something he enjoyed. But he knew it was important, so he handled it like everything else—with dignity. But it was all new to him. He didn't know how to be like Don Sutton and answer a question with a five-minute response. So, his press conferences were interesting, but nothing particularly memorable. I don't remember him ever getting upset during them."

There were more than a few people who believed Fernando actually understood English fairly well during Fernandomania but that he preferred Jarrín do the talking for him, embracing some of the distance it created between him and the press. "Even in the early years, I think he knew more of the English language than he let on," Brener suggested. "It was just easier for him to talk in his native language. He understood when a reporter asked him a question in English, but Jaime would translate it and Fernando would reply in Spanish anyway."

The question that often was asked about Fernando was how he could be so supremely confident and in total command on the pitcher's mound yet so shy and mostly reclusive off of it. A 1985 *Sports Illustrated* piece revealed an episode Valenzuela encountered at the earliest stage of his Dodgers career that may help explain this dynamic:

> Valenzuela, too, has never forgotten an embarrassing incident that occurred at a spring training English class in 1980. Barely 19 and less than a year out of the Mexican Leagues, Valenzuela was so shy he would only smile at the instructor when she called upon him. The day's lesson was a simple drill on phrases used in ordering breakfast. When the instructor insisted that Valenzuela reply, Dodgers minor league instructor Chico Fernandez leaned over and whispered an answer in the trusting youngster's ear.
>
> "Taco," answered Valenzuela.
>
> The room, filled mostly with veterans, broke up laughing. Valenzuela left the class and never returned.

Even through his remarkable run of victories to this point of the 1981 season, other than the occasional meal with Jarrín, the hottest commodity in baseball spent much of his free time on road trips alone in his room watching television. Word was that his favorite programs to watch were cartoons, which helped him learn some English.

And back in Los Angeles, prior to moving into a room next to Mike Brito's swimming pool at his residence, Valenzuela stayed in a downtown hotel room dubbed "Fernando's Hideaway" by his teammates because they hardly saw him socially once he left the stadium. But even his wish for solitude gave way to a bout of homesickness, which is why he left the hotel life for one to be shared with Brito's family. However, Fernando soon learned that the anticipated privacy of living in Brito's quiet residential neighborhood could easily be breached. "People would wait outside my house to see him," Brito recalled. "There were *a lot* of girls. We would have to leave my home through the back by the pool. It was crazy, and I couldn't believe it all happened so quickly. It was just incredible."

As excited as everyone was with Fernandomania, the Dodgers organization resisted the temptation to throw him to the wolves in terms of media and team promotions. Instead, they respected Fernando's much-needed quiet time away from all the pandemonium.

*

Valenzuela fielded questions at two New York press conferences by giving mostly very short answers in Spanish—which were often followed by much longer versions Jarrín gave in English. "Jaime was there to protect Fernando and to give structure to his answers," Garvey recounted. "One time a reporter asked Fernando the question that a pitcher always gets—'How did you feel today?' Fernando, as usual, gave a six- or seven-word answer. But Jaime's translation went well beyond that. So I said to him later, 'Jaime, good job today. Man, you gave them two minutes. You filled a lot on that one.' And he just looked at me and smiled. Jaime was a crutch, basically. But even after Fernando started getting more and more Hispanic and international press, it didn't matter. Fernando was smart. He had a very high baseball IQ, but he was also very sensitive, so he did a lot of watching and listening."

Because of Valenzuela's shyness and modesty, the question of how much English he knew at that time was always up for debate—even by his own teammates. "I thought he understood a lot more English than people caught on to," Garvey said. "There was one inning, maybe three or four games into the '81 season, when Fernando couldn't get the ball over the plate and Tommy was riding him. As a first baseman, I never went to the mound. Number one, when Tommy was on the mound, it got a little ugly sometimes in terms of language. So this one time I called time and I went over to the mound to Fernando. I said to him, 'So, first of all, I think you're a lot older than you look. And, second of all, just keep throwing. Keep challenging [the hitter]. Don't try to pick. Just throw that ball, put movement on it, and let him pop it up or ground it out. Let's go—be *confident*.' [One] of his virtues was a quiet confidence on the mound. So he smiled, I patted him on the behind, and he got himself righted again, finished up the inning, and went on from there. So I could already sense that he understood more and could speak more English, but having Jaime answer the questions the first couple of years took a lot of pressure off him. So, in that sense, it was a tremendous asset to have Jaime as an interpreter to answer the tough questions that could be setups or loaded ones in a big market. It helped Fernando a lot."

But the ever humble Jarrín gave Valenzuela more credit than could be physically seen by others regarding the left-hander's handling of the media storm. "I remember this kid from Mexico with long hair and a little chubby taking baseball by storm," Jarrín said with a sparkle in his eyes while reminiscing about that chaotic, yet exhilarating, period. "But while he was very quiet and shy, he was also very confident, calm, and intelligent."

To a great degree, Valenzuela was extremely fortunate to be surrounded by four perfect storytellers to share on his behalf his amazing tale with an eager public. "Listening to Tommy, Vinnie, Jaime, and even that scout character [Mike Brito] running around with the cigar and fedora talk up Fernando's first starts of 1981, it was like right out of a movie," Langill said. "Fernando was more than glad to give up the microphone to any of them to talk on his behalf. And I think the more he was quiet, the more he just had this intrigue in terms of how wonderful a mystery he was. Because he wasn't really offering that much in terms of emotion, you just had to use your imagination to figure out what he was thinking. I've asked him on occasion several times if, at any point, he was nervous and whether he could believe the circumstances he was under at that time. He'll just shrug his shoulders. He still just keeps those things to himself. So the funny thing was you had the center of attention barely speaking, but you had the four other guys doing his talking for him. Tommy spoke Spanish, so that was a big help. For Scully, this wasn't his first rodeo, after having gone through his years with the 'Boys of Summer' [Brooklyn Dodgers] and then Sandy Koufax, so listening to his shock over what he saw with Fernando added a lot of credibility. And thank goodness this phenomenon put Jaime on the national stage, launching his career after twenty-two years, and he ends up in the Hall of Fame. And you had Brito getting the credit as the scout who discovered Fernando—talking him up the whole time."

All the media attention being bestowed upon a rookie pitcher after little more than a month's worth of starts might normally get under the skin of the veterans on a star-studded ball club like the Dodgers. Lasorda, the seasoned baseball man, was wary of this becoming a problem. "Lasorda got concerned that with Fernando having press conferences . . . the other pitchers would bark about it," Jerry Reuss recalled. "So Tommy called Dave Goltz, Burt Hooton, Rick Sutcliffe, and me into his office. He said, 'I want you to know that you're all going to have press conferences, too. Hooton started laughing and said, 'Tommy, you know that's not true. We're not going to have press conferences because no one wants to hear about us. We've been here for years and never had a press conference.

Now, if this has anything to do with Fernando, all the attention he's getting is fine by me because when they're asking him questions, that gives me the freedom to go out and do the things I need to do in order to pitch a ball game.' I echoed pretty much the same thing, telling Tommy, 'I don't care about a press conference. If it were me, I probably wouldn't want to do it because it takes away from what I need to do in order to be successful. So, you know, Fernando having them is okay by me.' Once Lasorda understood that, after hearing from two of the veteran pitchers on his staff telling him 'What do we care?' he got the message that we just worried about winning some ball games and letting that be that."

Aside from the well over two hundred press credentials given out for the game in New York, world famous sports artist LeRoy Neiman was on hand to sketch Valenzuela. Neiman was known for producing brilliantly colored expressionist paintings of established superstars like Tom Seaver, Muhammad Ali, and Julius Erving. So for him to come out to Shea Stadium to begin painting a pitcher about to make just his seventh big league start exemplified the sudden grip Valenzuela had on the sports world.

The game itself would prove to be a television ratings bonanza in the United States and throughout Latin America, with a Mexico City network's broadcasters calling the game off the same feed as the Dodgers' network. KTTV in Los Angeles drew a 47 percent share—numbers that a World Series game back in those days could only dream of approaching. And it wouldn't be just the first time that Valenzuela's family would get to see him pitch on television but the first time for other Latinos south of the U.S. border as well.

For teenaged José Mota, his first glimpse of Valenzuela pitching a big league game was in the Dominican Republic that night via what was then a novel means. "A friend of my dad's invited me and my brother to this establishment in the Dominican that had a satellite signal," Mota recalled. "In 1981 games were not televised every day like they are now. They were aired maybe once a week, and you had to go somewhere to watch it. And this was in the Dominican, where there was a lot of sports betting, so the friend said if my brother and I wanted to watch Fernando pitch, he had a way of getting the satellite signal down for it. For us, it was like a big Mexican party when he pitched. Everyone had a great time with the music and the nachos and the churros."

For a young Nomar Garciaparra, watching Fernando pitch that night—and other nights—was a true family affair. "It was an *event*," Garciaparra told me. "Fernando meant and still means an awful lot to me and my family and my culture. My aunt and uncle came over from Mexico, didn't speak good English, and weren't sports fans. But whenever I'd go over to their house, everyone had to be quiet when Fernando pitched. That's what it meant to them. I had been to their house numerous times and had never seen a sporting event on their TV, even with soccer being the sport of Mexico. I never noticed *any* sporting event on TV or on their radio until Fernando was pitching. So for me, growing up, I obviously knew the voice of Vin Scully—and know what he means to Dodger fans. But for my family, it was all about Fernando, and Jaime Jarrín was 'the voice' to us when it came to the Dodgers. Jaime's voice was the one I heard growing up more than any voice on radio. When I met Jaime, I was like, 'Oh my God!' I got to know him [as a fellow Dodgers broadcaster], and to call him my friend is an honor for me. He's one of the classiest individuals that you'd ever meet."

Coming into the Mets game, Valenzuela was the Major League leader in wins (6), shutouts (4), complete games (5), earned run average (0.33), and strikeouts (50). So it should have been a breeze for Valenzuela against such an inferior club, but the young man from a Mexican town of fewer than a thousand would now be performing under the bright lights of the biggest city in the country—and perhaps, at least initially, he felt the weight of the moment.

"The place was *packed*," recalled then-Mets reliever Jeff Reardon, who pitched three innings of relief in that game. "It was nice to have a full stadium, so in that respect everybody looked forward to facing Fernando even though he was a very tough pitcher. Every player knows when a guy's undefeated at that point of the season, but I don't think any one of us realized all the mania about him until the Dodgers came to Shea. But then we saw all those people, and we were like, 'Jesus, this guy's really packing them in!' He comes to New York and packs an extra thirty thousand fans into the stadium. That's pretty good for a guy all the way from Mexico."

At Shea, just as at Dodger Stadium and in ballparks the Dodgers had visited to that point in the season, Mexican flags were proudly waved, and many fans in the crowd wore sombreros. José de Jesus Ortiz, who is of Mexican descent and was the first Latino to serve as president of the Baseball Writers' Association of America, believed the Fernando phenomenon was unprecedented in its impact. "I really do believe Fernando's significance, in terms of what he did to give Mexicans a feeling of belonging, and of telling Americans that 'we're here,' was remarkable," he said. "More than anybody, he brought Mexicans out of the shadows in the United States, because if you went to Houston, all the Mexicans came out and you saw them for the first time in the Astrodome. You'd go to Shea Stadium, and if you didn't realize that Mexicans were all over New Jersey, New York, and Connecticut, you finally saw them. When Fernando would pitch at Wrigley Field, you had no idea that there were so many large enclaves of Mexicans in Chicago. You saw the same thing in Milwaukee and everywhere else around the league. People were like, *Oh my gosh, there are Mexican flags all over the stadium.* And it wasn't just LA or San Diego. People in San Francisco who were diehard Giant fans would change their outlook for one day when Fernando pitched against them because they knew what a friend and a mentor he had become for Mexicans. So he took us out of the shadows and introduced us to a country that didn't realize we were here in such large numbers."

In the Mets game, Fernando struggled early with his control but would manage to escape bases-loaded jams in the first two innings completely unscathed. "What was striking to me right away was how great he was under pressure," Lyle Spencer recalled. "Even in other games during that April and May run, where there were a lot of base runners, he would bear down and elevate his game. And he was just as good on the road as he was at home. Wherever he pitched, he was comfortable." Baker credited Lasorda and the coaching staff for allowing Valenzuela to work his way out of a tight spot. "Fernando and the other great pitchers, they figure out a way to get out of trouble," Dusty Baker said. "Nowadays, they don't let guys do that. I remember when I was ten years old, climbed a tree, and told my dad to call the fire department. He said, 'No, you figure out a way to get down yourself.' It's the same thing with pitching. Sometimes we don't let them try to pitch their way out of a tough situation."

The Dodgers' patience with Valenzuela was once again rewarded. From the third inning on, he continued to get in and out of trouble yet still didn't give up any runs. He would allow a total of seven hits and five walks over nine innings pitched and clearly got better and stronger as the game progressed. "We were amazed to watch him pitch," Reardon said. "He wasn't really overpowering, but his windup is what I remember the most. He deceived most of the hitters with that great screwball he'd throw. He was not your best-built pitcher out there, but he sure knew how to pitch."

Valenzuela would go the distance, striking out eleven in a 1–0 win. Fernando was now 7–0 with a microscopic 0.29 ERA following a remarkable fifth shutout of the young season. He had survived the media crush and a pesky Mets effort that night.

After the last out was made, Vin Scully was dumbfounded on the air. "I can't believe it," Scully said incredulously. "It is the most puzzling, wonderful, rewarding thing I think we've seen in baseball in many, many years. It is puzzling because after all these years looking at this game, I know how tough it is. I know how tough it was for even the best that ever played. And somehow this youngster from Mexico with the pixiest of smiles on his face acts like he's pitching batting practice in Mexico and turns in his fifth shutout. He is the talk of the baseball world in English, in Spanish, in any other language that's close in hand."

Fernandomania and the winning streak were alive and well—and a story made for Hollywood was heading back to Los Angeles.

An International Frenzy 11

> The Mexicans now saw someone with the same face, the
> same eyes, the same body, and the same complexion out on
> the field. That's how he became so saviorlike to them.
>
> —JOSÉ MOTA, Dodgers broadcaster and son of Manny Mota

The cover of the following week's edition of *Sports Illustrated* blared a single word, in block capital letters, beside an action photo of Valenzuela: "UNREAL!" By the standards of the time, landing on the cover of the esteemed magazine, with readership numbering in the millions, was the pinnacle for any athlete. The honor was reserved for the most remarkable athletic achievements, so for a rookie pitcher less than two months into a season to grace this hallowed publishing ground was nothing short of extraordinary. In fact, in the then twenty-seven years since the magazine's inaugural issue, it was unprecedented.

Fernando's image was everywhere. That same week, he would also adorn the covers of other longtime iconic publications, including like *The Sporting News*, *Baseball Digest*, and *Sport Magazine*. But despite the massive amounts of publicity he was receiving, Valenzuela hadn't changed one bit from the shy, reclusive ballplayer he had presented to the media to that point. And his humble nature served to endear him only further to his teammates. "The other guys loved him," Mark Langill said. "He fit right in with them because they realized that *Wow, this guy's on the cover of every magazine and he's just a normal guy.* You can make the comparison to Koufax in this respect because Sandy, from all accounts, was the same way in terms of being down-to-earth despite everybody following his every move."

With Fernandomania at a fever pitch, the return to Dodger Stadium for Valenzuela's eighth start of the season, on May 14 against the Montreal Expos—a Thursday night game—had been sold out for a week. Attendance for the game was 53,906, the most for one of the Dodgers' regular season games since 1974. Walk-up sales skyrocketed to more than 12,000. The Dodgers quickly hired ushers who spoke Spanish to accommodate the newest Latino fans.

"Guys on the team, particularly the white guys, who weren't being racist or nothing, but they said [the games Fernando pitched] were 'dark hair days' because there weren't as many blond or white people in the stands," Dusty Baker recalled. "Most of them were from Mexico, Guatemala, Salvador, Venezuela, and Puerto Rico. If you were Latin American, you came out to see Fernando. Fernandomania was real! It was the damnedest! It brought excitement to the stands, excitement to the Dodgers, and it even pumped up the *other* team!"

Chances were, if you were Chicano and didn't make it into the ballpark on days Valenzuela was pitching, you were watching on television with the sound down and listening to the Spanish-language radio broadcast by Jaime Jarrín. "It was like a misdemeanor if you were caught on the streets of Los Angeles if you were Mexican and there was a game [with Valenzuela] going on," actor Danny Trejo said in the *Los Angeles Times* docuseries *Fernandomania @ 40*. As a result, the ratings for the Dodgers' Spanish-language broadcasts nearly tripled when Fernando pitched.

José Mota recounted how Valenzuela had become a source of pride for the community in and around Dodger Stadium on days he pitched. "Fernandomania was unreal. If you went anywhere near Dodger Stadium or downtown LA, you started to see the sombreros, Mexican flags, and the Mexican outfits. It was an event. On Olvera Street [a historic street that attracts nearly two million visitors a year and pays homage to the city's Mexican heritage] there was such pride and joy. The people there were like, *Our Mexican hero has finally arrived! We have one now! We've been identified in soccer, in music with Linda Ronstadt and others, in movies, but now we have a baseball player at Dodger Stadium that we can go see pitch all summer long!* There was so much joy all throughout LA infiltrating down to the San Diego area, where there are obviously so many Mexican [fans]. For so many Hispanic families, they enjoyed baseball the minute Fernando walked out on the field. It was like they saw a savior. He was so much more than just a pitcher to them."

The venerable former *Los Angeles Times* sports editor Bill Dwyre was blunt in the powerful assessment he gave on *Fernandomania @ 40* when he said, "[Valenzuela] made the Dodgers seem more relevant to all communities. It was easier to forget about people being shoved out of their homes when Fernando was winning games. That's a very shallow statement, but I think it's true."

On the stadium's message board that evening, while the lineups posted for each team had the usual first and last names of the starters, Valenzuela was listed only as "Fernando." It was as if he were receiving the "Elvis" treatment on a glittering Las Vegas billboard: no last name required.

The flags fluttering in the Southern California breeze throughout the stands no longer just represented Mexico but also many other countries. "Every Latin American country seemed to be represented," recalled Baker. "Not only Mexico. I'm talking El Salvador, Nicaragua—there were so many different flags."

People were left to wonder, after his 7-0 start, if the bubble would ever burst. The media coverage at Dodger Stadium for this game rivaled the one in New York, with camera crews coming from as far away as Sweden. Fernando was now international news far beyond the borders of the United States and Latin America. When asked by a reporter, tongue-in-cheek, in the pregame press conference if he thought he would ever lose a game, the usually shy Valenzuela, after the question was interpreted by Jarrín, deadpanned in Spanish, "That would be very difficult, but not impossible." The room broke up in laughter over the good-natured braggadocio in his answer.

While Valenzuela and, for that matter, Jarrín had become media darlings, not all of the coverage of the press conferences was necessarily glowing. Fernando's expanding waistline was targeted by some reporters, with one writing, "Valenzuela's nickname should be Pauncho," with another penning, "Maybe he'll overdose on burritos and beer." Fernando's agent, Antonio De Marco, a Mexican immigrant himself, relayed to *Sports Illustrated* at the time that his client was taking it all in stride: "[Fernando's] very grateful to the media, even when they make fun of him." Furthermore, De Marco stated, "he heard they would be cold

An International Frenzy

and mean, but they've been just the opposite. They give him affection and love. Fernando's shy, but he wants to learn English; he's listening to cassettes and his pronunciation is very good."

The media madness was not limited to the sea of reporters at Dodger Stadium that night. The Dodgers' Spanish-language radio network, which had but two outlets before Fernandomania and none outside of the Los Angeles listening area, now had *twenty-seven* Mexican radio stations joining in.

By now, the merchandisers outside of the stadium were hard at work hawking everything from "El Toro" toys to Fernando T-shirts to record albums with odes to Valenzuela. One of the record albums was called *The Saga of Fernando*, released, ironically enough, on the Screwball Records label.

Further evidence that Valenzuela had achieved pop culture status and had captured the imagination of fans everywhere were various tribute songs written about him. A Mexican American father-and-son duo, Mark and Lalo Guerrero, wrote songs entitled "'Olé! Fernando" and "Fernando, el Toro."

Another local singer-songwriter, who called himself "Larry from Redondo," called in to radio station KABC to perform a Fernando song, which included this verse:

The batters come up but they're helpless.
The reason is simple and pure:
If his fastball should miss, I will promise you this,
That his scroogie will get them for sure.

There was no foreseeable end to the hysteria surrounding Valenzuela. In an effort to enhance community relations, the Los Angeles Police Department had ordered one hundred thousand Dodgers baseball cards that bore the LAPD insignia on the back to hand out to children in the areas they patrolled. However, the cards had been ordered early in the season, and now the fifteen hundred Valenzuela cards that had been printed were missing. After several days, two officers came forward—sheepishly admitting to hoarding the entire allotment of Fernando cards for the Little League teams each sponsored. The officers were forced to return the Valenzuela cards in exchange for those of other Dodgers players.

The same week, Fernando would take part in his first clinic as a part of the Dodgers' community outreach program. Clinics such as these typically drew around three hundred people. However, with the venue for this event being City Terrace Park, located inside a predominantly Chicano neighborhood, more than ten times the usual number showed up. A security presence more appropriate for a president escorted Valenzuela through the enthusiastic crowd to a podium. After saying a few words to the crowd and demonstrating to them how he throws his screwball, much of the crowd lined up for his autograph. After a good deal of time, Fernando, clearly overwhelmed by the demands for his signature, slipped away and tried to hide in a women's restroom until the crowd dispersed. It worked to an extent, though some of his more persistent fans found him in there and successfully secured his coveted autograph.

"The mania over Fernando was incredible," Langill recalled. "I remember Bobby Castillo telling me dealing with the crowds away from the ballpark was tough for Valenzuela. Bobby could go out at night and not have to worry about anything. But if you were a private person right off the bat like Fernando was, it made things even tougher than usual to deal with."

But on this night, Fernando was back in his safe and controlled environment—the Dodger Stadium pitching mound—gunning for his eighth consecutive victory. And unlike the first two rocky innings in his previous start against the Mets, when he loaded the bases in each frame, he was perfect in this one—six up and six down—against the Expos' mighty batting order.

But then in the top of the third, with one out, Montreal's light-hitting shortstop Chris Speier, who batted just .225 with two home runs in 1981, took Valenzuela deep to give the Expos a 1-0 lead. Remarkably, it was the first time in the season that Fernando trailed in a game. Observers were anxious to see how the young superstar would respond to his first real test of "adversity." They quickly found out. The next eighteen pitches would be strikes, including strikeouts of the next three batters he faced.

Baker is still amazed by how the unflappable Valenzuela responded to the home run. "Fernando taught me to 'take the air off the ball,'" he said. "I was a basketball player long before I was a baseball player. Most of the action in baseball and basketball happens in about a minute or less. [With some pitchers], you can go to the bathroom and come back and there's four runs on the board. Suddenly, it's *boom, boom, boom,* a walk, another hit, and it becomes a feeding frenzy. I'd be like, *How many pitches has this guy thrown this inning?* And he'd have like twelve. And four runs are in. But with Fernando, I'd be standing in left field, and I'd see him when things got tough, and he would just walk around the mound and rub the ball up and then start pitching again. He could take the air off the ball."

The Dodgers would take a 2–1 lead in the bottom of the sixth on a two-run single by Steve Garvey. Meanwhile, Valenzuela was positively dealing, yielding just a lone single (after Speier's home run) through the eighth inning. But then in the top of the ninth, needing just one out to finish off a two-hit masterpiece over the Expos, future Hall of Famer Andre Dawson squared up a Valenzuela fastball on a 1–2 count with a blast into the bleachers to tie the game.

The sellout crowd was stunned, but Baker would learn something about Fernando months after Dawson's home run. "I knew Fernando could *pitch* when he gave up that home run to Andre Dawson in May," Baker revealed. "Because the Expos were in the East, we didn't see them again until [the National League Championship Series] that October. The next time Fernando faced Dawson with two strikes in the count, he threw him a screwball [instead of a fastball] and struck him out. He had total recall of everything, which was so important with pitchers back then. You may not know the guy's name, but you remember your sequence of pitches, you know his walk. Because, back then, there were no reports when a guy got traded; you had to remember a walk or a windup or something about a player. And that's why I feel sorry for the kids now because they don't have full recall. They don't have it because everything's given to them. But that showed me something about Fernando. He later told me that he used what he remembered about the home run to strike Dawson out the next time he saw him."

Following the Dawson home run, Valenzuela settled down and retired the dangerous Gary Carter to end the Expos' half of the ninth. This was no small feat, considering that the future Hall of Fame catcher was in the prime of his career and regularly shined the brightest in big spots. Most managers would have removed a young starter after giving up a game-tying home run with two outs in the ninth—especially with a southpaw like Valenzuela about to face a power-hitting right-handed hitter like Carter. But everyone in the park, most importantly Tommy Lasorda, knew that Valenzuela was the best option the Dodgers had in that critical juncture of the game.

"Nothing seemed to faze this young man," Brener recalled about Valenzuela's composure. "He came from the small town of Etchohuaquila, and here he was in the big city of Los Angeles. Fifty-three thousand people. And, incredibly, nothing fazed him. He just went out to the mound, went to work, and did his thing. He was sensational."

The now tied ball game set things up for one of the Dodgers' other rookie stars, outfielder Pedro Guerrero, who, with a team-leading .505 slugging percentage while substituting for an injured Reggie Smith, had a chance to be the hero. And Guerrero came through big time, belting a dramatic home run to win the game.

Valenzuela had his eighth straight victory, the longest such streak by a rookie to start a season since the end of World War II, when Dave "Boo" Ferriss did it with the Boston Red Sox in 1945. But even more impressive than Fernando's eight straight wins was the dominance he displayed in getting there with his seven complete games and five shutouts. Additionally, over that stretch, he struck out sixty-eight and had allowed just four earned runs over seventy-two innings for an unworldly 0.50 ERA. And with his two hits in this latest victory, he was now batting a team-leading .360, albeit with far fewer at bats than the regular position players. "Fernando's start was unprecedented," Claire said. "It was unmatched in not just Dodger history, but *Major League* history."

For a pitcher who had to earn a spot in the rotation out of spring training, his performance was nothing short of a fairy tale. But as awe-inspiring as it all was, the win over Montreal would prove to be the apex of Valenzuela's miraculous run, as he would lose the first game of his career in his next start at Dodger Stadium, against the Philadelphia Phillies, 4–0. While he certainly pitched well enough to pick up a ninth straight win—yielding just three hits over seven innings—it simply wasn't to be.

Fernando, true to form, showed little reaction, much less any outward disappointment, in the postgame press conference. "I knew [the streak] had to end," Valenzuela told the throng of reporters through interpreter Jarrín after the game. "I'm not sad. I knew it was going to happen sometime."

The muted response left even those closest to him to wonder what he was really feeling. "I would love to have known what was really going on inside of him," Rick Monday pondered four decades later. "Was it a volcano? Was it a hurricane? Was it a calm sea? To this day I'm not sure. But whatever it was, it worked for him."

Mike Brito, who knew Valenzuela as well as anyone in baseball back then, believed what people saw in Fernando was what you got—no more and no less. "Nothing upset Fernando," the super scout said. "He never showed much emotion. If he has any emotion, only he knows it. He always took it easy, and the attention [during Fernandomania] never went to his head."

On this night, even one of his most loquacious supporters, Lasorda, was short of words. "He had good stuff," the manager told the media. "He lost. We knew he would sometime."

Perhaps a column in the next day's *Los Angeles Times* described the situation best: "The ranks of the immortals, already slender, were reduced by one Tuesday night. Fernando Valenzuela is human after all."

The streak may have been over, but the fervor of Fernandomania lived on.

Manias   12

An excessive enthusiasm or desire; an obsession.

—*Oxford Languages Dictionary*

A few weeks into the season, the mania over Valenzuela was unprecedented. Kellogg's would even soon sign a deal to put his smiling face on a box of cornflakes. But while Fernandomania is unquestionably the most prominent of all baseball-related manias, it was hardly the first in popular culture. Going back to the seventeenth century during the Dutch golden age, tulipmania was in full bloom; prices for bulbs reached extraordinary heights before eventually collapsing after several years. In more recent times (the 1960s), there was Beatlemania—an extreme enthusiasm for the band that created a frenzy among its millions of fans worldwide.

In the second half of the twentieth century, baseball featured three manias—one before Fernando, one for him, and one after his—that captured the imagination of fans like no others.

In 1976 Mark "The Bird" Fidrych, a Detroit Tigers nonroster invitee out of spring training who only pitched one inning through mid-May that season, took the baseball world by storm by then going 9-2 (all nine victories were complete games) with a 1.78 ERA over the next two months—great enough for him to be named the starting pitcher for the American League at that summer's All-Star Game, to be played in Philadelphia. He became just the second rookie to start a Midsummer Classic. But what attracted far more attention than his success was how he talked to the baseball, pranced about the mound after each opposing hitter's at bat, and manicured the mound by patting it down with his hands. He was built like and acted like a big bird—hence the nickname. Although there was never a formal term used to describe the delirium over Fidrych—though we'll call it "Birdmania" here for the sake of argument—there was no mistaking that his '76 campaign qualified as a mania before injuries soon put an end to his brief career.

Nearly two decades later, in 1995, there was "Nomomania," named for Hideo Nomo, a Dodgers pitcher who came to Los Angeles as an already-established Japanese hurler, having starred in the Nippon Professional Baseball League. With a tornado-like windup and delivery, he burst onto the Major League Baseball scene in his first season to earn the honor of National League starting pitcher in that summer's All-Star Game. While he would go on to have a fine career, which included pitching two no-hitters and twice leading the Major League in strikeouts, he would never reach the heights of success or create the level of hysteria he did in his first year with the Dodgers.

Not surprisingly, all three pitchers won Rookie of the Year Awards in their respective inaugural Major League seasons. But more important, they each had a profound social impact that is still felt today.

As far as the influence each had on baseball, Fidrych's innocence and sheer love of the sport served as a breath of fresh air at the outset of the free agency era, when the perception of player greed had deeply sullied the purity of the game for many of its most ardent fans. It was indeed like the jolt that Valenzuela gave Major League Baseball during the strike season of 1981, when players and owners again grappled over money. To say that Fidrych *dominated* baseball coverage in the summer of '76 cannot be emphasized enough. Even players in the National League, like Dusty Baker, felt the tremors and aftershock of the volcanic games that "The Bird" pitched that year. "During that [late 1970s] era, to me, the greatest impact on the game by any player was from Mark 'The Bird' Fidrych," Baker stated. "I didn't really get to see him play because there were no interleague games back then, but the hype and everything I heard about him—how he pitched, how he excited people—was amazing. He had a similar impact as Fernando in that respect."

One person who not only observed Fidrych pitch but also got a rare glimpse of him on a personal level was Lyle Spencer. "The only thing comparable to Fernandomania that I experienced was with Fidrych," Spencer explained. "I was there one night [in '76] in Detroit when he beat the California Angels with a complete game. He was so dominant.

There were usually ten to fifteen thousand fans at Tiger Stadium games, but because it was Fidrych, the place was completely jam-packed—a capacity crowd. It felt like a night very similar to what Fernando was doing in '81. Fidrych was completely outgoing—an eccentric. He did all the patting down of the mound, talking to the ball, and everything else, but I do think it was all genuine. It wasn't staged. He wasn't doing that for any purpose I don't think—it was just who he was. We had never seen anything like this guy before. So after the game I'm sitting there with him, just him and me, in the dugout, and he's got the headphones on doing an interview with the TV guys upstairs. I look out of the dugout and noticed nobody's left the stadium. It was still packed. This was ten or fifteen minutes after the game ended. He finishes the interview, and I asked him, 'What's going on?' And he said, 'Check this out.' So, he jumps up out of the dugout, goes out on the field, waves his cap to all the different corners of the stadium, and the crowd roared—and only then did they start leaving. That was unlike anything I had ever experienced.

"Like Fernando, Fidrych turned out to be the most normal, down-to-earth guy you could ever meet," Spencer continued. "I *loved* that guy. We really bonded. We had similar attitudes, and I even kind of looked like him with the Afro then. So after the game he won we went out to a restaurant/bar called the Lindell Athletic Club. Of course, it's jammed with fans. And people were coming up to him, and he treated fans like they were his friends. He did not separate himself from people. Fernando had the same kind of fundamental kindness and generosity about him, and that's why, when he came along, I could reference that night with Fidrych. And that was the only night I had spent with Fidrych because I wasn't actually doing the baseball beat—I was covering hockey then—but I would take an occasional trip covering the Angels. So my experience with Fidrych was all by chance."

The Tigers, who finished in fifth place in a then six-team American League East, would draw nearly a million and a half fans in '76—registering the fourth-highest attendance total in the twelve-team league—pretty much solely because of Fidrych.

It wouldn't be a stretch to believe that on some level "The Bird" had saved the game. "It was not a great time for baseball," Spencer recalled. "They were losing fans at that time to football, and the NBA was starting to gain in popularity. And people were upset about money intruding on baseball. *Big* money. It doesn't seem big now, but it was then. Fidrych absolutely—100 percent—helped save the game."

As a result, Fidrych wasn't packing just Tiger Stadium but also ballparks throughout the American League. "Very few players had the universal respect [that Fernando received], and it was the same way with Fidrych," Mark Langill suggested. "With both of them, it was bigger than baseball. They didn't have the types of personalities that you could manufacture. And even though they were complete opposites in personalities, Fidrych and Valenzuela were true to themselves. And the fans saw that. No matter how much in the spotlight you put them in, they were still going to be their own person. That was the great part of it all."

But while Fidrych was one of the game's great characters, in the same vein as Dizzy Dean decades earlier, shaking hands with everyone—even police officers, umpires, and batboys—on the field after a victory, Valenzuela seemingly couldn't get off the field and into the clubhouse quickly enough. Thus, the demeanors of the two pitchers couldn't have been more different, but the two were equals in invigorating the game and distracting fans from the greed and negativity that surrounded it.

With Hideo Nomo, the first Japanese-born player in the Major Leagues, his greatest impact on the game was a cultural one. "I never sensed Nomomania reached the overall level of Fernandomania because *nothing* did," Spencer opined. "Fernandomania was a full-on festival every time he pitched. I think Nomomania was definitely 'a thing,' but its importance was opening doors [to other Japanese players] to play in the Major Leagues—just as Fernando did [for Mexican players]. While not on the same level, Nomo was obviously important. He opened doors for Koreans to play here, too, starting with guys like Chan Ho Park [the Majors' first South Korean-born player]."

Remarkably, Valenzuela, Nomo, and Park were all signed and started their careers with the Dodgers—further proof of the organization's longtime trailblazing efforts in promoting diversity and breaking through barriers, an effort that began with the promotion of Jackie Robinson to the big leagues in 1947. "Even though Hideo, who I signed, had been pitching professionally in Japan for several years," Fred Claire said, "players weren't coming from Japan to play Major League Baseball. Signing Hideo broke a barrier and set the stage for other [Asian] players. In the case of Fernando, other players had come from Mexico—like

Bobby Ávila—but the reaction of the Hispanic fans for Fernando was classic. When you think about players from other countries, you certainly had the great Roberto Clemente, but there were players from Puerto Rico before Roberto, and you've had great players from the Dominican Republic like Ramón and Pedro Martinez and Juan Marichal before them. But with Hideo and Fernando, these were epic stories in the baseball world. And the two were so much alike from the standpoint of their personalities. Both were very quiet. But they also both had a lot of confidence in their abilities."

Claire sometimes reminisced about a pledge he made to Nomo when he first signed him to a Dodgers contract—and the self-assuredness the pitcher showed him that day. "I can remember sitting in my office, in January of '95 [before Nomo's first season], negotiating with Hideo's agent Don Nomura and how he was pushing for a Major League contract. I said, 'Major League contracts are earned, not given.' I asked Nomura to explain that to Hideo—which he did. And I could see Hideo nodding, and then Don said, 'Hideo has a question. He asked if he signs with you, Fred, will he be given a chance [to make the club]?' I said, 'Don, if Hideo signs, I can assure you he will be given an excellent chance. And, furthermore, I won't sign another pitcher the rest of the off-season.' I was confident in saying that, because I didn't have any money left to sign anybody else anyway. But I also thought that might help reassure Hideo, though, strikingly, he had a quiet confidence about himself. You could see it. He was like, *I have done this. I will do this.* And in many respects, Hideo was taking somewhat of a greater risk than we were—or even greater—because he had been a star in Japan, and he could have stayed there. I always felt in my own mind that Hideo was willing to take everything he had, put it on the line, and say, *I'll show you what I can do.* Fernando did that, too. There were great similarities between the two. I was so fortunate to have been there to see both during their time [in Los Angeles]."

In terms of box-office appeal, Valenzuela's first twelve starts at Dodger Stadium in 1981 were sellouts and his road starts attracted an average of nearly fifteen thousand more fans than Dodgers games in which he didn't pitch—a staggering differential. Meanwhile, Nomo's drawing ability, while impressive, didn't meet Fernando's lofty impact at the gate. A Nomo start in 1995, when he began the season with a remarkable

ERA of just 1.93 through his first fifteen Major League outings, brought in "only" an average gain of around five thousand spectators, both at home and away.

"It's hard to compare *anybody* to Fernando," opined Ken Gurnick, who reported on both Valenzuela and Nomo throughout his four decades of covering Dodgers baseball. "He was one of a kind. Nomo is a tough comparison to make because he was already a superstar in Japan—a professional—and by the time he came over here, he was twenty-six years old and had five or six years under his belt—almost half a career. Fernando didn't have that age or experience when he got called up. So it's an unfair comparison there, because they came up at different stages of their careers. But there was that same kind of cultural worship and respect for both."

In the final analysis, one could say Valenzuela was a hybrid of the innocence of Fidrych, as well as the unabashed joy they both delivered to baseball fans, and Nomo's far-reaching cultural influence. Fernando was a crossover, making his overall impact and contribution to Major League Baseball and society the most significant of the three iconic players.

Mr. Valenzuela Goes to Washington   13

While it can be debated that the apex of Fernandomania occurred when Valenzuela notched his eighth straight victory and appeared on the *Sports Illustrated* cover in mid-May, it would be hard to argue if some believed the peak of the phenomenon occurred on June 8—an off day for the Dodgers. It was on that afternoon that perhaps the most glorious chapter of Fernando's storybook season transpired. Under the heading of "Only in America," the rookie pitcher from the tiny Mexican village of Etchohuaquila with just three months of big league experience was President Ronald Reagan's guest of honor at a White House state luncheon honoring Mexican president José López Portillo. Mexican immigration was a major political issue for Reagan early in his first term, and it was his administration's hope that the luncheon could help soothe some of the tensions over Mexican workers living in the United States during that period.

Accompanied by Jaime Jarrín and Antonio De Marco, Valenzuela finally displayed some astonishment over the whirlwind events that had taken place in his life in such a remarkably short period of time. "It is like a fairy tale story, with the fact I am in the Major Leagues first," he told reporters prior to his flight to Washington. "I never dreamed I'd be with the Dodgers. Since they signed me, I'd been longing to come to the Major Leagues. The success I have had at the beginning is like a fairy tale. All the press and commotion are something out of this world. I am so deeply emotional—it is hard to explain." Then, after arriving at the White House, he beamed, "I'm very proud, and I'm very honored, to be invited by the president of the United States. And it's doubly important for me because we have my president here, also, and I'm looking forward to seeing both of them."

"Fernando was usually quiet and shy, and that was one of the few times I remember him being really excited," Jarrín recollected. "Being at the White House with Fernando and Antonio De Marco, his agent, was my *greatest* experience. I had been in the White House twice before that, so I knew what it meant to be there. When you are walking through the White House, something very unique, something very special surrounds you. I can't describe the feeling that you really feel when you go there. When I went with Fernando, it was my greatest experience because, for one thing, I saw this kid, just nineteen years old from Mexico—no English, a little bit chubby, long hair—being in the [center of] attention of the most important people in the country in those days—President Reagan, then–Vice President George H. W. Bush, Secretary of State Alexander Haig, Secretary of Defense Caspar Weinberger. So you had probably the most powerful people in the world there waiting for this kid to sign a baseball or something else from them. That was an experience I will never, ever forget."

Reagan and his Cabinet members were hardly the only ones who sought Valenzuela's attention that day. Scores of representatives from both sides of the political aisle wanted an autograph or, perhaps even more important to their livelihoods, to have their photo taken with the Mexican pitcher to take back to their home states to show their Latino constituencies. And it wasn't like it was a slow day around the White House. Haig, as excited as he was to meet Valenzuela, was dealing with the media's questions over whether the United States would cut off military aid to Israel after that country's bombing strikes against an Iraqi nuclear reactor. The notoriously tough-as-nails Haig dodged the press inquiries long enough to enjoy a lengthy lunch with the two presidents and the three guests from Los Angeles. But as uncanny and dreamlike as the White House visit seemed, the feeling held by many within the Dodgers organization was that Fernandomania simply had no limits.

"It didn't seem surreal at all," Fred Claire recalled. "The story that was unfolding was of such a national magnitude. And certainly, if anyone understood Hollywood, President Reagan *understood* Hollywood. So I was never like, *Oh my goodness, the White House!* I never had that feeling at all. It was just, with all due respect, just another major point in the journey wherever Fernando went—whether it was Houston or New York or San Francisco or Chicago. With all the major press conferences, the White House trip didn't strike me as something that was out of the question."

Reagan, of course, had made his imprint in Hollywood over many years as a lead actor in motion pictures and then later as the president of the Screen Actors Guild. But he was also a huge baseball fan, with one of his most famous acting roles being his turn as the epileptic Hall of Fame pitcher Grover Cleveland Alexander in *The Winning Team* (1952). Prior to embarking on an acting career, he had worked as a sports broadcaster for WHO radio in Des Moines, Iowa, during the 1930s. Reagan would re-create Chicago Cubs games by reading slips of paper on which a telegraph operator had transcribed plays sent by Morse code. Legend has it that in a contest between the Cubs and the Cardinals, the communication line to the game went dead, but rather than lose his radio audience Reagan improvised a streak of foul balls that lasted nearly *twelve minutes* until the wire came back. Reagan would share this amusing story with audiences for the rest of his life.

"Ronald Reagan was a Dodger fan," Steve Brener said. "And Tommy [Lasorda] had a great relationship with the Reagans, so I'm sure Reagan was following everything that was going on with the Dodgers and Fernando. Valenzuela was the talk of the nation. Everybody was talking about him, so that was a rather impressive time."

De Marco, a former actor who had emigrated from Mexico, also had ties to President Reagan, having worked on his first political campaign in California in the mid-1960s. He had since gotten completely out of politics to focus on a career as an entertainment producer and film distributor—while representing Valenzuela as his business adviser. He also acted as a mentor to the twenty-year-old phenom—looking out for him in formal situations like this day at the White House. However, Fernando proved to be as unflappable at the presidential luncheon as he was on the pitcher's mound. "I think *I'm* the one who's supposed to help Fernando," De Marco told *The Sporting News* shortly after the White House visit. "So, when President Reagan lifted the champagne glass for a toast, I was helping to make sure Fernando had the right glass. He had the right one, all right. But I didn't. I had the wineglass. So, who's helping whom? I probably learn more from Fernando than he learns from me."

A strong case can be made that Fernando's visit to the White House was far more than the friendly meet-and-greet that it certainly was. It may have helped pave the way for the Immigration Reform and Control Act that President Reagan would sign five years later. According to a *Washington Post* piece in 2014, "The IRCA granted legal status to individuals residing in the United States without legal permission who met certain conditions; this provision of the law applied only to individuals who had entered the country before January 1, 1982. Ultimately, 2.7 million individuals were granted legal status under the law." It was widely believed that Valenzuela's White House visit and his backstory may have raised Reagan's awareness of an immigration issue he had been all too familiar with when he was governor of California. While it's unknown if Reagan actually discussed immigration issues with Valenzuela during the nearly three-hour luncheon, there was no denying that Fernando was all too familiar with the topic—and could speak to them (albeit through an interpreter). Nevertheless, Chicano historians give credit perhaps where it's due, referring to what preceded the legislation as the "Fernando Factor."

What the "Fernando Factor" may have also accomplished in more immediate terms was to ease Mexican immigration into the United States. One of the beneficiaries of this shift was Teresa Romero, who arrived in California from Mexico in 1982—at the height of Fernandomania—and ultimately became a living, breathing example of the American Dream by becoming the president of a large labor union, the United Farm Workers. "When I arrived in California, I was absolutely aware of Fernando," Romero told me. "I never met him, but, like Cesar Chavez, he seemed very humble, hardworking, and likable. I enjoy sports, but when it comes to baseball, I enjoy going in person. But when Fernando Valenzuela pitched a game, I would watch him on television. He was someone who had the charisma, the humbleness, obviously the talent, and I would watch him at every opportunity. And I wasn't the only one—my family members in Guadalajara all knew about him, too. In Mexico my parents would talk about how everybody was talking about Fernando, saying how good he was. Everybody was so proud about how he was pitching for the Dodgers. The entire country of Mexico was talking about him with pride and happiness that somebody from their country had become such an important figure."

Romero then relayed how she saw Valenzuela as a symbol of Mexican hope—a role model. "When you see someone you can relate to, when you see a simple, humble human being, I was very proud that he had accomplished what he did," Romero remarked. "He affected us Mexicans in a very positive way. At that point, I had just come to the United States and was very proud, as a Mexican, how Fernando was bringing a different, polished image to the world. And he was appealing to the younger Mexicans—as well as the Latino population in general. We, as human beings, especially when it comes to sports, there is always somebody who we idolize—be it in basketball, football, baseball, or any sport. But if you ask me as a Mexican, with Fernando, the appeal was that he was somebody like me who spoke Spanish and some English with an accent. I could relate to him and all the immigrants from Mexico because, at some level, Fernando was experiencing the change of being in another country at the same time I was. But it's mostly being able to relate because he looked like me—because he's from Mexico like I am. It's different when we talk about the Tom Bradys, Magic Johnsons, or Kobe Bryants of the world."

Romero's initial assessment of Valenzuela's character was on point. Just a week before the White House visit, he had visited with a terminally ill Mexican teenager who had less than a month to live. Valenzuela granted the boy's dying wish of having his picture taken with him. And Fernando had agreed to begin doing public service radio spots to encourage kids to stay in school—mostly targeting Spanish-speaking Mexican American children in Southern California. After just a few short months in the limelight, Valenzuela was already using his celebrity to set a good example for youth, both in the United States and in Mexico. He had become an ambassador of goodwill.

Following his White House visit, Valenzuela, together with Jarrín and De Marco, took a flight to rejoin the Dodgers in St. Louis for their series against the Cardinals. Upon entering the visiting clubhouse, a few of his wisecracking teammates had just one question for him: "Just how many Ronald Reagan autographed pictures did it take to get one Fernando?"

Struck Out   14

As Fernando's significance [added] the culture of the Hispanic player
to the game, Marvin Miller changed the face of economics in it.

—STEVE GARVEY

The unthinkable was becoming a reality. The prospect of a baseball
strike that would interrupt one of the most thrilling seasons in years—
and stifle a sport that had reached an all-time high in popularity both in
the United States and globally—was looming large. And in Los Angeles,
that possibly meant that Fernandomania would stall—at least for a time.

"It wasn't easy," recalled Jerry Reuss, the Dodgers' player representative, of the labor strife. "The challenge for me was to compartmentalize
everything that I could. And once I understood what the responsibilities
were, then I could keep the labor issues on one side and then focus on
pitching on the other. That way I didn't have to mix them. So, it worked
okay for me, but it was tough."

Reuss's primary responsibility was to keep the players informed of
any developments in negotiations between Marvin Miller, who was
executive director of the Major League Baseball Players Association,
and the owners' chief labor negotiator, Ray Grebey. The major issue
at hand was the owners' demand for compensation when losing a free
agent to another team—a form of compensation that players believed
would adversely affect the value of the free agency market. But even as
little progress was made in the talks and tensions rose to a fever pitch,
the Dodgers and the rest of baseball marched on.

Fresh off Fernando's White House visit and before the second-largest
crowd at St. Louis's Busch Stadium all season long, Valenzuela pitched
masterfully in his June 11 start against the Cardinals—allowing just three

hits over seven innings. But a George Hendrick inside-the-park home run in the very first inning was all St. Louis needed in a 2-1 victory. The loss cut the Dodgers' lead in the NL West to just a half game over the Cincinnati Reds. With the players going on strike that night, it would prove to be the last game the Dodgers—or any other team—would play for two months.

It would be a lost summer for baseball; the strike would force the cancellation of 713 games—a staggering 38 percent of the schedule—and gut the middle part of the regular season.

As painful as it was financially and career-wise for the Major League players, the strike proved, somewhat ironically, to be a blessing in disguise for the Dodgers' prospects of returning to serious October baseball. The Dodgers were banged up at the time, and their fragile hold on first place could have easily slipped away without a work stoppage.

Steve Garvey, who was in the midst of his National League record consecutive game streak that had begun on September 3, 1975, could barely grip a bat. "If you had to have a lockout, it was a good time both personally and for the team," he told me. "In that last game in St. Louis, I had checked my swing and strained my wrists. I told Tommy [Lasorda], 'If I was you, with Reginald [Smith] on the bench, you should pinch-hit for me because I can't swing the bat like I should.' And Tommy looked back [at Smith], because he knew if I told him something like that, then, yeah, there's something wrong."

Lasorda would pull Garvey and put in Smith in the ninth inning of this one-run game with the Cardinals' future Hall of Fame closer Bruce Sutter on the hill. Garvey, a player who lived for big situations like this one—and made a living at thriving in them—was seriously concerned about the injury and his streak. "So the game's over," Garvey recalled, "and we're all waiting around before hearing that we're going on strike. Then I looked up, thanking the Lord. I thought, hopefully, the strike was going to be five days or, at most, a couple of weeks. But it turned out to be two months. I put my wrist in just a regular elastic-type of clasp. After we came back from the strike, I was 100 percent better."

The other notable Dodgers star who needed a break—albeit not an eight-week one—was Valenzuela himself. Although he pitched well in that final game against the Cardinals, Fernando had hit a rough patch—

losing two of his previous three decisions. In fact, in losses to the Atlanta Braves and Chicago Cubs—both road games—he didn't make it past the fourth inning and yielded seven earned runs in each outing. His 8-0 start with the microscopic 0.50 ERA to begin the season had somewhat ballooned to a 9-4 record with a 2.45 ERA. But even after the recent losses, he was still tied for the National League lead in wins and was first in innings pitched, complete games, shutouts, and strikeouts, while his ERA still ranked seventh best in the Senior Circuit.

To better focus on his pitching and get back on track, Valenzuela had suspended his press conferences. "He never admitted there was any pressure from the press," Antonio De Marco told *The Sporting News* that summer. "He didn't mind the interviews. He understood. He said he was tired sometimes, but not mentally, not because of the press conferences. He doesn't blame the media for anything that happened. He's unflappable in any situation."

Instead, it was Valenzuela's heavy workload on the mound that was clearly starting to have an effect on his performance. For Fernando, the break was welcome. "I've always maintained that [the] strike helped Fernando," Mark Langill offered. "He is still the only player since 1945 to win his first eight starts. And to have seven of them be complete games and to go nine innings in the other game, that's a workload suddenly approaching Koufax in the '60s. And I don't know if you necessarily have a happy ending in '81 if that pace is maintained throughout an entire season. I don't know if a guy in his first full year in the Majors could have sustained that pace. As far as the trust that Tommy had in him, it was obviously a compliment. But that's a whole lot of innings to ask of a rookie pitcher."

But while the work stoppage would allow the Dodgers to reset and heal, the backlash from baseball fans was swift and severe. The United States, mired in a serious economic downturn triggered by tight monetary policy to fight mounting inflation, was in no mood for millionaire players and owners to squabble over money. The fans' ire was split fairly evenly. There were those who blamed the players for striking during the regular season instead of waiting until after the season to work out any labor issues with the owners. And there were others who believed the owners had provoked the players into striking by trying to put an end to the binding arbitration process whereby an arbitrator was, more and more, siding with a player's higher salary demands than the lower offers coming from the team's owner.

No matter which side fans were on, there was no debate over the players' allegiance to Miller, who had served as director of the MLBPA since 1966 and had reshaped the players' union into one of the strongest in the country. Many in baseball believe Miller should be on the Mount Rushmore of the most impactful people in baseball history—right there alongside Babe Ruth and Jackie Robinson. His greatest legacy, without question, was his work in putting an end to the reserve clause, which had previously bound a player to his team for all eternity, and in ushering in free agency in the process.

"He was brilliant," said Bill Lee, the talented and eccentric former Red Sox and Expos pitcher who served as a head player representative for both the American and National Leagues. "Back in '72 [at the time of the first players' strike, which didn't result in the cancellation of any games], his first words to us were, 'The relationship between players and owners is always going to be *adversarial*.' And the greatest thing about that was 80 percent of the ballplayers did not know what that word meant! But anyway, Marvin Miller was the most powerful man and the right man for the job at that time. He basically said, 'You guys have to do it yourselves. I can't do it for you. You've got to stick together.' It was the old 'either hang together or you hang separately thing.' And his tone—he never got angry. He never got mad. He never belittled the players in their position. And we became a very strong union because of him."

Lee, as intelligent as he is humorous, once famously referred to the advent of baseball's free agency era as its own emancipation proclamation in how it enabled players the freedom to change teams. "It's 'Workers of the World Unite,'" the fierce defender of unions said.

Out of respect for Miller, the iconic union head, Lee made the trip from his home in Vermont to Cooperstown to attend the 2021 Hall of Fame ceremony in which Miller was inducted posthumously. "I was in the press rows," Lee said. "And every time I heard a good point, I would raise my hand in solidarity just like Lee Evans did at the 1968 Mexico Olympics" (to protest racism, Evans had given a Black power salute during the medals ceremony).

Bill Lee was hardly alone among his peers in terms of the respect and affection he felt toward Miller. "If I was in agreement with how he handled the [1981 strike], I was lockstep," Rick Monday said. "That's because I had been on those committees in New York in the past—being not just in the room but across the table. Things were said back and forth, and Marvin told us ahead of time, 'Don't take any of it personally. This is all negotiating. There's going to be a lot of fluffing of the feathers.' And when we broke for lunch the first day, we came back and before we went into the room, Miller goes, 'Okay, here's the deal. We're going to get denials this afternoon of things we've already talked about. And I don't want you to blink. I don't want you to say anything. I'm just telling you this is what's going to happen. And it's going to be a different scenario on what the other side is going to say we even talked about this morning. It's fluffing of the feathers. We have some other issues we're getting closer on. But I don't want anyone to get mad. I don't want you to throw your pens or anything else. They're going to test all of you.'

"I had great admiration and respect for the man in what he was able to do, but more so with the way he conducted the meetings that we had with the different teams," Monday continued. "Nothing was hardline. It was, 'Hey, guys, here are the issues. Here's our stance. Here's their stance. Here's the probabilities. And, at some point, we're probably going to have to make a decision between this and this and this.' Miller was always open to listening to people. But his knowledge of what was going on was impressive. He was a very bright man and he heard everything that we said."

Garvey was even more passionate when reminiscing about Miller: "Back when he came and joined the union, it was a time where we needed a strong, knowledgeable leader. And if you look at all he accomplished, he essentially changed the business of sports. He should have been in the Hall of Fame the year after he retired."

Garvey then touched on the reasons why the baseball establishment waited until after Miller's death to enshrine him in the Hall of Fame. "You could see the prejudice against him. It seems it was a great testimony to how that traditional business and ownership of baseball felt about the emergence of the union and agents. My first agent was Jerry Kapstein in '74. You could really see the nervousness [from team executives]. They weren't used to dealing with agents. And they didn't really know what to expect, but they knew free agency was coming, and they knew agents were there to stay. So along with Marvin Miller, the emergence of the agent, and then the freight train that was coming called free agency, it started to change the whole economics and business of the game."

Dusty Baker recalled how ugly things got for Miller as the union head. "You know how many *death threats* that he had? The negative comments?" Baker asked me rhetorically. "We were told then that if the players kept insisting on making more money that the players were going to drive the game broke. And that was *forty years ago*. Does the game feel broke to you?! The [salaries] today are mind-boggling to me. And I have no jealousy or envy at what the players are making now. *Zero*. And I don't know where it's going to end. All I know is you got the most intelligent businessmen in the world in the game, and I don't know any boss, unless [a worker] is on commission and sales, that's going to pay an employee more than he pays himself. So my question is, *How much is the boss making?*"

*

As the strike went from days to weeks to more than a month, tensions began running high within the ranks of several teams—including the Dodgers. Players' livelihoods were being compromised by the strike, and a lot of misinformation and rumors were flying around, which only fueled in-fighting and strife among the Dodgers. Davey Lopes, for one, had become critical of his own union bargainers based on hearsay information he received from *the owners*, of all people, and other sources. But Lopes was not entirely to be blamed for his outbursts, and he was hardly alone, as the talks had temporarily been moved to Washington at the urging of Secretary of Labor Ray Donovan and had been conducted under a news blackout. Aware of dissension in the ranks, Miller would get on a plane the following week and attend separate meetings in Chicago and Los Angeles and then brief players on what was really going on, finally bringing the players back to a united position. Lopes would later admit that airing his frustrations publicly was a mistake. His comments, and those from others, like Detroit Tigers pitcher Dan Schatzeder, temporarily jeopardized negotiations and gave owners hope they could break up the union if there was enough discord among the players.

"We didn't have the same stream of information that you can have today," Monday said. "One of the bigger things that eventually came out was a suggestion that we do not comment about things, because they may have already been settled in New York—that we just hadn't heard about them yet. It was a distraction, and having been on some negotiating councils and committees myself as a player years before, it's dangerous when you begin to comment on things in meetings three thousand miles away. Regarding [the infighting], everybody's entitled to their own opinion, and everybody had them."

Even the media faced challenges in getting accurate information—or even *any* news at all. So some newspapers, like the *Los Angeles Herald Examiner*, got creative in filling sports pages left blank by the baseball strike. "Somebody at our newspaper, which was a little eccentric in its own way at the time, dreamed up the idea of doing something we called 'Strike Ball,'" Lyle Spencer recalled. "I was creating imaginary games on a fairly daily basis which, of course, allowed Dusty [Baker] to have an amazing season. He was probably the MVP of 'Strike Ball.' Or maybe Reggie Smith. I loved Reggie, too, because he gave the best quotes I've probably ever seen. Reggie was honest to a fault."

So while some newspapers, like the *Herald Examiner*, had their fun printing fictitious fantasy baseball games to give fans something to read and while negotiations continued in New York, many of the Dodgers worked to stay in shape. "Most of us that were in the LA area were working out at USC," Monday said. "And, mysteriously, bats and balls would appear there every day. Damn same thing every day."

"I knew that baseball couldn't afford not to come back [that season]," Baker believed. "But after working out with some of my teammates at USC for the first couple of weeks of the strike, guys started dropping out—boom, boom, boom. They figured it was over. Well, I kept working out with my nephew, playing Wiffle Ball, I was swimming, I was running the stairs at Pierce College, and was taking batting practice at a place called Buddy's Bat-a-Way [in Van Nuys]. I ended up having one of the highest batting averages in the league after the strike."

As for Fernando, he made the most of each day during the strike. He went to Mexico and played the part of the returning conquering hero— bouncing around to destinations like Mexico City, Hermosillo, Yucatán, Navojoa, Tijuana, and Mexicali, often giving pitching clinics or playing in games. It was reminiscent of the barnstorming days of Babe Ruth and Lou Gehrig during the late 1920s.

But the highlight of his time back in Mexico was in the country's capital. He received the "key to the community" from the mayor of Mexico City before giving a pitching clinic to more than twenty-five thousand youngsters. He then spent some time with President José López Portillo as his guest at the palatial presidential residence.

Everything about Fernando's visit to Mexico City was grandiose, even what was supposed to be a low-key dinner at his agent's sister's house. "Word got around the neighborhood that Fernando was dining with us, and a hundred kids surrounded the house," De Marco said. "The kids started chanting, *Val-en-zue-la, Val-en-zue-la.* Fernando went outside to talk to the kids and throw the ball around with them."

The next day, he concluded his visit to Mexico City with a police motorcycle escort back to the airport. After a quick stay in Los Angeles, his next visits would be to Tijuana and Mexicali, where he would take part in a two-game semipro exhibition series set up by Mike Brito. But there was a major problem with this. Playing games anywhere or for any team other than his own was a violation of his—and any other Major League player's—contract. But for Valenzuela, who made just $42,500 in salary that season and wasn't getting paid during the strike, he had to earn a living somehow. And he wasn't the only Dodger to play in those games. Outfielder Pedro Guerrero and infielder Pepe Frías did as well.

"First of all," Guerrero told me, "I didn't agree with the strike, but I couldn't do anything about it. Me and Fernando—we didn't have any money. Fernando lived close by, so we went to talk with Mike Brito, the guy that signed Fernando. He put together a couple of games in Mexico and we went down there. That's how we got a little bit of money."

After word got out, Dodgers general manager Al Campanis was incensed, telling the *Orange County Register*, "I'm not going to comment because I just can't believe it happened." Brito immediately came to Valenzuela's defense. "That guy with the Angels [Mike Witt] pitched five innings in Mexicali," he noted to reporters. "Fernando only threw three, but nobody said nothing about [Witt]."

Brito was also in hot water with Dodgers brass over his involving Valenzuela, Guerrero, and Frías in the tournament. But Brito's father figure–like closeness to Fernando unquestionably kept him from receiving any disciplinary action from the Dodgers—or outright termination of his scouting position.

The appearances by Valenzuela, sanctioned or not, would turn out to be a positive for both himself and the Dodgers—ultimately serving as his way of staying in pitching shape. To that point, he had mostly just gotten his running in each day—with the act of throwing a baseball somewhat sporadic throughout the strike.

Perhaps what was most remarkable during the work stoppage was how the continued fervor over Fernando never waned. That wasn't generally the case with the rest of Major League Baseball. The fans weren't just angry about the perceived greed-induced strike but were showing a good deal of apathy as well. But with Fernandomania, it was almost as if the strike had never happened. "All the ingredients are still there," De Marco remarked as the strike was nearing a conclusion. "The people still love him, and he still loves the people. The commercials and all, we've been very low key because of the strike. We want to keep everything under our hat until things get back to normal. We didn't think it would be right, with the strike and all. But you can imagine, when people found out Fernando Valenzuela was available [because of the strike], he was very much in demand."

Just how much demand? While in Mexico City, he did an endorsement for a bread company that reportedly paid him $10,000. Another deal for Fernando posters (of which seventy-five thousand were printed) guaranteed Valenzuela $50,000 for the U.S. rights alone. Other entities with potential deals, among the twenty to twenty-five offers that De Marco claimed to have received on behalf of his client, included Kern's Beverages and Coca-Cola, as well as various bubble gum, soft drink, and automobile companies. Prior to the strike, De Marco claimed to have rejected more than $200,000 worth of endorsements—the rough equivalent of five times Valenzuela's salary—so El Toro could better focus on his pitching. "They want him for commercials in English and Spanish," De Marco said at the time. "He'll talk English soon. He picks up everything very fast. I would say that things look very bright for him—even during the strike. Two studios, MGM and Columbia, have contacted us about the possibility of doing his life story." The last part of that statement was striking—the offers of a movie deal for a lifetime *nine-game winner*! If you had to choose just one of the many accolades he received in 1981 to exemplify the hold he had on people at that time, it would be hard to find a better one.

For other promising young players around baseball, their options for making a livelihood were far more limited during the strike. Yankees pitcher Ron Davis, who set a Major League record for relief pitchers that May by striking out the last eight California Angels he faced in a game, worked as a waiter at Smith & Wollensky, a steakhouse in Manhattan. The Mets' lead-off hitter, Mookie Wilson, worked a couple of days a week as a maître d' at a place called Joe's Seafood in Queens, New York. Phillies pitcher Marty Bystrom had a sales job at a car lot. These were far different times. Today, in part because of the strength of the players' union, the Major League minimum salary is $700,000, making it fair to assume if there was a strike today that none of the players would have to wait tables or sell cars to get by.

The strike would mercifully end on July 31—just as the owners' strike insurance ran out—with a compromise between the owners and the players. It was agreed that the teams that lost a "premium" free agent (defined as a player statistically ranked in the top 20 percent for his position) would be compensated by drawing from a pool of players left unprotected by *all* the clubs instead of just from the team that signed the free agent. The players' union also agreed to restrict free agency to players with six or more years of Major League service time. As it turned out, this provision was pure genius by Miller. The owners were thrilled at the time—thinking that controlling a player for six years was a major victory. But what it ultimately did was escalate salaries further by creating higher demand for the free agents. The last part of the agreement—which ultimately closed the deal for both sides—had the owners granting the players service time for the two months they were on strike in return for the players agreeing to extend the collective bargaining agreement by one year.

"The owners won't underestimate the players anymore," Miller told reporters. "That's probably the most important thing to come out of the strike. If there was any victory, it was a victory for the spirit of the players."

Talks had been so contentious that Miller and Grebey refused to pose together for photographers once an agreement had been reached. Instead, Grebey was photographed holding up a copy of the *New York Daily News* blaring the front-page headline "PLAY BALL!"

Major League Baseball decided to split the season—awarding those teams in first place in their respective divisions after the June 11 games a first-half title, which guaranteed them a divisional series at the conclusion of the regular season. The teams with the best second-half records in their divisions would be declared second-half champions. Should the same team finish first in both halves of the season, the club with the second-best overall record would make it to the divisional series.

The Dodgers were a happy recipient of this decision—having held a half-game lead over the Reds in the first half. For Cincinnati, there was little justice in this ruling, as they played one fewer game than the Dodgers. Even worse, the Reds were leading a May 26 game against the San Francisco Giants, 6–0, in the third inning before the game was called for rain. Cincinnati would also finish in second place behind the Astros in the second half. So, despite having the best all-around record in the NL West by four full games over the Dodgers and six games over Houston, they didn't qualify for the postseason. For the Reds, it would be a bitter pill to swallow.

"That was a really sad year all around for every Red," Cincinnati pitcher Bruce Berenyi lamented four decades later. "We got screwed so bad, it is *still* with me. I may have made the All-Star team, Tom [Seaver] would have won twenty games. We should have won the West."

The Dodgers of course were overjoyed. "The most important outcome of the strike was us getting into the playoffs," Garvey said.

Embarrassingly for the Major Leagues, St. Louis, just like the Reds in their division, would end up with the best overall record in the NL East, but because the Cards didn't have the best mark in either half of the season, they also missed out on postseason baseball. Cardinals manager Whitey Herzog was outraged, saying at the time of the playoff qualification decision in August—well before the outcome of the season—"the entire concept is so stupid I can't believe we're going to ask the American public to buy it."

Esteemed *Sports Illustrated* columnist and MLB Network commentator Tom Verducci wrote in 2020, "What Watergate was to the presidency, the 1981 strike was to baseball. Never again would we look at either institution with the same amount of faith."

The strike, and the fallout from it, would prove to be the beginning of the end for Bowie Kuhn, the beleaguered baseball commissioner. The work stoppage caused owners to suffer losses of more than $72 million in ticket sales, concessions, and broadcast revenues. The cancellation of 713 games was also devastating to the players, who lost an estimated $28 million in salaries. So maligned was Kuhn during the strike that, at that summer's Hall of Fame induction ceremony, he was roundly booed by those in attendance. Less than two years later, Kuhn's efforts to renew his contract failed, and he would be replaced by Peter Ueberroth in 1984.

Play would resume on August 9 with the All-Star Game—and another opportunity for Valenzuela to bask in the glow before a national audience after he was named the starting pitcher for the National League.

But even the greatest player in the game had his concerns about how the strike had negatively impacted the game. "I think the fans will stay away," George Brett told reporters. "I would."

If baseball ever needed a heavy dose of Fernandomania, it was in the wake of the strike.

A Star-Spangled Return

The public address announcer at the old Municipal Stadium in Cleveland waited patiently for the rounds of booing to subside after announcing the National League's number-eight hitter, Davey Lopes, during the pregame player introductions along the third base line. Most all of the National League lineup had received similar receptions from the American League crowd of 72,086 fans—the largest in All-Star Game history—for two reasons. First, they were the opposition. And second, the crowd was making loud and clear their outrage over the strike. But then, in a sharp contrast, the PA announcer's next introduction was drowned out by cheers: "Batting ninth and pitching . . . from the Los Angeles Dodgers . . . he's tied for the league lead in victories as a rookie . . . warming up in the bullpen . . . Fernando Valenzuela."

In a clear signal of Valenzuela's universal appeal, a rousing and lengthy standing ovation ensued. Only the cheers given to hometown Indians manager Dave Garcia, catcher Bo Díaz, and hurler Len Barker, who had pitched the Major Leagues' first perfect game in thirteen years earlier that season, would be louder than what the Mexican kid from the Dodgers got. "The reception to Fernando in Cleveland was both surprising and very nice," recalled Steve Garvey. "You can see if it was in LA, or maybe a New York or someplace like that, but it was great to see that [Cleveland] people knew who he was, knew what he was doing, and appreciated how he was doing it in a very topsy-turvy season."

Whether or not Fernando realized how odd it was to be cheered like that in an American League park, he now represented something more than the most exciting pitcher in Major League baseball—he was also the most transcendent. Nobody was in a bigger spotlight than Valenzuela at this All-Star Game. "I think most All-Star Games have a theme," said Garvey, who would certainly know, having played in ten of them. "That year [in 1981] it was about the Hispanic player and Fernando, because of how he started the season. In 2021 the theme was [Japanese standout pitcher *and* hitter] Shohei Ohtani."

"That was the largest crowd Fernando had ever pitched before," Mark Langill noted. "With a sellout in Cleveland, that was just a wonderful way to be able to bring baseball back, as opposed to having a staggered start to the second half. That idea to start the second half with an All-Star Game I think was very powerful, because it had been the worst summer for the sport. Suddenly, on that night, that's when the healing began."

The NBC television broadcaster Joe Garagiola, commenting on the loud receptions—both the cheers and the boos—exclaimed emphatically, "Baseball is back!" With the fallout from the strike, Major League Baseball had a tremendous amount riding on this nationally televised Sunday night game. If it was played sloppily after the long two-month hiatus, the product would suffer mightily. But an exciting, well-played game would help a lot of fans forget a summer largely without their baseball. Thus, this All-Star Game was the most important in a generation. Baseball clearly was on trial. For some, however, the timing of it was seen as simply a money-grab, as the players had only had eight days since the official end of the strike to work out with their teams. "What an utter farce," Hal Lebovitz opined at the time in the *Plain Dealer*, Cleveland's largest newspaper. "To charge top prices for what has to be a charade, a workout, a non-contest is sinful. Talk about greed."

The Dodgers would be well represented at this All-Star Game with a total of six players on the National League roster. Besides the starters in Valenzuela and Lopes, Garvey, Baker, Hooton, and Guerrero were on the NL team. Only the Yankees had as many representatives. For Baker, it was the first All-Star Game appearance of his then-ten full Major League seasons—and he was going to make the most of the opportunity. "I remember [National League manager] Dallas Green and Pete Rose had a lot to do with me being on the All-Star team," Baker recalled. "It was truly my *first* All-Star team. I did make one in Little League, but I was an alternate in the Pony League for two years. Later, I did make the All-Star team in Triple-A but couldn't go because I had military duty. I was in the Marine Reserves, and I had to go to summer camp. So making that All-Star team was a big deal for me. And when I walked into the ballpark and into the clubhouse, Pete Rose was the first one to greet me. And then Dallas Green was the second one and said, 'Hey, man, I chose you on this team because I know you're a winner.' Then Pete Rose comes by and goes, 'Hey, we ain't lost to those American League cocksuckers in nine years—and we ain't losing to them today!' He said that because there was a lot of pride playing for the league you represented. We [the National League] were the dominant league. We also had the most Black and Latin players, too, which nobody wants to say or talk about."

Baker is certainly on point regarding how the two leagues had differed historically on racial inclusion to that point. Starting with the first African American to break the Major Leagues' color barrier, Jackie Robinson, who joined the Dodgers in 1947, National League teams continued to sign most of the standout minority players over the next two decades—including all-time greats Hank Aaron, Willie Mays, Monte Irvin, Larry Doby, Roberto Clemente, Frank Robinson, Ernie Banks, Roy Campanella, Willie McCovey, Tony Perez, Willie Stargell, and Joe Morgan. And into the 1970s, superb Black players like Dave Parker, George Foster, and Andre Dawson were added by National League clubs. In 1971 the world champion Pittsburgh Pirates fielded a team with Black players at each of the nine positions—the first time that had occurred in Major League history. By contrast, the American League's most dominant team in the two decades after integration, the Yankees, had just one star player who was Black, Elston Howard, who debuted for the club in 1955. The Boston Red Sox were even more pathetic in this regard. They didn't even sign a single Black player until 1959, when they inked Pumpsie Green, and wouldn't have a great Black player until Jim Rice—nearly *thirty years* after integration—after their original sin of passing on the opportunity to sign Jackie Robinson in the mid-1940s.

But on this night, while the bright lights were on Valenzuela, there was also much focus and intrigue on Rose, who would be playing in his fifteenth All-Star Game. "Charlie Hustle," as he was called for his hard-nosed play on the diamond, entered the so-called second season needing just one hit to break Stan Musial's National League record for hits. While All-Star Game statistics didn't count toward any regular season records, there was still tremendous anticipation for any at bat involving the man who would one day become the all-time Major League Baseball hit king. Rose, who had talked Green into putting him rather than Lopes in the lead-off spot by asking him rhetorically, 'Who would the fans rather see as the first batter after a seven-week strike? A guy hitting in the .100s or a guy who will break Stan Musial's record with his next hit?' was the first batter of the game. After taking the first pitch offered by American League starter Jack Morris low for a ball, Rose, along with everyone else in the ballpark, was stunned to hear some ten thousand whistles that fans in the stadium were blowing to express their frustration and anger over the greed that had overtaken the national pastime. The exercise was part of a campaign called "Blow the Whistle on the Players," the brainchild of a bartender who had handed them out to fans prior to the game. The whistles would continue to sound throughout the game, after the first pitch of every half inning, but they proved not to be a distraction to Rose, as he served a 2–0 pitch from Morris into left field for a single. However, that was where any potential early rally for the National League would die, as Morris retired Dave Concepción, Dave Parker, and Mike Schmidt in order to end the top of the first.

Valenzuela would then walk out to the mound to face the greatest collection of hitters he had ever opposed to this point in his young career. Facing the top half of an American League lineup that included three future Hall of Famers—Rod Carew, George Brett, and Dave Winfield—he didn't disappoint. After yielding a pair of infield hits to Carew and Willie Randolph, he escaped the inning unscathed—even helping himself with a quick-as-a-cat assist on a come-backer off the bat of Brett to put up a scoreless inning.

Fernando's start that night, which would be the first of six consecutive Midsummer Classic appearances for the left-hander, would end right there, as Tom Seaver, who had been warming up in the bullpen since the top of the inning, came in to relieve Valenzuela to start the second. But with millions watching in the United States and throughout Latin America, Fernando had made a tremendous statement on the prime-time stage. He proved he could pitch against the highest level of talent with the entire baseball world watching. "To have Fernando go out there and deliver like he did was a really good way to come back from the strike and kick off what was the second half of the season," said Garvey, who wrapped a double off Dave Stieb in the game.

The game itself would prove to be a thriller, albeit with the usual outcome of that era—a tenth-straight National League victory. But the tight

5-4 NL win, with all the Senior Circuit's runs coming by way of the long ball—courtesy of Schmidt, Parker, and Gary Carter (twice)—would be a boon to Major League Baseball. Along with a photo of the game's MVP (Carter) slapping the hand of National League third base coach Dick Williams, the following week's *Sports Illustrated* blasted the header "A Big Hand for Baseball."

Only time would tell if the lift the All-Star Game gave to baseball would be a lasting one.

The Lasorda Effect　　16

I bleed Dodger blue, and when I die,
I'm going to the big Dodger in the sky.

—TOMMY LASORDA

What kind of manager did a pitcher as quiet, shy, and reclusive as
Valenzuela need? Well, the larger-than-life Tommy Lasorda was simply made to order. As Fernando's manager from the time he was called
up to the big leagues in the fall of 1980 through his entire ten years in
Los Angeles, no single individual shielded him more from the media
and celebrity limelight and had a greater impact on Valenzuela's career
than Lasorda.

But for all the positives Lasorda bestowed on Valenzuela's psyche and
development throughout his rookie season, a strong argument can be
made that the baseball strike saved the manager from himself in terms
of potentially burning out his young pitcher. After all, Lasorda's use of
Valenzuela—a pitcher who had never even started a Major League game
before being thrust into the cauldron of his Opening Day assignment—in
the first half of 1981 was by any measure excessive. Fernando had already
thrown 109⅓ innings in just fourteen starts, a hair under an average of
eight innings per game. As a result, Valenzuela had already shown signs
of a tired arm in the two weeks preceding the strike, but that didn't keep
Lasorda from sending him out to pitch every fourth day.

"In retrospect, Tommy absolutely overworked Fernando," Lyle Spencer said. "But at the same time, there wasn't much awareness of those
things back then. You had guys like Nolan Ryan who were just getting
warmed up at 150 pitches. So, while Tommy was responsible [for over-
use] in some respects, you also have to put it in the context of the time.

Even [Mets manager] Davey Johnson, if you want to look at Dwight Gooden's first two years, did the same thing. Dwight pitched around five hundred innings at age nineteen and twenty—same as Fernando. It was very similar, and it was only four years later. Managers didn't think long term back then about their players because they felt they had to win now. I think, looking back, Tommy didn't serve Fernando well long term. But you know, even more striking is what a guy like Sandy Koufax did. He was striking out three hundred guys a season—it was the nature of the game. But I do think if Tommy had known what we know now, he would have been more conservative with Fernando. And plus, throwing that screwball was another factor. I don't think we know how damaging and stressful that pitch is on the arm when thrown as often as Fernando threw it."

But despite the fact pitchers of that time didn't have much in the way of a pitch count, Lasorda did have a reputation around baseball for overusing starting pitchers. In fact, the common phrase for any pitcher being overworked back then was "being 'Lasorda'd.'" Perhaps his philosophy came from his own legendary work ethic. Lasorda pitched endless sessions of batting practice well into his sixties. So perhaps his thinking was that if he could work himself like he did on the mound as a senior citizen, then why not have a professional pitcher in their twenties complete games?

"Fernando was being left in games in the sixth or seventh innings in bases loaded situations where a pitcher would ordinarily come out," Dusty Baker recalled. "And you look at it over a ten-year period, that's an additional three hundred innings or so. But it was probably hard for Tommy, because Fernando was still his best option in many of those situations when compared to bringing in a reliever. He could help you in so many different ways. Besides being a great pitcher, he could hit, he could field his position, he never threw the ball away. He could do everything except run, which I really think might have hurt him."

Lasorda also loved to win and hated to lose. There was never a middle ground with him. "Fernando obviously made it a lot easier for Tommy to win in the '80s," Ken Gurnick said. "And Tommy took wanting to win to levels unlike anyone I've been around. I've been around some amazing managers—even those that managed the Dodgers after Tommy [retired], like Davey Johnson and Joe Torre. So I've been around some World

Series winners in covering the Dodgers. But nobody was as tenacious [about winning] and as bitter in taking defeats as Tommy. In fact, Al Campanis once told me, 'I've been around a lot of managers, and with most of them, you have to teach them how to win. But with Tommy, I had to teach him how to lose.' So Tommy was a really bad loser."

Lasorda was also cocky. And brash. And a fighter. He had to be. Nothing was ever given to him. He had a most unremarkable Major League pitching career, posting a lifetime mark of 0-4 with a 6.48 ERA over three seasons with the Brooklyn Dodgers and Kansas City Athletics. After his playing career ended in 1956 and before he became Dodgers manager at the end of the 1976 season, he managed in the Minor Leagues for eight years and was that club's third base coach for four more. Nobody in baseball worked harder than Lasorda did at eventually achieving his ultimate goal of becoming the manager of the Dodgers.

"Tommy Lasorda was the obvious choice to follow Hall of Fame Dodger manager Walter Alston," former Dodgers owner Peter O'Malley told the *Los Angeles Times* in a 2021 piece. "He was well known to everyone in the organization from the days he pitched in the minor leagues to his scouting to managing our farm teams to third base coach under Alston. I thought Tommy handled the constant inquiries about when he would be the manager very well. I never promised him that he was the heir apparent[,] but fortunately we were good friends from the very earliest days. I traveled to the Dominican Republic to see him manage winter ball, to Ogden, Utah, where he managed a rookie team, to Spokane, Washington, where he managed our Triple-A team, and our relationship was very honest and frank. When Tommy was asked how difficult it might be to follow the legendary Walter Alston, his reply was 'no problem, but the guy following me will have a big challenge.'"

While taking over the managerial reins from an icon like Alston might have been a daunting task for most first-time big league managers, Lasorda was very comfortable with the transition. It was as if, in his mind, it was the job he was always meant to do. He felt it was his time.

Steve Garvey played parts of his Dodgers career for both Alston and Lasorda, and for him the differences between the two Hall of Fame managers were stark. "Walt was much more stoic than Tommy," Garvey told me. "He was 6 foot 3, very strong, a smart baseball man, and was comfortable and obviously confident in himself, as accepting twenty-three one-year contracts would show. But that's basically what a lot of managers got back then—whether you went to the World Series every year like he did or not. But when Walt said something, you listened, because you knew he had watched and watched and was going to tell you what was going to be best for you. So there was no extraneous conversation. He gave us a few rules—be ready to play, get there on time, get the signs, do all the little things and do them the Dodgers' way.

"Tommy was different. He came to baseball out of high school, learned the Dodger way, played that way, played it with a different flare, a different attitude, different persona, worked his way to the Minors [as a manager] to where he was in the on-deck circle [as the Dodgers' third base coach] when Walt retired and stepped in. And by that time, a whole group of us were really Tommy's boys. He was like a second father to me. He was my manager in Ogden, Utah, when I signed in '68. We had just a great relationship. So a bunch of us, we're sitting there having put four or five years together, and Tommy now steps in. He was taking over a very familiar group of guys. And the Dodgers every year would add somebody during this sort of pre-free agency era—a Jimmy Wynn, a Dusty Baker, a Reggie Smith—and these additions kind of kept us right up there for a ten-year period."

The change in personalities and styles at the helm would have initiated an adjustment period for most clubs. But not this Dodgers team. "The Dodgers went from a reserved Walter Alston to Tommy, the rah-rah motivator during that time," Steve Brener said. "Of course, Tommy managed so many of his players on the Dodgers in the Minor Leagues. He worked with them day in and day out and then he got to manage them when he was granted to manage the Dodgers."

Lasorda was a Dodgers lifer and wasn't afraid to show his passion for the organization and his players. He had spent practically his entire youth into middle age working his way up to the "throne," and he would soak in his elite status and embrace every precious moment of it. "Tommy wasn't lying when he said that he bleeds blue, because that was the only team he ever talked about," longtime Dodgers clubhouse manager Mitch Poole told me. "He played in other organizations, but they weren't his true love. He had a love for this team, and he showed it to me all the time."

As a result of his obvious exuberance and passion for the ball club,

Lasorda instantly became a Dodgers fan favorite. "There was this one time when I picked Tommy up at the airport," Poole recounted. "I was bringing him back to Dodger Stadium. On our way, he's messing around with my car radio and finds a station playing Sinatra. I thought, *How in the world did he get Sinatra on my radio?* Anyway, as we're going up the Interstate 110 Freeway, he falls asleep. He's got his head back, and people were driving next to us and going, *Oh my God! That's Tommy Lasorda!* You could read their lips. It was like, *Oh my goodness!*"

Lasorda had also become a media darling—someone the press could always count on to give them lively and entertaining quotes—while deflecting attention from his players so they could concentrate on their game. A Lasorda press conference was *never* boring—albeit at the expense of sometimes being contentious. In what is now YouTube gold, Lasorda's answer to KLAC reporter Paul Olden's question about Dave Kingman's three-home-run performance following a tough fifteen-inning loss to the Cubs on May 14, 1978, was perhaps the most entertaining of all—except for poor Olden, who bore the brunt of the manager's profanity-laden response.

The exchange went as follows:

OLDEN: What's your opinion of Kingman's performance?
LASORDA: What's my opinion of Kingman's performance? What the fuck do you *think* is my opinion of it? I think it was fucking *horseshit*. Put that in . . . I don't give a fuck! Opinion of his performance?! Jesus Christ! He beat us with three fucking home runs!

After some uncomfortable laughter from the press, Tommy continued his rant.

LASORDA: What the fuck can you mean, "What is my *opinion* of his performance?" How can you ask me a question like that, "What is my opinion of his performance?" Jesus Christ, he hit *three* home runs! Je-sus Christ! I'm fucking pissed off, to lose the fucking game, and you ask me my opinion of his performance? Je-sus Christ! That's a tough question to ask me, isn't it? "What is my opinion of his performance?"
OLDEN: Yes, it is. I asked it, and you gave me an answer.
LASORDA: Well, I didn't give you a good answer because I'm mad.

Perhaps hoping he could defuse Lasorda's long and painful answer, Olden backtracked.

OLDEN: Well, it wasn't a good question.
LASORDA: That's a tough question to ask me right now—"What is my opinion of his performance?" I mean, you want me to tell you what my opinion of his performance is . . .
OLDEN: You just did.
LASORDA: That's right. Je-sus Christ . . . guy hits three home runs against us . . . shit. I mean . . . I don't mean to get pissed off or anything like that, but, you know, you asked me *my opinion*. I mean, he put on a helluva show. He hit three home runs. He drove in, what, *seven* runs?

Incredibly, the twenty-four-year-old Olden had the courage to correct Lasorda at that tense moment.

OLDEN: *Eight.*
LASORDA: *Eight* runs. So what the hell more can you say about him?

The rant had mercifully concluded at that point, but consider this: how would Valenzuela have answered a question about an opposing team's hitter belting three home runs in a game? It probably would have gone something like this: *He's a great hitter. Give him credit.* Would the media, much less Olden, have preferred *that* boring answer?

"I kind of learned what kind of questions to ask or how to ask them to get your job done," Gurnick told me when we discussed this infamous Lasorda tirade. "Yet, when Paul Olden asked that question about Kingman, I mean, he got one of the *greatest* interview answers ever. But it could have gone a different way. Tommy could have said, and I've had managers say, 'We're done,' and you get nothing. And some managers handle it that way. But with this interview, Tommy blows up, and it is the greatest interview of *all time*! He was just a unique individual, and he was great for the game."

As for Olden, despite being on the receiving end of Lasorda's outburst, he saw it in a similar way. "Long before the internet era, Lasorda could often add a touch of 'showmanship' to his dealings with the media that equally included newspapers, TV and radio (where the infamous Kingman response made its debut and found it's [sic] legs on a legendary popular local nightly program that was a 'must listen' for the movers and shakers in Southern California)," Olden wrote to me in an email. "Tommy and I had many pleasant and professional interactions long after that 1978 post-game response. I last saw him in Japan in 2004 when MLB opened its season there. He was in the capacity of MLB Ambassador, and I was there to broadcast the game for Tampa Bay, as I was a broadcaster for the team. We chatted on the field before the game. When I turned fifty that same year, Tommy signed a ball to me, saying, '*What's my opinion of Paul turning 50? What do you think . . . ?*' If there was a Happy Face emoji back then, he would have used it to finish that salutation."

The idea that Lasorda remembered exactly what he said to Olden in his infamous Kingman response from twenty-six years earlier and used the spirit of it to wish him a happy fiftieth birthday speaks volumes about how he could make light of a situation and not hold a grudge against a reporter, especially one as respected as Olden. "Tommy had one of those personalities where he would say whatever was on his mind and would cuss you out and all that," Gurnick recalled. "And the next day, it was like it never happened. That took some time getting used to for me, because I had never been around a person like that before. For me, my first year [with Lasorda] was tough because when he came after me, I went after him. And that went on day after day after day. We went at it the whole first year. Tommy was very tough on me, as he was on a lot of rookie reporters. Other baseball people were the same back in the day. They wanted to see what you were made of, and they tested you. And Tommy tested me that whole season. But after that, we were fine, and I enjoyed Tommy and feel lucky that I got to cover him. He was always very nice to me and my family after that."

The ultimate beneficiaries of Tommy Lasorda's love of the spotlight and how he embraced the media's attention were the players themselves—a factor that can't be understated in a sports-obsessed media market like Los Angeles. "No manager has every tool in the kit," Gurnick said. "What Tommy might have lacked in other tools, his ability to deflect attention and set a comfortable tone in the clubhouse for his players should never be underestimated. It was a big part of Tommy's success—to make the players feel comfortable and be able to focus on their job. And I think Tommy's ability to speak Spanish and to deflect media attention were both very helpful to Fernando."

"The focus was *always* on Tommy," Brener said. "Although the players got their fair share of media exposure, Tommy liked the limelight and loved being in it, so it certainly took something away from the players. But the players still got their accolades."

In some situations, Lasorda's attention-seeking behavior could benefit the team, as when fans of rival teams grew hostile. "The public just saw this guy they thought was coming off as brash," Monday reflected. "But some of it was orchestrated to take away tension from the club. Like when we would go to San Francisco. [Lasorda] would blow kisses and everything else [to the Dodgers-hating crowd]. He wanted the attention and boos going at him—not to us. So, while they're getting on his ass, they're leaving us alone. Not that [Giants fans] were giving us ice cream sundaes and things like that, but at least temporarily they were busy concentrating on pissing Tommy off."

If Lasorda blowing kisses to opposing fans seems like something one might see in a circus-like atmosphere, it's precisely how some of his own players saw him. "To me, Tommy was the P. T. Barnum of baseball," Garvey told me. "He was the ringleader, controlled the three rings under the big tent, and did that for the Dodgers, he did it for the National League, did it for baseball—here and internationally."

"Tommy was certainly the ultimate promoter," said Brener, who would know that better than anyone, as he was the Dodgers' director of publicity. "He was a publicist's dream. He loved to go out and make appearances. He loved to deal with the media. He loved his players. And he loved Hollywood."

It's that last part that allowed Lasorda to transcend baseball and become a household name. His office at Dodger Stadium was often like a West Coast version of the Friars Club, with legendary Hollywood stars like Frank Sinatra, Dean Martin, Jack Lemmon, Gregory Peck, Mike Douglas, Jonathan Winters, and Don Rickles as his pregame guests. "Tommy was a prominent figure in Los Angeles at a time where he was as popular, if not more so, than the Hollywood crowd who adored and adopted him as one of their own," Olden recalled.

"Lasorda was a part of all the stuff that was around in LA," said Danny Heep, who was a part of the Dodgers miracle '88 world championship team. "I never had another manager like Tommy. He was a part of the LA experience. He's what they want out there. It's Hollywood, and he fit right in. And he liked and enjoyed managing that way. His coaching style worked there very well. Tommy did a lot of stuff outside of practices. Or, while we were practicing, he might have movie stars around the batting cage. And he did a lot of speaking engagements. Tommy was a part of Hollywood. He was an actor himself and was just all over the map. But I would think, *Hey, he's won world championships, so it works*. It just proves that there's not just one way of doing things."

Lasorda was, in fact, an actor—and a memorable one—in his recurring role as "The Dugout Wizard" on the wildly popular children's show *The Baseball Bunch*, which aired for five seasons in the early 1980s. But this was just a sampling of his many television and film appearances. His IMDb page lists more than a hundred roles and appearances on everything from soap operas to comedies to documentaries. And it all started with his becoming manager of the Dodgers.

"The Dodgers, from their beginning in Los Angeles, always were embraced by Hollywood," noted Fred Claire. "You look back and you'll see Bob Hope with Don Drysdale, Sandy Koufax, and Tommy Davis in any number of times and ways—and it's continued since then. When I joined the Dodgers, 'Hollywood Stars Night' was bigger than it was as time moved on, because there were different types of personalities. We had the Jackie Gleasons, the Dean Martins, to the whole gamut of people. Again, Hollywood loved the Dodgers, and Tommy certainly loved that part of it."

But while Lasorda was viewed as a character, what often gets lost or isn't known widely to the public was his innate motivational skills. "Tommy was a hell of a motivator," said Rick Dempsey, the 1988 Dodgers backup catcher. "This guy was so good, he could talk the devil out of hell. He was just so good at talking to players, motivating them, and getting everyone in a good, positive frame of mind. That's what Tommy's strength was. You just had to buy into the bullshit—the hugging and stuff—which was fun because we made it work for everybody. You buy into the bullshit, and he was positive about winning. That's all we were there to do."

Dempsey would know a good motivator when he saw one. He played in twenty-four Major League seasons and for two of the most high-profile managers in baseball history—Billy Martin and Earl Weaver, two of Lasorda's contemporaries to whom he was always compared. Of Lasorda, Martin, and Weaver, it seemed clear which one Dempsey enjoyed playing for the most. "Tommy was a lot of fun," Dempsey said. "I grew up with Billy Martin and Earl Weaver, and they were not easy people to get along with. They wanted to win; they were *vicious* about winning. To put up with an Earl Weaver for as long as I did wasn't easy. And trust me, he was the best manager I ever played for, but he was miserable if you dropped the ball playing catch on the sideline. He would *scream* at you. And we just got used to dealing with that kind of treatment. Talk to any Oriole about Earl Weaver, and they'll tell you the same thing. Billy Martin was a fighter, too, and he didn't like losing either. If you didn't play the game the right way, he would jump your ass in a heartbeat. Today's game, players can't handle that sort of thing because they'll go right to their agent and ask to be traded. But my father was hard on me growing up, and I just learned to deal with it long before I became an Oriole with Earl or a New York Yankee and a Minnesota Twin, where I played for Billy. Tommy was just so much more positive with his players than those two."

Garvey recalled the beginning of a two-week Major League Baseball goodwill tour in Japan in 1979 in which Lasorda, managing the National League, could hardly stand the idea of the opposing American League manager, Earl Weaver, receiving the attention he was getting for being ejected from the first game of the trip.

"We play the first game in Yokohama," Garvey began. "The first inning, the first batter, Bert Campaneris, gets on, and on the second pitch, he attempts to steal second base. The umpire calls him out, but he looks safe. And out comes Earl Weaver, running out there to argue the call. He's really putting on a show—throwing his hat down and everything. This is going on for *five* minutes. So, the Japanese umpire throws him out of the game. I'm sitting next to Lasorda on the bench, and he goes, 'Arghh.' I asked him what's the matter. And he goes, 'That should have been *me* out there.' I said, 'That's funny. You've gotta give Earl one thing in these fourteen days that the press can go to him for, because you're just going to suck the air out of every stadium. It's all about how you really mentored Sadaharu Oh, and you're the reason he hit over 800 home runs and stuff like that."

But while Garvey may have rolled his eyes over Lasorda's craving for attention, he acknowledged his effective, if unique, way of motivating his players versus the way one of his other Hall of Fame managers, Dick Williams, did. "Tommy was Tommy," Garvey explained. "You'd have these clubhouse meetings, and there would be thirty expletives from him in seven minutes. Rick Monday would have his clicker, and he would count them. He was something. I remember spring trainings, late afternoons, and he'd be out there on the field, yelling and screaming and pitching batting practice for two and a half to three hours. He was an excellent baseball man, an excellent entertainer, a Type-A personality, and he was probably ADHD before anybody ever talked about that. But he just really loved the game. But Dick Williams, my manager in San Diego, while his record speaks for itself, was more of a drill sergeant. He was a very good Xs and Os guy but didn't really care to be the psychologist that Tommy perfected. Williams was the kind of guy that used a little more fear in the way he managed. Tommy's fear was a little different. It was almost a tongue-in-cheek fear. Not that you didn't respect and listen to Tommy, but there was so much humor involved with it, as a rule. Dick was different."

Garvey would then share why Lasorda was an ideal manager for a young, rookie pitcher like Valenzuela compared to someone like Williams and other old-school skippers: "If you were a rookie pitcher under Dick, and you walked two guys in a row, he would come out there to the mound and just stick his hand out. The rookie would just give him the ball, walk off the field, and that was it. With Tommy, that pitcher might be able to argue a little bit [to stay in the game] because Tommy knew that the camera was on him and he was mic'd up, so he was going to put on a show."

Rick Monday recalled how Lasorda's psychological skills made him a master at figuring out how to best motivate each one of his players. "Tommy knew the buttons to push for all of us," Monday said. "He knew that he could push a button in me—and it would motivate me. And he could push another button, and it would piss me off. And he knew that he had to push different buttons with you to motivate you and maybe two buttons over here to *really* piss you off. But he knew all the buttons for all the guys. So each of us on the team got a letter from him before we went to spring training in '81. And in the first paragraph, first sentence, he basically wrote, 'Hey, we've got a challenge in front of us, and we expect to win, and so forth . . .' But then the second paragraph was to push the buttons of the player that he sent the letter to. So when you ask about Tommy and what he meant, and what were his methods, he knew the buttons to push. I'm sure he knew which buttons to push with Fernando [in '81]."

And aside from knowing which buttons to push in motivating Valenzuela, Lasorda also knew how to communicate them verbally—just well enough—in Fernando's native language. "Tommy could speak enough Spanish that made Fernando comfortable enough that he didn't have to speak English," Gurnick recalled. "That was *really* good. If Fernando had had an old-school English-speaking manager, it might have been a tougher thing for him—especially coming out of Double-A ball as a teenager really speaking very little English. So Tommy speaking some Spanish was probably a big thing."

Others on the team, like Dusty Baker and Mike Scioscia, also were able to communicate with Fernando in Spanish, but his being able to converse with Lasorda in the language carried more weight—even if, as Valenzuela would admit later, his English was better than his manager's Spanish. "Fernando had mentors in Mexico and [mentorships] with others," said Garvey. "But he knew that Tommy was somebody that he needed to listen to and was probably going to be his manager for as long as he was with the Dodgers. I think that was a big part of their relationship."

"As an authority figure, Tommy's coming from a different place than others on the club," Spencer added. "That's more of a boss-worker kind of relationship. But Tommy had a vibrant personality, and some people responded to that better than others. I'm sure that was helpful to Fernando in the sense that Tommy could joke with him and be light with him."

Lasorda's manner with Valenzuela no doubt played a major part in keeping Fernando loose and able to relax in even the most stressful of circumstances. "Tommy and Fernando had a great relationship," recalled Brener. "Tommy was sometimes Fernando's interpreter. Fernando would be answering a question in Spanish and then Tommy would 'make up' an answer for Fernando and say something like, 'Tommy Lasorda's the best manager I've ever had!' They had fun together. It was quite a relationship."

"Tommy's jokes were impeccable," recalled Poole. "He knew how to deliver them. You could listen to it, and, even if you heard that joke a hundred times, the way he delivered it was always so good it would make you cry. I don't know anybody like that. I don't know anybody that could carry himself the way he did."

Valenzuela wasn't the only young Latino player with whom Lasorda worked hard to cultivate a rapport in the early 1980s. "It was fun to play for Tommy," Pedro Guerrero said. "I had a good time with him, and he treated me real good. Plus, he liked the Latin guys—the Dominican players—because he used to go every winter to the Dominican. And every time he went down there, I used to come see him and he would give me 100, 150 bucks—so we had fun."

Lasorda clearly had empathy for players coming to the Dodgers from other countries, as he himself had spent long periods of time scouting and coaching players wherever baseball was played. "There was such attention on Hideo Nomo [when he joined the Dodgers in 1995], and it helped that Tommy had been in Japan to do clinics there [with the Dodgers] in '65," Mark Langill noted. "He knew what it was like to be a player in another country because of his experience as a player and a manager in other countries."

Lasorda was also a staunch defender of Valenzuela after the south-paw's weight surged from 190 to 204 pounds due to a diet of strip steak, pizza, tortillas, soft drinks, and beer during the first half of the '81 season. When asked about it by reporters after Valenzuela's eighth straight win, Lasorda shrugged and said, "Babe Ruth did pretty good with a bulging waistline. Why fight success?"

It was a classic Lasorda response that immediately extinguished a potentially combustible topic for the young pitcher and exemplified why there might not have been a better manager in baseball for Valenzuela at that time.

FIG. 1. Dodger Stadium sits in Chavez Ravine, once home to three Mexican American neighborhoods. A side of Chavez Ravine, part of the San Gabriel Mountains, is visible beyond the stadium's outfield pavilion. Photo by Erik Sherman.

FIG. 2. (*opposite top*) Jaime Jarrín was a respected member of the news media and longtime Spanish-language Dodgers broadcaster prior to 1981. It was only after serving as Valenzuela's interpreter during Fernandomania that Jarrín, a future Ford C. Frick Award winner, would become a recognized figure and international celebrity. Photo by Erik Sherman.

FIG 3. (*opposite bottom*) Legendary Dodgers scout Mike Brito not only signed Valenzuela to his first big league contract but served as a father figure to the reserved young pitcher. Photo by Erik Sherman.

FIG 4. (*above*) Nomar Garciaparra, a Mexican American All-Star shortstop and then Dodgers television analyst, said Valenzuela's impact on him and his family was immeasurable. Photo by Erik Sherman.

FIG 5. Longtime Dodger Stadium clubhouse manager Mitch Poole made sure that no Dodgers player would wear Valenzuela's uniform number 34 after Fernando left the Dodgers in 1991. Photo by Erik Sherman.

FIG 6. The gregarious Dodgers manager Tommy Lasorda (pictured with, from left, Hollywood voice actor David Marc Bronow and author Erik Sherman in 2019) deflected much of the media spotlight from the shy Valenzuela. However, his over-use of Fernando didn't serve the pitcher well over time. Photo by Erik Sherman.

FIG 7. (*above*) Dodgers historian Mark Langill considered Lasorda's decision not to start Valenzuela in the 1980 one-game playoff against Houston a blessing in disguise, as it preserved Fernando's anonymity going into the next season—thus setting the stage for Fernandomania. Photo by Erik Sherman.

FIG 8. (*opposite top*) More than forty years after Fernandomania began, Valenzuela jerseys are still worn in great numbers at Dodger Stadium and on the road by fans who hadn't even been born when he was pitching. Photo by Erik Sherman.

FIG 9. (*opposite bottom*) In the aftermath of the forced removal of Mexican American families from Chavez Ravine neighborhoods during the building of Dodger Stadium and in the years leading up to Fernandomania, less than 10 percent of the fans at Dodgers games were Latino. After Valenzuela arrived on the scene, that figure skyrocketed to roughly 50 percent, where it remains today. Photo by Erik Sherman.

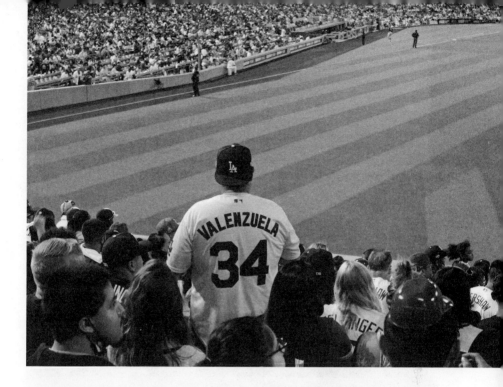

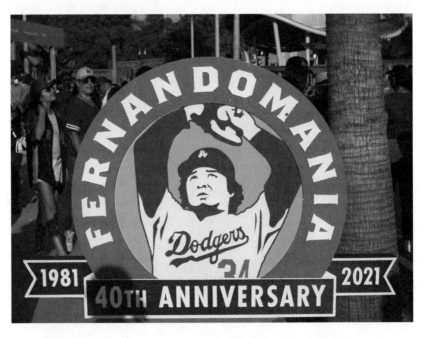

FIG 10. (*opposite top*) Rick Monday hit one of the most celebrated home runs in baseball history in the Dodgers' 1981 pennant-clinching victory over the Expos. Valenzuela pitched the game of his life that afternoon, overcoming almost wintry conditions in Montreal. Photo by Erik Sherman.

FIG 11. (*opposite bottom*) The Dodgers and the Los Angeles media celebrated the fortieth anniversary of Fernandomania throughout the 2021 season. Photo by Erik Sherman.

FIG 12. (*above*) Fernando revolutionized the ballpark experience at Dodger Stadium. Because of his impact on the fan base, mariachi bands are a regular presence at Dodgers games. Photo by Erik Sherman.

FIG 13. In homage to Valenzuela, photos, souvenirs, newspaper headline clippings, and advertisements featuring him in his playing days adorn a wall at Dodger Stadium. Photo by Erik Sherman.

FIG 14. Murals of Valenzuela can be found across the United States, from Los Angeles to Jersey City. In this one at Dodger Stadium, Fernando's remarkable rookie season of 1981 is celebrated. Photo by Erik Sherman.

FIG 15. Pedro Guerrero, who had once been Valenzuela's Dodgers teammate and had remained his friend, made the final out of Fernando's 1990 no-hitter against the Cardinals. Guerrero revered Valenzuela and said he wouldn't have felt good if he had broken his friend's no-hitter. Photo by Erik Sherman.

FIG 16. Steve Garvey suggested that Valenzuela set off a cultural change within Dodger Stadium that rippled throughout all of baseball. Photo by Erik Sherman.

Houston Has a Problem 17

With baseball's ruling that the clubs leading their respective divisions at the onset of the 1981 strike would be guaranteed a spot in a "divisional series" after the conclusion of the regular season, the Dodgers got to spend the final seven weeks of the campaign tuning up and staying healthy for the postseason—without worrying about winning the second-half title. For Fernando, with a Dodgers playoff berth guaranteed, it allowed for a much-needed reprieve from the heavy workload he endured throughout the entire first half of the season—a reprieve that would prove both welcome and fruitful.

While there was no shortage of effort displayed by the Dodgers, who might have felt they had little to play for in the second half, the organization did take advantage of the opportunity to give playing time to what Lasorda referred to as his "Kiddie Corps"—a bounty of young players brought up from the club's rich farm system. And just as the Dusty Bakers and Rick Mondays of the club had been mentors to Valenzuela, now Fernando was given the opportunity to be a leader-by-example to the young pitchers promoted to the big leagues for the first time. He had them believing that, if a twenty-year-old kid like him could succeed at the big league level, then why not them?

After struggling a bit in his first two starts of the second half—taking no-decisions in games the Dodgers would split—Valenzuela went on a season-ending roll beginning in an August 22 game in St. Louis, where he struck out twelve Cardinals in a 3–2 victory, his National League–best tenth of the season. He followed that effort up with a 6–0 complete game four-hitter over the Chicago Cubs at Dodger Stadium. His next outing was more of the same; he hurled ten innings while giving up just one run in a 3–2 fourteen-inning win over the Pittsburgh Pirates. Valenzuela then continued his late-season dominance with a 5-0 complete game shutout of the Cardinals back at Dodger Stadium.

Despite a baseball strike that had taken a huge bite out of attendance figures and despite pitching in games that meant little more than spring training to the playoff-bound Dodgers, Valenzuela starts continued to pack stadiums to near capacity. Fernandomania only intensified as the season wore on and the postseason approached.

As the season drew to a close, Lasorda inexplicably began pitching Valenzuela on just three days' rest with no clear incentive other than to perhaps build some momentum heading into the playoffs. After Valenzuela pitched an absolute masterpiece three-hit complete game for a 2-0 shutout over the Atlanta Braves on September 17, he was back out on the hill just three days later, this time losing to the Giants, 5-2. He would then fall victim to a Don Sutton two-hitter in a 4-1 defeat in Houston. With two straight defeats for Fernando, many believed he could use some rest as the playoffs beckoned, though Lasorda had him out there again—pitching on short rest to wrap up his regular season—this time tossing eight innings without yielding an earned run in a 1-0 loss to the San Diego Padres.

Valenzuela had given up an average of less than two earned runs a game over the last six weeks of the season. But now he would have to face the biggest challenge of his young baseball career—serious October baseball, beginning with the divisional series against the Houston Astros, the second-half NL West division champion.

*

Over the years, I've asked scores of players from the modern era which pitcher they least liked facing. Without debate, the name that pops up again and again is the flame-throwing Hall of Famer Nolan Ryan. By 1981 Ryan was a thirty-four-year-old veteran of fourteen big league seasons. Most pitchers at that age are looking to retire from the game. But for Ryan, despite a career that by that point would have punched his ticket to Cooperstown, the so-called "Ryan Express" was impossibly just getting into full gear. By the time he eventually hung up his spikes in 1993 at the ripe old baseball age of forty-six, he had struck out an all-time record of 5,714 hitters and thrown seven no-hitters—both records that likely will never be broken. In fact, one of those seven no-hitters had come in his last regular 1981 season outing against the Dodgers just eleven days before the start of this divisional series.

By contrast, Valenzuela had but fifteen career wins to his credit but had been the most exciting and transcendent athlete on the planet that season. And this reality was evident at the box office in Houston, a city located a day's drive from the Mexican border. Attendance had taken a hit because of the strike, and this newly formed first round of the playoffs was not selling out stadiums like the playoff series of the past. However, of the two divisional series games played in Houston, this first one featuring Valenzuela as the exciting new headliner was significantly better attended than the following night's contest. "Everyone was aware of Fernando's dynamic," Houston closer Joe Sambito said. "It was Fernandomania, and everybody in Houston knew what he was doing and the numbers he was putting up. And while he was an opponent, he was good for baseball. And while he rallied the Mexican Americans in Southern California and brought them out to Dodger Stadium, Houston had a large Latin American population, too. Our Latino fans always had come out for [longtime Astros All-Star outfielder] José Cruz. Cruz was their favorite guy. And they rallied around most of the other Latin American players we had on our team, but José, because of his longevity as a steady everyday player there, was a fan favorite. With Fernando coming into Houston as a visiting player, the Astros would market him that season and would get an extra five to ten thousand people in the stands because of it."

For "El Toro," facing Ryan in Houston in the first game of a short best-of-five series would be a daunting and critical task. Falling even a game behind in the series would put the Dodgers in a major hole. The pitcher's duel between the veteran and rookie aces was everything everyone expected in the early innings. Both pitchers struck out five through five scoreless innings, and each allowed just two runners to reach base. If Valenzuela was the least bit starstruck by opposing Ryan in a postseason game, he wasn't showing it. "Fernando's performance in that game didn't surprise me, because he'd been showing what he can do pretty much all year," Jerry Reuss said. "I also think because of the language barrier and the fact that he didn't follow Major League Baseball to the degree that most people do, [the significance of the game] might not have had an effect on him. But I can't say what he was thinking for sure. I just go by what I see, and Fernando pitched the same way in that playoff game as he did pretty much throughout the entire season."

The Astros would break the scoreless tie with a bloop RBI single by Tony Scott into short right-center field in the sixth inning. But the Dodgers answered right back. In the top of the seventh, Steve Garvey, a postseason superstar who would end his storied career with eleven home runs and a .338 batting average in eleven playoff series, took Ryan deep with a solo home run just over the orange homer line beyond the center-field fence to knot the game at 1–1.

In the bottom half of the seventh, the Astros seemed primed to retake the lead. César Cedeño led off the frame with a double to left field and then promptly stole third base. But Valenzuela got out of the inning unscathed by retiring both Art Howe and Kiko Garcia on short fly balls to the outfield—neither deep enough to entice Cedeño to tempt fate and try to score on a potential sacrifice fly—and then, after intentionally walking Alan Ashby to face Ryan, retired him with a harmless ground ball to Lopes at second to end the threat.

With the game still tied in the top of the ninth and Valenzuela still going strong, Tommy Lasorda made a questionable move by pulling Fernando from the batting lineup and getting journeyman Jay Johnstone to pinch-hit for him. It was a highly debatable decision by the Dodgers' skipper because Valenzuela likely had another two innings in him and was likely the best-hitting pitcher in the National League that season. The move failed, as Johnstone would hit a harmless come-backer to the mound for the first out of the inning. Ryan would then retire Lopes and Kenny Landreaux, to retire the Dodgers in order for the seventh time of the game.

"Nolan probably threw as good tonight as he did in the no-hitter," Astros catcher Ashby would tell reporters after the game. "Actually, I think he had *better* stuff. His curveball was even better. I think he only made one mistake all night and that was the pitch that Garvey hit for the home run. He was in command all night."

The Astros would win the game in the bottom of the ninth against Dodgers reliever Dave Stewart, a promising, hard-throwing rookie who would years later become the ace of the Oakland A's staff with four straight twenty-win seasons. With two outs and nobody on base, a single by pinch hitter Craig Reynolds was followed by a game-winning two-run homer by Ashby into the right-field bleachers to give Houston a 3–1 victory and a 1–0 lead in the divisional series.

If that first game was heartbreaking for the Dodgers in that they wasted an outstanding performance by Valenzuela, the second game of the series would prove to be more of the same. Again the Astros would start an experienced, highly successful veteran pitcher—Joe Niekro. The knuckleballer was coming off twenty-win seasons in '79 and '80, and in '81, despite a 9–9 record, he had the lowest ERA of his career, at 2.82. The Dodgers countered with Reuss, the thirteen-year veteran who was pitching the best baseball of his life with a career-best 2.30 ERA in 1981, which followed a 1980 campaign in which he was 18–6 with a 2.51 ERA and a National League–best six shutouts.

Like in the first game of the series, the two elite pitchers lived up to the backs of their baseball cards, as they matched zeros inning after inning—Niekro going eight shutout innings, Reuss nine. The game would remain 0–0 going into the bottom of the eleventh inning, when, as in the first game, Lasorda again summoned Stewart from the bullpen and again the young pitcher didn't have it, surrendering singles to Phil Garner and Tony Scott before the manager removed him from the game. Three batters later, now with Tom Niedenfuer in the game and the bases loaded, pinch hitter Denny Walling won the game for the Astros with a single over the head of Derrel Thomas in right field. The Dodgers had yet again wasted a magnificent pitching performance, this time leaving two or more men on base in four different innings. In the series, they had now put up just one run against Houston in twenty innings.

Down 2–0 in the divisional series, the Dodgers would take the somber flight back to Los Angeles, knowing they needed to win all three games at Dodger Stadium to avoid elimination. But not everyone on the team's charter plane was down or worried about the prospect of an early off-season. "On the flight back, Dusty comes over to me and asks, 'What are you going to be doing this winter?'" Niedenfuer recounted. "I told him, 'Well, the team wants me to go to winter ball.' And he says, 'Well, don't worry. Even though we're down two-nothing, we're going to still have three or four more weeks of playing here.' Dusty was a very positive guy with the young players. And that was a real big key; how he and all the veterans treated us twenty- to twenty-four-year-olds was great."

While the Astros were riding high, some of them, like Sambito, the game two winner in relief, believed the divisional series was far from over due to the issues the Astros had winning games at Dodger Stadium. "There were definitely some thoughts in our club about how, the year before, we couldn't win at Dodger Stadium in the final three games of the regular season to clinch the division," Sambito said. "We lost three straight there and had to win the one-game playoff game, which we did. But in the back of our minds, we knew we didn't play well there. So, there we were again, in pretty much a similar situation in '81—needing to win one out of three. But we knew it wasn't going to be easy. We always played close, low-scoring games against them. It was more of a trademark of Astros-Dodgers baseball at that point."

But while it was true that the Astros had struggled mightily at Dodger Stadium—heading into the divisional series, they were losers of eleven of their last thirteen games there—the combination of the Astros' dominating pitching staff mixed with a Dodgers lineup that had experienced a scoring drought for the better part of a month didn't bode well for the men in blue-and-white.

The Astros would start All-Star selection Bob Knepper, a six-year veteran enjoying by far the best season of his career with a 9–5 record and a minuscule 2.18 ERA. For the Dodgers, in desperation mode, they would go with the more experienced Burt Hooton on short rest over regular-rested Bob Welch. No one could debate the move. Hooton's numbers were impressive, and his 2.28 ERA was the lowest of his ten seasons as a full-time starting pitcher.

Home cooking never tasted so good for the Dodgers, as they would waste no time in jumping all over Knepper in the bottom of the first inning. Lopes walked, Landreaux sacrifice-bunted him to second, Baker drove him home with a double to left field, and Garvey then topped off the inning by belting a two-run homer to give the Dodgers a very quick 3–0 lead. Hooton would pitch masterfully over seven frames, with the only mistake coming in the third, when he gave up a home run to Howe. The run would prove insignificant, especially after the Dodgers broke the game open with three runs in the eighth off Sambito, to win the third game of the divisional series by the score of 6–1.

Now, with the fourth game presenting an opportunity for the Dodgers to knot the series, all eyes were once again turned to Valenzuela, who would once again be pitching on just three days' rest. On Houston's side,

Bill Virdon opted to give Ryan his full four days' rest before a possible game five with everything on the line; he chose to go with yet another veteran from his talented stable of pitchers, Vern Ruhle. As a spot starter who also worked out of the bullpen, Ruhle was coming off two of his most impressive seasons of his eight in the big leagues, posting a 12–4 record with a 2.37 ERA in '80 and a 2.91 ERA in '81. While not a dominating pitcher like Ryan, Ruhle was more than capable of beating any team in the league. And in this game, he would prove it.

Game four would be more like what was expected in an Astros-Dodgers match-up rather than the rout by the Dodgers in the previous contest. Both Valenzuela and Ruhle were tossing perfect games through the first four innings. However, with the game still scoreless in the bottom of the fifth, Pedro Guerrero belted a two-out solo home run for the Dodgers' first hit of the game, giving them a 1–0 lead.

With Valenzuela positively dealing through the middle of the seventh, having given up just a lone hit to Cedeño in the fifth inning and then proceeding to pick him off at first, the Dodgers added to their lead in the bottom half of the inning when Bill Russell rapped a clutch, two-out single to right field to bring home Garvey to make it 2–0. But with the dominance and poise Fernando was displaying on the mound, it might just as well have felt more like 10–0 to the Astros. "When you get to play with an elite pitcher like Fernando was, even at that young age, the day he was pitching—especially in the postseason—we expected to win," Niedenfuer said. "And I'm sure the other team expected that they might not win. He was just that dominant. He definitely raised the expectations on our team. And the guys enjoyed playing behind him because he was around the strike zone so much and he worked fast."

Only a cut Valenzuela developed on the middle finger of his left hand in the ninth inning could stymie his mastery of the Astros. Terry Puhl took advantage of it with a one-out double to center field and would score a couple of batters later when Tony Scott hit a two-out RBI single to left field to trim the Dodgers' lead to 2–1. But despite the cut and a rising pitch count, Tommy Lasorda stuck with Fernando and was rewarded for it when Valenzuela retired Cruz on a pop-out to catcher Mike Scioscia to end the game and knot the division series at two games apiece. "His performance was just so impressive," recalled Sambito. "His mound presence and confidence were impressive—he never got rattled. He knew what he was doing out there at all times. The only thing he was lacking was experience, but I guess he showed that sometimes you don't need experience."

In the two games he pitched in that divisional series, Valenzuela posted a 1.06 ERA over seventeen innings—an astounding performance by a rookie pitcher under the bright lights of the postseason. And just as the Dodgers had done at the end of the 1980 regular season in keeping Houston from clinching the division title on their home turf, they were doing it again by keeping them from winning that one, final, elusive game to win the divisional series. Los Angeles was now just one victory away from moving on to the National League Championship Series, and Valenzuela's superb and gutsy performance had made it all possible.

But a tremendous hurdle stood in their way—a fully rested and ready Nolan Ryan. Ryan had downright dominated the Dodgers over his last two starts against them, giving up a mere *two hits* over his last eighteen innings pitched against them. Reuss, who would pitch this game on short rest, also had had remarkable success versus his opponent, thus setting up this fifth and final game at Dodger Stadium to be a classic confrontation between two of the game's elite pitchers.

The decisive game would live up to expectations, with nothing but goose eggs on the scoreboard for each team through five innings. But then the Dodgers would finally break through against Ryan in the bottom half of the sixth, scoring three runs with RBI singles from Monday and Scioscia and then another when Russell knocked the ball out of Walling's glove on a wide throw to first base to give the Dodgers a 3–0 lead. Ryan would strike out Reuss to end the inning, but he was done for the day; a pinch hitter came in for him in the top of the seventh inning.

With Reuss still dealing zeros, the Dodgers added to their lead with a Garvey RBI triple off Frank LaCorte in the bottom half of the seventh to take a commanding 4–0 lead. It would prove insurmountable for the Astros, as Reuss continued his stellar work and went the distance to complete a five-hit shutout—a remarkable culmination of eighteen straight scoreless innings in his two starts—to win the NL West division series for the Dodgers. "I was just trying to get one out at a time and pitch the game accordingly," Reuss recalled. "If I was behind in the count, then I had to keep in mind the pitch selection. If I'm even up, same thing. And then when I was ahead, there was a little more room for margin of error. But in the postseason, there's a little more at stake, so there's no way that you can possibly let your guard down and take anything for granted because the team that you're playing, well, it's no accident that they're in the postseason for a good reason—they've earned the right to be there."

The Dodgers would now take on a far superior all-around team in the Montreal Expos in the National League Championship Series. And Valenzuela would have another series in which to shine in front of a national and international audience.

Blue Monday

18

> We had Fernando on the ropes early, but we didn't
> get him. And then he was just unbelievable.
>
> —Expos pitcher BILL LEE on Valenzuela's game five
> performance in the '81 NLCS

The irony was rich. For all the hysteria, accolades, and praise heaped upon Valenzuela throughout Fernandomania, arguably the most impressive outing of his *entire career*—the fifth game of the 1981 National League Championship Series—will forever be overshadowed by one dramatic swing of the bat from his teammate Rick Monday. And in the annals of baseball history, the outcome of this historic game—dubbed "Blue Monday" for how sad the Dodger blue slugger made Montreal Expos fans on a Monday afternoon that October—would further cement the legacy of greatness for one of the game's most storied franchises while contributing to the eventual demise of another team's long-term viability north of the border.

Reputation-wise, the two clubs couldn't have been more different. While the Dodgers, at least publicly, projected a pristine, buttoned-up image among the masses, the Expos were like a Canadian version of the Yankees—loads of talent, inflated egos, and plenty of infighting. "We were always fighting amongst ourselves," Bill Lee recalled.

Another way they were like the Bronx Bombers was how, late in the season, they too saw their manager fired—in their case, the brash future Hall of Famer Dick Williams. "Dick was a Napoleonic type of manager," Lee said. "It was his way or the highway, but he was always good in the late innings. He was acerbic. He was brilliant. And boy, he could get you mad. He was like Hannibal Lecter. He could wiggle his finger and cause you distress."

Despite Williams's vinegary personality with his players and staff at times, there was no denying that, after taking over an awful sixth-place club that lost 107 games in 1976, he improved the team each year, ultimately leading the Expos to back-to-back second-place finishes in 1979 and 1980—winning 95 and 90 victories, respectively—the best combined record in the National League over those two seasons. But in 1981 they had underachieved, finishing with a record of 30–25 in the first half, in third place behind the NL East–leading Phillies, and they began the second half with just a 14–12 record. For as much angst as Williams brought to the organization, the Expos players, at least initially after his firing, were a dysfunctional team at best and one talking mutiny at worst without him. "Williams got into a fight with [owner Charles] Bronfman and [general manager John] McHale, and they got rid of him," Lee recalled. "And then the next thing you know, they bring in Jim Fanning and we lose three games early on. Warren Cromartie calls a [players] meeting in Philadelphia and goes, 'We have no coaches. No nothing. Does anybody know Dick Williams's phone number?' And I go, 'Marti,' you hated Dick Williams.' But he knew he was an effective manager. And then I turn to Steve Rogers and say, 'You pitch well because you hate Dick Williams.' With Rogers and Williams, it was like the adversarial relationship that Earl Weaver and Jim Palmer had [in Baltimore]."

Expos closer Jeff Reardon, who pitched to a remarkable 1.30 ERA over forty-one and two-thirds innings after arriving in a trade with the Mets that season and would go on to have more career saves than Hall of Fame relievers Rollie Fingers, Goose Gossage, and Bruce Sutter (and who as of 2022 is still not in the Hall of Fame), further elaborated on the abrasiveness of Williams. "Dick was a prick," Reardon said bluntly. "I hate to say it like that, but it didn't seem like anybody liked the guy. I remember one time sitting in the dugout, which I did the first couple of innings of a game before going to the bullpen because I liked watching the hitters, and [Coach] Vern Rapp said, 'Dick, maybe we should try to hit-and-run.' And I'm thinking, *Not a bad idea.* Dick says to him, 'Vern, go take a piss.'"

It drove McHale crazy the way Williams handled Reardon, whom the Expos obtained from the Mets for a heavy price in young five-tool outfielder Ellis Valentine just before the strike. Reardon hadn't allowed a run in his last seven appearances before Williams's firing, but McHale felt his manager went longer than he should have with relievers Bill Lee, Elías Sosa, and Woodie Fryman rather than Reardon. Reardon felt certain that a combination of irritability and ego were Williams's undoing, ultimately leading to his dismissal from the Expos. "Williams used me as a set-up man," Reardon recalled. "But he went on ripping me [after he got fired] because he thought I complained about not being the closer to the front office. He called me a crybaby. But I never even knew where the front office was. I wasn't that type of player. So I was very upset when I read that stuff he was saying about me. After he got fired, I heard the story of what went on and I'll tell it to anybody, and swear by it, because the guy was in the room when it happened. John McHale said to Dick, 'Why aren't you using Reardon as a closer? This is the reason we traded for him.' And Dick said to him right away, 'Don't tell me how to fucking manage.' And McHale said, 'Yes I will. *You're fired!*'"

Williams would be replaced by "Gentleman Jim" Fanning, whose disposition was the polar opposite of his predecessor's. "It was almost like a librarian taking over as the manager," Reardon said. "There wasn't a whole lot of respect for Fanning, because he was a front office man, not a field man. But you know, he did the best he could." In fact, Fanning hadn't worn a baseball uniform or managed a team at any level in nearly twenty years. And it was his first time managing in the Major Leagues. But what he had going for him was an association with McHale since 1961, when McHale was president of the Milwaukee Braves. Even Fanning, who was the Expos' vice president in charge of player development at the time, was surprised by the move, telling reporters, "I'm excited obviously. I suppose it's something every guy wants to do when he starts managing in the minor leagues. But I need to get *acquainted* with my team."

Reardon recalled incredulously how out of place Fanning seemed his first day as the Expos' new skipper. "When Fanning took over, we're in Philadelphia, and in the middle of the locker room, there were picnic tables. Well, I always went to the ballpark early to do my running, and I see this guy getting dressed in his uniform by one of the picnic tables. I'm like, *Who the fuck is this guy?* He sees me, comes over, shakes my hand and goes, 'Jeff, my name's Jim Fanning,' because I had never met him before. 'I'm your new manager.' I said, 'Hey, you got an office, you know.' He goes, 'I do?' I said, 'Yeah, you've got a big office back there.' He goes, 'I didn't know that!' I'm saying to myself, 'This guy's a winner.' But I ended up liking him because he said to me, 'I'm just telling you right now, from now on, you're my closer.'"

The Expos may have had turmoil and controversy, but they were also supremely talented. They were more than capable of turning things around quickly. "I felt that Montreal had the best team in the world," exclaimed Dusty Baker. "Over a five-year period, Montreal and Philadelphia, in that order, had more talent than anybody. The Expos had speed, they had power, they had outstanding pitching. God! With Gary Carter, Ellis Valentine, Andre Dawson, Tim Raines, and Steve Rogers, they could have gone to the World Series four or five times during that period."

Despite a slow start in baseball's "second" season of 1981, the Expos won eleven of their last fifteen games of the campaign—including a timely seven-game winning streak in late September—to capture the second-half NL East crown. They would then shock the defending world champion Phillies three games to two in their division series, with Steve Rogers outdueling Hall of Famer Steve Carlton in both the first and the fifth-and-deciding game. It was now off to Los Angeles to take on the Dodgers in the National League Championship Series. But even the flight to the West Coast wasn't without controversy. Bill Lee, the Expos' last pitcher to win at Dodger Stadium (Montreal had remarkably lost eighteen of its last nineteen games in Los Angeles), was facing possible disciplinary action by club management for skipping the team charter because he was irked that girlfriends weren't permitted to accompany the players but wives were. Lee, nicknamed "Spaceman" for his countercultural activities in the conservative, buttoned-up world of baseball, was ridiculed—if somewhat humorously—by McHale for his actions. "We're waiting to see if he arrives by parachute or spacecraft," the general manager told the press in Los Angeles. For the record, Lee landed by way of commercial airliner.

Despite the distraction, the Expos were raring to go—even if a bit concerned about a certain Mexican southpaw. "After we beat the Phillies, our confidence went way up," Reardon recalled. "But while we were excited to play the Dodgers, we were also worried. We knew that we could face Valenzuela twice, and he would be tough to beat. They had other good players, too, but Fernando was the key for us to get around."

The Dodgers were also getting back Ron Cey, inactive since his left forearm was fractured by a Tom Griffin pitch against the Giants a month earlier. Dr. Frank Jobe, the orthopedic surgeon made famous for performing the first "Tommy John surgery," had previously predicted that Cey would be in a cast for six weeks—and thus likely to miss the entire postseason. But Cey shed the cast after just three weeks and would give the Dodgers a tremendous boost to the middle of their lineup in this championship series. With Cey back at third base, Pedro Guerrero moved to right field, and the two paid immediate dividends for the Dodgers in the first playoff game. Cey had two hits, including an RBI double to score Steve Garvey with the Dodgers' first run of the game. And in the eighth, Guerrero slammed a two-run homer to turn a close game into a commanding 4-0 Dodgers lead. Burt Hooton was masterful on the mound, tossing seven and two-thirds innings of shutout ball and Los Angeles took the opener, 5-1.

With Hooton's performance, the Dodgers' starting pitching had continued its domination of the postseason. And next up was Valenzuela. So, with the combination of the Dodgers' home field dominance over the Expos and with El Toro taking the mound for LA in playoff game two, Montreal's prospects suddenly looked bleak. And when the Expos slated a journeyman, Ray Burris, to pitch next, it raised a few eyebrows. Over the previous two seasons, Burris had been waived by the Yankees and released by the lowly Mets. But under the heading "Anything can happen in baseball," it certainly did for Montreal in NLCS game two. Burris, he of the lifetime 4.26 ERA over nine seasons, pitched the game of his life, baffling the Dodgers with a five-hit shutout. Valenzuela, to his credit, pitched well enough to win, giving up three runs over six innings, but it clearly wasn't a vintage Fernando outing. And while it was his third start in nine days and he was clearly feeling some fatigue, credit the Expos' lineup for breaking through like they did against Valenzuela— especially in Los Angeles, where he had been so unhittable all season. "We laid off the screwball, because he throws those for a lot of balls," said Tim Raines, who led the Expos' attack with three hits in the game.

With the series now deadlocked at one game apiece as the clubs flew east to Montreal, forecasts called for temperatures dipping into the high thirties for the remaining games of the championship series. Much was being written about how the elements might affect the warm-weather Dodgers.

*

Olympic Stadium, sometimes called the "Big O," was generally a miserable environment in which to play baseball. Designed for track events to be held in the 1976 Summer Olympics, it was hardly ideal for baseball games or the players. The stadium was designed by French architect Roger Taillibert to be a state-of-the-art facility featuring a retractable roof, which was to be opened and closed by cables suspended from a 574-foot tower, making it the tallest inclined structure in the world. But at that time in 1981, the retractable roof was not yet completed, creating an opening smaller than the playing field and making the stadium a very chilly place for spring and fall games.

Lee, not surprisingly, had a most colorful description of the Big O's oystershell-like open roof: "It looked like a giant bidet, like a place where Paul Bunyan's wife squatted to take a leak." But it didn't mean Lee didn't love pitching there. "It was good for me because when it was sunny, it had an ellipse around it. It was not a round circle. It was how the planets go around the earth—very Copernican. And when the light would come down when I pitched, it was great to change speeds because hitters couldn't really respect speed change. If you just threw hard, you got hit. If you just threw hard and breaking balls, you got hit. But if you were a three-pitch pitcher like I was, it was really good."

But while the opening in the roof helped Lee, the hard playing surface was unforgiving and shortened the careers of some Expos players. "It was damaging," Andre Dawson recalled. "It was like playing on a gymnasium hardwood floor. It really took its toll and put my career at risk. But I didn't dwell on it too much. I just tried to block it out and play however my body allowed me to. And it wasn't until I left Montreal and went to Chicago and played on a natural surface over half of the games that I really noticed the difference. It's just one of those situations when I look back on it, you can't do anything about. It's just what the game was at that time with a lot of multipurpose stadiums with the AstroTurf in mind for weather purposes. But a lot of times I just went out and bit the bullet, took my medications, and played as well and as often as I could."

"It was like playing in a parking lot," is how Reardon described it. "I can see why Andre Dawson and Gary Carter were so badly affected by it. Carter was catcher, but he still had to run. I think he told me he had like twenty knee operations after he was finished there. And I don't know how Dawson or even Tim Raines lasted as long as they did playing on it. It really was a carpet on a cement floor."

But for as bad as the stadium was for the players' well-being, they loved the Montreal fans. "The people up there were so nice," Reardon said. "We didn't know what the hell they were saying because it was all in French, but they cheered a lot for us. In my first game playing there in '81, there were forty-three thousand people in the stands. I'm like, *Oh my God!* Compared to Shea Stadium, where they would be lucky to get fifteen thousand fans on a Saturday, it was a huge difference. Montreal drew great, and those fans were nice and polite. It's just too bad they didn't have a better stadium. It was already ancient from the time they built it."

To make matters worse, cold weather had already made its presence known in Montreal by mid-October. For some of the Dodgers used to playing in the warm temperatures of Southern California, the frigid conditions would represent a major challenge, while others, like Cey, were ready for it. "When I was growing up in Tacoma, Washington," he said, "I played baseball in rain and snow. It's cold in Montreal, but I'll be ready."

Another Dodger accustomed to blustery weather was the Missouri-bred Reuss, who would start the third playoff game by facing off against Expos ace Steve Rogers. The two would pitch brilliantly into the sixth inning, when, with the Dodgers leading 1-0, the Expos finally got to Reuss. Montreal third baseman Larry Parrish ripped an RBI single to tie the game. Then the next batter, light-hitting Jerry White, belted a three-run homer, giving the Expos all the runs they would need in a 4-1 victory. "Everybody says, '*Jerry Who?*' Well, I'd like to stop that '*who stuff*,'" White told reporters after the game.

Now the Dodgers were in a serious bind—down two games to one. In the fourth NLCS game, it was either win or go home. The two clubs put out their game one starters—Burt Hooton and Bill Gullickson—with similar results. Both starters, as they had in their previous outing, pitched well and kept the game close into the late innings, before the

Expos' bullpen surrendered a bunch of runs to the Dodgers. In this one, with the score tied 1-1 in the top of the eighth inning with one out and Baker on first, Garvey belted the first pitch he saw from Gullickson for a two-run homer to put the Dodgers on top 3-1. The "Iron Man" all but admitted he was trying to go long—something most hitters rarely try to do. "You try to do something to break up a situation like a 1-1 tie," Garvey said. "After the sixth inning, I'll usually try to drive the ball for a home run on the first two strikes. After that, I just tried to make contact." The Dodgers would tack on four more runs in the ninth against three different Expos relievers—Fryman, Sosa, and Lee—to round out the scoring of their 7-1 victory.

The Dodgers, as they had done in the previous series against the Astros, had staved off elimination to live another day. The Dodgers would now pin their hopes for survival—and a trip to the World Series—on the twenty-year-old Valenzuela in the fifth and deciding game of the league championship series.

*

A cold rain descended on the city of Montreal for the scheduled Sunday game. After a three-hour delay, the contest was postponed until the next day—giving game two starters Valenzuela and Burris a full rest between starts. That evening, before the biggest start of his young career, Fernando went out on the town to grab dinner with a few of his Dodgers teammates. But for Valenzuela, it would be a short evening. "At the restaurant, Fernando said to me, 'Pete, I'm out of here. I'm going back to the hotel,'" recalled Pedro Guerrero. "And I said, 'Why? It's still early.' And he said, 'No, I'm pitching tomorrow and I'm going to beat those guys. Not even the cold is going to save them!' So I said, 'Okay, go for it!' He was positive—*very* positive."

The next day, the rain tapered off to a drizzle with temperatures barely above 40 degrees Fahrenheit. But this time, after a rain delay of just half an hour, there would be a ball game with the resilient, never-say-die Dodgers looking to win their fifth sudden-death postseason game, one in which a defeat would have ended their '81 season. "We were always a team that had a controlled aggressiveness," was how Garvey described the Dodgers of that era. "Controlled aggressiveness means taking your time, staying within yourself, exerting effort at the right time, staying focused, not doing outlandish things, not wasting energy, not overthinking, and not losing control of your emotions."

But standing in their way was an Expos team that was supremely confident. "Oh, we felt sure we were going to win," Lee said. "Burris was throwing so good. We believed there was no way we were going to lose. And then we were going to beat the Yankees in the World Series."

Burris may have been on a roll, but the Dodgers had Fernando. Yet, much of the talk surrounding Valenzuela revolved around how this kid from Mexico would handle the freezing conditions. "The cold was terrible," recalled Monday. "But before the game, Fernando and I were walking out towards the outfield and, with his mouth, he's creating bubbles on his tongue and blowing them into the air. And then there was a little snowflake that's coming down, and he's catching it with his tongue. He was *really* uptight [sarcasm]. So I asked him, 'Fernando, have you ever seen snow before?' And he goes, 'Oh *sí*, in the mountains.' And I'm thinking, *We ain't in the mountains*."

Garvey recalled Lasorda using the elements to play up the underdog card with the press: "Tommy announces Fernando as the starter, thinking people will probably say things like, 'He's this kid from Mexico up in Montreal. You know, he's probably not going to do that well with the cold weather and so forth.' But despite the cool day, with everything that Fernando had accomplished, there was no question that Tommy was going to ride him."

The crowd of partisan Expos fans, many of whom had sat in the cold rain the previous day for hours until the game was postponed, had come back revved up. "Oh, they were going nuts," Reardon recalled. "The place was packed. They were pretty excited, so I really thought we were going to do it." One of those fans was a young Anson Tebbetts, who became Vermont's secretary of agriculture in 2017 and who on that game day in 1981 had played hooky from school with his history teacher, Don Marcus, and two of his high school friends. "It was quite common for Expos games to be filled with Vermonters," Tebbetts recalled. "Getting across the border was always interesting back then. Pre-9/11, border patrol officers might be eating a donut and just wave you through. That particular day, we didn't see anyone in the booth, so we just drove across. About two hundred feet later, we heard sirens going off and were chased down by border patrol. The officer goes, 'What the heck were you doing?

You should have stopped. We could have *shot* you!' I remember thinking we weren't going to make it to the game because we were stopped. I was just a high school kid that didn't leave Vermont very much to go to the big city, so that left an impression on me." After some quick explaining to the border patrol officers, they continued their journey to Olympic Stadium. "It was fascinating," Tebbetts said. "We were sitting in the top row of the center-field bleachers, and it was *really loud*. The fans would bang on the classic hard plastic seats that went up and down and made an incredible noise. They would bang them when Expos' rallies would start or if they got two strikes on a batter. And throughout the bilingual stands, you could hear the beer vendors shout, '*Bière froide!* Cold beer!' Maybe our teacher got in trouble for playing hooky with us. We didn't know. But it certainly was worth it. I think I probably learned more on that day than I would have learned in class—that's for sure!"

The pumped-up crowd's enthusiasm reached thunderous levels in the bottom of the first, when the Expos started to rally against Valenzuela. Lead-off hitter Raines belted a double off the center-field wall to get things started. Rodney Scott followed with a sacrifice bunt, but when Fernando's throw to try to get Raines at third base was late, the Expos had runners on the corners with nobody out and their best hitter, Andre Dawson, coming to the plate looking to bust the game open early. Dawson, looking for Valenzuela's screwball all the way, instead got jammed by a slider and hit into a double play to plate Raines and give the Expos a 1–0 lead. Fernando would get Carter to hit a harmless fly ball to center field to end the inning relatively unscathed. In a prelude of things to come, as Valenzuela walked off the mound toward the dugout, he smiled, as if to signal that was all the Expos were going to score off him that day.

"I think he showed his composure getting out of that first inning jam," Lyle Spencer recalled. "His composure came with competing with older guys at a young age back home [in Mexico], and I think that was extremely helpful to him. He never felt overwhelmed by a situation. He was just able to lock in. And I think that's true of almost all great athletes. They have a special gene that allows them to just block out everything around them and focus on what they have to do. And, to me, that was most evident in game five in Montreal. I have always felt that was his greatest performance because of the weather conditions and that unbelievably powerful lineup with three future Hall of Famers

[Raines, Dawson, and Carter] and all the other right-handed hitters the Expos had. It was *freezing* that day. He's blowing steam on the mound from the cold. It was unbelievable watching him getting through that Expos lineup with everything on the line. I don't think many people experienced anything like that, and he was still just a kid from Mexico. That's when it hit me how special and how extraordinary Fernando was."

And even though Valenzuela was still just a young, rookie pitcher, his teammates and manager never had any doubts about him. "Getting out of that jam—that was Fernando," Garvey said. "He stayed within himself. He never got too high or too low. Tommy was going to let him work his way out of jams, and I think Fernando knew that. When you know that you can't make a lot of mistakes, it's normal to find yourself always looking into the dugout or out at the bullpen instead of knowing that you're going to have to push your way out of jams."

The Expos knew they had missed out on a tremendous opportunity. It's often said in baseball that with the great pitchers, you've got to knock them out early because they get stronger as the game goes on. "If we get Fernando down three runs in the first had Dawson hit a ball out, everything changes," lamented Lee. "One big hit there and Lasorda might go into his bullpen."

Still others, like Reardon, saw getting on the board first against Valenzuela as validation they could beat him. "After we almost got him in the first inning, we realized that we might have a chance to beat those guys," Reardon said. "It gave us a lot of confidence."

And that confidence would grow as Burris continued to pile up scoreless inning after scoreless inning against the Dodgers as a follow-up to his shutout over them in game two. The scoreless streak would reach thirteen, as the Expos held on to their 1–0 lead through four innings.

But then in the top of the fifth, the Dodgers would at last break through against Burris. Monday, inserted into the lineup to replace a slumping Kenny Landreaux, singled to start the frame. After fouling off a pitch on a hit-and-run and then fouling off a bunt attempt, Guerrero singled to right, putting runners on first and third with nobody out. After Scioscia lined out to second, Valenzuela came to the plate looking to help his own cause. During his at bat, a short wild pitch moved Guerrero to second, giving the Dodgers two runners in scoring position. Then, on a 2–2 pitch, Fernando grounded out to the left of Expos second baseman Rodney

Scott to bring home Monday and tie the game at one apiece. For a pitcher hitting in that vital situation, Fernando did a remarkable job of bringing the run home any way he could. He proved he could beat a team with not just his left arm but with his hitting skills as well.

Valenzuela would return to the mound and dominate the Expos, retiring the next eight batters in a row before surrendering a two-out double to Larry Parrish in the bottom of the seventh. After an intentional walk to White, he got out of that inning after Cromartie popped out harmlessly to Scioscia behind the plate. Raines's proclamation after the Expos' game two victory that the key to their success was laying off Valenzuela's off-the-plate screwballs wasn't the case this time. Fernando wasn't just throwing strikes with his signature pitch but "painting the black" on both sides of the plate. "Fernando had movement like [Luis] Tiant in that game," Lee said, making the comparison to his former Red Sox teammate. "He could throw the ball by you, and you didn't like that. And then he'd fool you with that changeup. We started swinging at bad pitches, at too many balls out of the strike zone."

On the Expos' side, Burris was equally up to the task at hand, retiring the Dodgers in order in both the sixth and seventh innings. "Both Fernando and Burris were matching each other pitch for pitch," Dawson said. "And facing Fernando early in his career was tough. He was as dominant in that game as he had been at any other time he took the mound."

As the game moved into the eighth inning, tensions were rising at Olympic Stadium. "It was just so nerve-racking," recalled Reardon. "When we were hitting, the fans were so quiet until something happened, and then they went nuts. Everybody was on edge every pitch."

And the elements were becoming increasingly challenging for the players, with the mercury dropping with each passing inning. "As the game goes on," Garvey recalled, "you've got this great pitching and it's getting colder and colder. I tried never to wear long sleeves—not that I wanted to show off my muscles—but because they were constrictive to me. But I did in this game. By the late innings, boy, it was starting to feel chilly."

But while the young Mexican could be forgiven for being affected by the increasingly chilly weather, he seemed unfazed by it. "I'm not sure to his day that he understood it was cold," Monday said. "For Fernando, it was just like another game. He put his pitching hand in his back pocket to keep it warm. Other than that, he was like, *Okay, who's hitting next?*" On the Expos' side, they were astonished by Valenzuela's performance under the circumstances. "I'm thinking, *Boy, this guy is really something,*" said Reardon. "You would never figure the guy was from Mexico. We figured by this point in the game with him pitching up in actual snowy weather that he wasn't used to that it would affect him. So to see this rookie go out there in a game five and deal like he was—it was simply mind-blowing. I knew right then that he was going to have a good, long career. There were all these jokes about who knew how old Fernando really was—like there always were about other guys from other countries. Anyway, he was holding us in check that whole game."

If any team had an advantage under these adverse conditions, it would certainly seem that Montreal would, having been used to these elements at home games both early and late in the season. But the Dodgers clearly held an edge with their vast postseason experience over the younger Expos. "As good a team as Montreal had—and they really had some great players—they had never won a game that would put them in the World Series before," Garvey observed. "And it was just the opposite for us, having won pennants in '74, '77, and '78. Yet, with the history and the culture of our group, we still hadn't won the world championship yet. So there was a lot on the line for both teams."

After the Dodgers threatened in their top of the eighth with a one-out infield single by Lopes, who then promptly stole second base but was ultimately erased on a fielder's choice groundout at third to end the potential rally, Valenzuela went back out to the mound to pitch the bottom of the frame of this tight 1–1 game. Not only was the level of pressure increasing, but so was Valenzuela's pitch count—swelling to more than a hundred, as was the case in most of his starts. But as he breezed through the Expos' three hitters (including Tim Wallach, who pinch-hit for Burris), removing him from the game was the last thing anyone on the Dodgers' side was thinking about. "There was no pitch count that day," Baker said. "There was a *performance* count. We had to think who we could bring in from the bullpen that was going to be better than who we had out there in Fernando. That's no slight against any bullpen guy. That's a tribute to who you got out there. You weren't going to take out a Fernando—just like you wouldn't take out a [Tom] Seaver or a [Steve]

Carlton. Later on, I think those high pitch counts might have shortened or affected Fernando's career and his earning power. But like I've said, for five or six years there, he was Sandy Koufax."

With Burris now removed from the game, Fanning went for the jugular by bringing in his ace starting pitcher, Steve Rogers, to face the Dodgers in the top of the ninth. But while Rogers had been outstanding in winning three postseason games that October, it was seen as a very risky move. After all, the Expos had an outstanding bullpen led by Reardon. Additionally, starting pitchers have different mind-sets than relievers do—a tendency to go out and throw strikes—and can be less careful as a result. The move to bring in Rogers was downright shocking to Reardon himself. "I figured Fanning didn't have a choice—we're talking the playoffs, ninth inning, and he had me warming up first anyway," Reardon said. "So when Fanning brought Rogers in, I thought he was actually calling for me. Cy [the nickname given Rogers by his teammates for perennially being a Cy Young Award candidate] was warming up too, but I thought he was getting ready for Game One of the World Series (if we won). I'm thinking, *Maybe we're being pretty confident here.* Anyway, [right-field umpire] Dutch Rennert makes the motion for the beard, so I start walking in. But Rennert goes, 'No, Jeff, not you.' I asked, 'What do you mean?' And he said, 'He wants Rogers.' I said, 'You sure?' See, Steve had a beard then. So Rennert goes, 'Yeah, I'm sure. He said he wants Rogers.' So I stayed out there in the bullpen, still trying to throw and stay warm. I remember how damn cold it was and how the baseball felt like a snowball. I have nothing against them putting Steve in. But he started games—he was no reliever. And I was sure the cold weather wasn't going to help him. When you're sitting on the bench like he was and probably never thinking you're going to go in the game, it's not easy. [As a starter], he probably didn't have enough time to get warmed up."

Still, with Rogers in the game to keep the Dodgers at bay, this epic game for the ages had now seemingly taken on a higher dimension—like the first eight innings were a series of aperitifs for the delicious main course to come. With the Montreal crowd chanting "Steve! Steve! Steve!" in unison, Rogers retired Garvey easily enough on a pop-out to Scott at second base. But then Ron Cey temporarily silenced the boisterous fans with a high and deep drive to left field. Off the bat, it looked like it had a good chance to leave the park, but it ultimately died in the glove of Raines on the warning track for the second out of the inning.

That set the stage for one of baseball's all-time classic moments.

*

The Expos believed they had dodged a bullet. A slightly warmer day and Cey's shot to left would have given the Dodgers the lead. Yet, Fanning left the right-handed starter out there to face the always dangerous left-handed-hitting Monday. For as stunned as some of the Expos were that Rogers was even in the game to begin with, leaving him in to face Monday left some of them utterly flabbergasted. "Rogers had been tremendous in the playoffs, but in a situation like that, you've got to bring me in," said Lee, the left-handed reliever. "I'm warming up in the bullpen, ready to go. I touch my hat. Fanning sees me, gives me a smirk, and leaves Rogers in. I even know how I would have pitched Monday— sinkers in, breaking balls away. I would have gotten his attention inside and then pitched him away. That way, there's no way he can hurt you. If I had come in, gotten Monday out, and we went on to win the game, they would've made me president of Canada!"

Reardon was just as miffed that *he* wasn't in the game, considering how comfortable he said he felt pitching against Monday. Statistics of their head-to-head match-ups would on paper appear to back him up on that sentiment. In the ten times the two faced one another from 1980 through 1984, Monday was hitless in nine of those at bats—striking out four times—with one walk. In fairness to Monday, by this point the two had only faced one another twice—with the other eight confrontations coming in the twilight of Monday's career. "If it were today with saber-metrics, Fanning may have let Cy [Rogers] pitch first and then bring me in to face Monday," Reardon said. "That's how baseball is now. But even then, the writers after the game were all wondering why the hell I didn't go in the game."

In any event, it was Rogers—and not a relief pitcher—who would face Monday, and he would fall behind 3-1 in the count. Not wanting to put the go-ahead run on base, Rogers would throw him a fastball up and over the heart of the plate. Monday feasted on it, belting an arcing line shot to the deepest part of the ballpark in center field. The only issue for the Dodgers slugger was knowing where the hell it went! "Depth perception for me was kind of weird, anyway, in Olympic Stadium," Monday said. "They didn't have the roof on back then. Behind the center-field fence it went back, it seemed, for miles of nothingness in that stadium. There were no stands out there. It was truly a weird situation of depth perception. It was just the opposite for a center fielder or right fielder looking in, but from home plate looking out, it went so far beyond the fence that depth perception was always kind of goofy for me. So I didn't watch it sail—or the flight of the ball. I caught a glimpse of it just as it disappeared. I knew it was hit well, and I went down the first base line initially thinking, *Damn it! Did I hit all of it?* And then I was watching Andre Dawson in center field, and he kept running, kept running, and I'm thinking, *Well, maybe it's off the wall.* It was a very high wall. And then Dawson started to run out of room, got closer to the fence, and that's about the time that I saw the ball, and then didn't see the ball in play. I saw it disappear. Home run."

Monday, who would later tell reporters it was the first time in his career that he was unable to follow the flight of one of his home runs, was hardly alone in losing the ball in cavernous Olympic Stadium. "I'm going to be honest with you," Reuss said. "If anybody says they could follow the arc of the ball off [Monday's] bat, at least from our bench, they had better eyes than I did because I couldn't see it at all. In that stadium, at least back then, they had a row of lights that were between the bleachers and the top of the ballpark. When the ball gets hit into the outfield and up into those lights, you lose it as the ball arcs and comes back down through the lights again. That's exactly what happened with Monday's home run. What I did was watch Dawson go back to the fence and look for his reaction. He was poised to jump for it, but he never had to because the ball cleared the fence by plenty. And that was when I knew it was a home run. I never did actually see it go out, though."

There was one person in Olympic Stadium that afternoon who knew exactly where the ball was. "It wasn't deceiving to me at all," Dawson recalled about the flight of Monday's home run ball. "I felt that I had a bead on it. It was just a matter of how far the ball would carry, but I knew Monday hit it well. He had hit another pitch deep down the right-field line earlier in the game, so I backed up to make sure I didn't give up a double on this one. But once the ball took flight, I did feel that, *Okay, I've got a good bead on it*, and I went back to the wall, but it just kept carrying."

Monday's home run—by far the most important of the 241 he hit throughout his career—gave the Dodgers a 2–1 lead and ignited a wild celebration at home plate as his teammates swarmed out onto the field. Monday was exultant as he circled first base, punching the air while leaping in midstride—a reaction that would be replayed countless times during the introduction to NBC's *Game of the Week* broadcasts for years to come.

Rogers would end the Dodgers' half of the ninth inning by striking out Guerrero, but the crowd of 36,491, whose excitement had reached a fever pitch just before Monday's home run in anticipation of the Expos batting in the bottom of the ninth of a tie game with the chance to win the pennant in dramatic fashion, sat silenced and stunned. They knew the hill the Expos would have to climb, how a one-run deficit felt more like five. Valenzuela had blinded Montreal since his rough first inning, spinning a three-hitter to that point.

Fernando would start the bottom of the ninth much as the demoralized Expos faithful had feared—two up and two down—by retiring Scott on a grounder to Garvey and then Dawson on a fly ball to Landreaux—in for defensive purposes for Monday—in right field. Valenzuela was now just one out away from putting the finishing touches on an absolute masterpiece that would put the Dodgers back in the World Series after a three-year hiatus. But the Expos would prove their worth as the ultra talented, resilient team they were. After walking Carter on a full count, Valenzuela got ahead of Parrish 0–2 but then ended up walking him as well, to put the tying and winning runs on base. This development left Monday, who must have known he would never again have to buy another meal in LA if the Dodgers held on to win, to think to himself, *Yeah, my home run was a big deal, but it didn't mean as much when the Expos had the tying and winning runs on base. That was just a number that went over the fence. Now we need an out in order to get to the next step, because the World Series begins tomorrow night.*

The suddenly worrisome situation was enough for Lasorda, who came out to the mound and signaled for Bob Welch, now a successful starting pitcher after a time in the bullpen that saw him famously strike out Reggie Jackson to end Game Two of the 1978 World Series. Even Fernando, who despised coming out of games, knew he had given every ounce of effort from his golden left arm and exited the mound with a big grin on his face. Valenzuela had been magnificent, allowing only three hits over eight and two-thirds innings that included a streak of twenty outs among twenty batters.

Welch would face White, the hero of game three of this series for his three-run homer to break open the game for the Expos. Again with two men on base, would he repeat his heroics? It wasn't to be, as he bounced the first pitch he saw to Lopes's left, where the Dodgers captain made things interesting with a low throw to Garvey at first to end the game. "Davey threw me a sinker," Garvey said. "When I saw it coming, I go, *Oh no!* But one of my real skills was digging balls out of the dirt. With Lopes's throw, I got it just before it went down in the dirt, getting down on my knees to catch it." Another wild celebration for the Dodgers ensued, as the players and coaches jubilantly surged toward Welch and Garvey near first base. The National League pennant was theirs, and they were going to New York to battle their longtime nemesis, the Yankees, in the World Series.

Three hours after the game ended, it snowed in Montreal. The long winter would begin both literally and symbolically for an Expos franchise that would never again get this close to a World Series berth. "I think if we had won, we would have beaten the Yankees because we had a better team that year," Reardon lamented. "And I think beating the Yankees would have rewritten the books for Montreal. I think you would still have a team up there. Because if we won the World Series in '81, I think we would have won another one after that. It seems like when a team wins the first one, they try to build the team even better. All the baseball writers said we were going to be a team to be reckoned with in the '80s, but our group never finished higher than third place. When Carter got traded, I realized that they're kind of giving up, because he was still in his prime, still an All-Star catcher. Then two years later it was Dawson leaving through free agency. I was like, *Oh shit, they're going to get rid of us all.* And then I got traded. In '81 we reached our biggest height and then everything went down the chute."

Lee pinpointed the beginning of the end of baseball in Montreal to when owner Charles Bronfman named Claude Brochu to replace McHale as team president in 1986; five years later he sold the team to a consortium led by Brochu. "[Brochu] is the one who did not take any of the money from the luxury tax and put it back in the ball club," Lee said.

"Then, the next thing you know, that asshole used-car dealership guy from Milwaukee [former MLB commissioner Bud Selig] took the team away [the Expos moved to Washington DC and became the Nationals in 1995]. The killer straw that snapped the neck [of the franchise] was Brochu. His relationship with Selig was the end of the Expos."

But in this moment, in this year of Fernandomania, the Mexican icon registered his greatest victory. Some would argue his greatest performance was still to come—in the World Series or even nine years later, when pitching his only no-hitter—but for this twenty-year-old, pitching in freezing temperatures with a pennant on the line and going up against a lineup with three future Hall of Famers in it, *this* was his finest hour. "His most prominent game was in Montreal," was how Baker described it. "If he doesn't win against the Expos, we don't even go to the World Series."

And about that World Series, with Valenzuela on his side, Lasorda was nothing but optimistic about the Dodgers' prospects when speaking with reporters after the game. "How can we lose with him out there?" Lasorda rhetorically asked the gathered throng of scribes. "The kid's done everything right all season. It's his year. We're going to the World Series. If you threw Fernando in the bottom of the river, he'd swim out the other side with a fruit salad!"

Speaking "Catcherese"

19

The Dodgers' desperation was as thick as the smog that hovered over downtown Los Angeles. The Yankees had won the first two games of the World Series in New York by playing every facet of the game flawlessly. From the magnificent starting pitching of Ron Guidry and Tommy John, the jaw-dropping defensive clinic put on at third base by Graig Nettles, the clutch hitting of Bob Watson and Lou Piniella, to the dominance of their closer Goose Gossage, the Yankees appeared every bit the team on a mission to capture its first World Series title in three years.

Now back at Chavez Ravine for Game Three, the Dodgers once again turned to Valenzuela to save their season. And for a team that appeared to be on the cusp of a major transitional phase, there was an awful lot riding on this must-win contest for LA. "There was a sense with the 'core' that this might be their last shot together," Lyle Spencer said. "And, as it turned out, it was. They had been through those gut-wrenching World Series in '77 and '78 where they thought they were better than the Yankees and lost, so they had a lot of back history for that reason. A failure under pressure. So that's why it was so meaningful to them. Most of the guys had been there in '77 and '78 and understood the pain. They didn't want that again. They also were coming through in the clutch now, with Monday's classic home run being an example of that. It was a combination of things that gave them hope. It wasn't just Fernando, but in a sense, it was, because he was the catalyst."

Pedro Guerrero, a member of the Dodgers' "Kiddie Corps" and thus a player who hadn't been around during the previous World Series match-ups between these two longtime October rivals, was brimming with confidence. "When I was in the Minor Leagues in Arizona in 1978, I remember watching the Dodgers lose the World Series to the Yankees for the second straight year and said, 'Hey they're not going to win the World Series until I get there!'"

Still, it appeared these Yankees were peaking at just the right time—crushing teams like a runaway freight train. Like the Dodgers, they had clinched a spot in the divisional series by finishing the first half of the season atop the American League East. But with little to play for in the second half, they performed listlessly—posting a losing record of 25–26. Then, after taking the first two games of the divisional round against the Milwaukee Brewers, they dropped the next two at Yankee Stadium to force a decisive game five. Even in that game, they trailed 2–0. But then, as if on cue, they caught fire. Reggie Jackson, the man they called "Mr. October," crushed an upper-deck two-run homer to tie the game. Then, the very next batter, Oscar Gamble, gave the Yankees the lead by stroking a home run into the right-field bleachers. From there, the Bronx Bombers piled on and won going away, 7–3, to advance to the American League Championship Series. From there, they pummeled their once and future manager Billy Martin and his upstart Oakland A's in as dominating a three-game sweep as there ever had been in a postseason, outscoring them by a 20–4 margin in the series. And now, they were up two games to none over the Dodgers in the World Series—even without the services of an injured "Mr. October."

If not for the promise of Valenzuela being on the hill at Dodger Stadium for Game Three, as well as the Dodgers' uncanny ability thus far into the postseason to come back after being down in both the Houston and Montreal series, the prospects of an LA championship for the first time since the days of Koufax and Drysdale, dating all the way back to 1965, seemed bleak at best. But because of the way things were playing out for the Dodgers that October, they still had hope. "After dropping the two games in New York," Steve Garvey recalled, "we're on the plane flying back to LA and the guys are standing in the aisle talking. I say, 'Well, we've got them right where we want them. We've had leads in the past. We've blown those. We were up 2–0 in the '78 World Series and that didn't work. So, why not? Do you see a pattern here—even destiny?' And everyone was like, *Yeah, maybe there is.*"

"We didn't read too many papers or turn on the television while we were down 0–2 to the Astros," Monday added. "And we didn't listen to too many of the experts when we had to win two in a row against

Montreal. And we didn't read the papers after we lost the first two to the Yankees. We were just either stupid enough to believe that we could do it or cocky enough to believe that we could do it."

Valenzuela would be matched up against the Yankees' own rookie left-handed sensation—Dave Righetti—who compiled a record of 8-4 with a 2.05 ERA during the regular season and a 3-0 mark in the postseason. The two young stud pitchers could have been teammates in New York had the Yankees outbid the Dodgers for Valenzuela's services with their offer to Yucatán, of the Mexican League, two years earlier. The Yucatán team's owner, Jaime Perez Avilla, told the *New York Times* in 1981, "When the Yankee scout [Wilfredo Calvino] talked to me about [Valenzuela], he didn't make a good offer. He told me, 'The boy is good, but I'll be doing you a favor by signing him.' Naturally, he was bluffing to see if he could get him cheaply." The difference in the Dodgers' purchase price of $120,000 and the Yankees' reported offer of $50,000 was significant back then for an eighteen-year-old pitcher, though the idea of how just a $70,000 margin would alter the history of the Dodgers, their Mexican American fan base, and the club's fortunes is mind-boggling.

Alternatively, the hurlers could have *also* been teammates in Dodgers uniforms. As noted in the book *They Bled Blue*, the Dodgers almost traded for Righetti in 1980, offering Don Sutton in exchange—but the Yankees got cold feet and offered the less-talented pitcher Mike Griffin instead. The Dodgers turned that deal down cold.

The premise that the World Series would likely come down to the left arms of two rookie pitchers wasn't lost on Righetti. "[Valenzuela] has to get our hitters out; I have to get the Dodgers out," Righetti told reporters before the game. "But it's great. It adds excitement to the Series. But I think there's more pressure on him than me. It's a shame that they're in their biggest game they've had all year and that he's a rookie and it's all in his hands. But they say he's their savior."

The Dodgers' savior, who had been magnificent in the postseason to that point with a 1.71 ERA in four starts, would catch a break with Jackson still ailing and now Nettles also out of the Yankee lineup after badly spraining the thumb on his glove hand while diving for a Bill Russell hot smash single in Game Two. But neither Valenzuela nor his counterpart in Righetti would be sharp at the outset of what was deemed to be a glorious pitcher's duel between the two aces. Fernando escaped trouble in the top of the first when he induced Piniella to hit into an inning-ending double play ball after walking lead-off hitter Willie Randolph and then Dave Winfield, and Righetti yielded a three-run homer to Cey in the bottom half of the inning. But the Yankees then battled right back in the top of the second when Watson continued his torrid hitting with a solo home run, which was followed by a Rick Cerone double and then, one out later, an RBI single by Larry Milbourne to cut the Dodgers' lead to 3–2. An inning later, Cerone blasted a two-run homer to give the Yankees a 4–3 lead.

This was clearly not what *anybody* expected—especially out of Valenzuela pitching at Dodger Stadium. "The extra round of postseason games and pitching on three days' rest may have started taking its toll on Fernando," Jerry Reuss theorized. "But it was the postseason, and in a lot of cases the adrenaline takes over. So you're allowed a rough ball game occasionally. Everybody understands that, because this is the Major Leagues—it's supposed to be that way. It's not easy all the time. So if you have a rough game and you still can battle your way through it, like Fernando was doing in the third game, it's impressive. I imagine every time Van Gogh picked up a paintbrush, he didn't create a masterpiece, that there were some that he looked at and probably said, 'No good, I've got to start again.'"

Valenzuela, unlike Van Gogh, couldn't start his work over again, though, as Reuss suggested, he could still grind it out. But Lasorda was nervous. Going down 3–0 in the World Series was not an option, and he quickly got Dave Goltz up in the bullpen. Lasorda was known for his quick hook in pivotal World Series games. In what has become more Lasorda YouTube gold, the Dodgers manager was mic'd up when he removed starting pitcher Doug Rau in just the second inning of Game Four of the 1977 World Series. Rau and Lasorda famously jawed at one another on the mound and all the way back into the dugout. But Fernando's pitching, especially in 1981, was far superior to Rau's, and Lasorda clearly was going to give him more rope than he usually would a struggling starter.

"I think Lasorda's mind-set was, *I'm going to leave him out there. I'm going to win or lose with him*," Garvey said. "It was kind of a safe pick, because guys went nine innings back then and threw 150 pitches. So it was smart leaving him out there to pitch through it. It was very comparable to having him work out of [trouble] like he did in the first inning of the last game in Montreal. Because if we lose this game, we're down 0–3. And even if we win the next two, then we've got to win two more in New York and the odds get exponentially greater against us."

Luckily for the Dodgers, Righetti continued to struggle as well, surrendering a Garvey single and a walk to Cey to start the bottom of the third inning. Yankees manager Bob Lemon had seen enough and removed the left-hander from the game. The move, at least initially, worked well, as LA couldn't cash in that inning, because Yankees reliever George Frazier shut them down to maintain New York's 4–3 edge. But the inning did generate an interesting development that would pay immediate dividends for Valenzuela. When Lemon removed the left-handed Righetti in favor of the right-handed Frazier, Lasorda went to his bench and had the left-handed Mike Scioscia pinch-hit for and replace Steve Yeager as catcher in the game. By all accounts, Valenzuela was more familiar with and comfortable pitching to Scioscia. Because of Lasorda's platoon system with his two catchers, with playing time contingent on whether the opposing pitcher was a left-hander or right-hander, Fernando pitched most of his games with Scioscia behind the plate. Additionally, because the two were close in age, Scioscia spoke at least some broken Spanish, they were both more in sync with pitch selections, and Scioscia was less demonstrative than Yeager, they were a perfect fit.

The move paid immediate dividends. Fernando settled down and retired the Yankees with scoreless fourth and fifth innings. "[Scioscia] would say, 'Let's throw this pitch,'" Valenzuela told MLB.com in 2021. "I would just go, 'No, no, no,' and he already knew what I wanted to throw. There was very good communication, very timely. In a game, that understanding is very important between the catcher and the pitcher."

However, through five innings, Valenzuela's pitch count had already surpassed the century mark and there was activity once again in the Dodgers' bullpen, with both Goltz and Tom Niedenfuer up and throwing. "I was warming up in the sixth, seventh, eighth, and ninth innings," Niedenfuer said. "So, I was ready." But Lasorda continued to stick with Valenzuela, even when it would have been completely understandable to have someone pinch-hit for him in the bottom of the fifth after the Dodgers took a 5–4 lead with an RBI double from Guerrero and a run-scoring double play hit into by Scioscia. The obvious question then became, *If*

Lasorda didn't get a pinch hitter for Fernando at a hundred-plus pitches in the fifth and with Guerrero standing on third with a valuable insurance run, when would he? "I always had confidence every time Fernando pitched that he would go nine innings no matter what," Guerrero said. "That was always a good thing because it gave us confidence. It didn't matter what kind of trouble he got into because he could always get out of it and then, *boom, boom, boom,* he starts striking out hitters. He was something else. That's why we called him 'El Toro!'"

As Fernando returned to the mound to pitch the sixth, he looked invigorated—nothing like a pitcher looking to come out of a game. "He was such a fierce competitor to stay in that game," Spencer said. "And people weren't aware of pitch counts back then. There's no way he would have stayed in that game now."

Still, after Fernando walked lead-off batter Randolph, Lasorda came out for a mound visit. As legend has it and as reported in numerous pieces on the encounter, the Dodgers manager told Fernando in his native language, 'If you don't give up another run, we're going to win this ball game.' To which Valenzuela, realizing they led by a run, answered back drily in English, 'Are you sure?' As Lasorda would explain later, it was his way of giving the pitcher something to strive for, knowing that his pitcher wanted to keep battling and try to finish what he started. "There were several [mound conversations] that I don't remember," Valenzuela told MLB.com. "But to stay in the game and to not be taken out, I was always trying to evade him and give him the runaround or go someplace else to avoid having him approach me and have that conversation."

Lasorda's trip to the mound proved effective, as Scioscia would proceed to throw out Randolph on his attempt to steal second base and Valenzuela would then finish off the inning with a strikeout of Jerry Mumphrey and a groundout of a now seriously slumping Winfield. "Fernando pitched well beyond his years, from Day 1," Scioscia told MLB.com in 2021. "When he came up in 1980, you saw there was a composure that he had, a poise that sometimes players have to work into. He had it right away, and I think it was exemplified in Game 3 against the Yankees. The confidence that we had in him, along with what Tommy and the coaching staff had in him was very real and we just knew that, somehow, he was going to get it done."

Scioscia's own solo trips to the mound as Valenzuela weaved in and out of trouble seemed to have a soothing effect on Fernando, as well. "They talked, so they must have understood each other," Reuss said. "Maybe they speak a third language—'Catcherese!'"

Valenzuela would pitch effectively and economically over the next two innings but with some major help in the eighth from an outstanding play at third by Cey. After Aurelio Rodríguez (filling in at third base for Nettles) and Milbourne started off the Yankees' eighth with back-to-back singles to put runners on first and second, Bobby Murcer was sent up to bat for relief pitcher Rudy May. Murcer popped up a sacrifice bunt attempt slightly into foul territory along the third base line. Cey charged in and dove head-first to snag it, then sprang to his feet and fired to first base to double up Milbourne for a double play. It was easily the defensive gem of the game. Valenzuela then retired Randolph on a fielder's choice grounder to third base to end the inning.

The score remained at 5–4 heading into the top of the ninth with Valenzuela—considering his pitch count and his unflattering line of nine hits and seven walks—somewhat miraculously still in the game. But Fernando would finish strong—a groundout by Mumphrey, a flyout by Winfield, and a swinging strikeout of Piniella to close out a 147-pitch performance for the ages to get the Dodgers back in the series. "[Lasorda] knew what I could do, and I think that's one of the reasons why he let me finish that game," Valenzuela said.

"I've talked with Fernando about which game in his career was his favorite," Spencer said. "He said it was Game Three of the '81 World Series, when he had sixteen base runners out there and still won the game. It was a game in which he had to pitch through trouble all night in his World Series debut that set the Dodgers up to win the world championship. For the team, I think it was liberating. You can't overstate the importance of that game, just like you can't in the final game he pitched in Montreal. He just put the Dodgers on his shoulders. And I think that's why he was just so beloved the rest of his career. Because if you're an athlete, you understand how remarkable those kinds of performances are. Basically, he saved the Dodgers' season repeatedly. They could not have gotten to the World Series or won the World Series without him. And every player on the team knew that and appreciated that for the rest of their lives. What he did in Game Three just capped off the most amazing season by a baseball player I've ever witnessed. What more could he possibly do? The only thing comparable would have been one of Koufax's seasons—in '63 or '65—in terms of putting a team on your back and willing them to championships."

For Fernando, the final pitch of Game Three—a screwball, of course—would end up being the last of his magically historic 1981 season. But his last pitch capped off far more than a World Series game. It sealed his legacy as the perfect hero with the imperfect body that inspired millions of Latinos to aspire not just to become baseball players but to pursue whatever their dreams might be. *If he could do it, then why not them?* Valenzuela had also single-handedly made it cool—or at least acceptable—for Chicanos to become Dodgers fans, or at least baseball fans, for the very first time. Fernando Valenzuela had sealed his legacy as a legendary figure on the baseball field and a transcendent one off it.

Comeback Kids 20

Basking in the afterglow of a resilient performance by Valenzuela the previous night, the Dodgers still had much work to do. Down two games to one, and with Reggie Jackson, who lived for October baseball, making his debut in this 1981 World Series, Game Four was another critical contest for Los Angeles. It would start out disastrously. Dodgers starter Bob Welch didn't retire a single Yankee in the top of the first—facing just four hitters—before Lasorda took him out of the game. Dave Goltz came in relief and provided it—retiring the three hitters he faced in the frame to limit the damage to just two Yankees runs. But after Goltz gave up two runs of his own over the following two innings, the Dodgers found themselves in a deep 4–0 hole as the game moved to the bottom of the third. The Yankees were threatening to blow out the Dodgers and take a commanding lead in the series.

Could LA's "Comeback Kids" rally as they had throughout the postseason when their backs were against the wall? As it turned out, with timely hitting and all-around sloppy play by the Yankees, both on the base paths and defensively in the outfield, yes, they could. The Yankees, a shining example of professionalism throughout the postseason to this point, had suddenly morphed into the Bad News Bears. Their play the rest of Game Four was not what the game's creator, Abner Doubleday, had in mind—and the Dodgers took full advantage. The game would take on the feeling of a fifteen-round heavyweight fight, with both clubs emptying their benches and bullpens to find an edge. In all, the two teams used ten pitchers and a total of thirty-six players. And despite runs being scored aplenty, twenty runners were left on base. The Dodgers would eventually tie the Yankees at 6–6 with a three-run sixth—highlighted by a two-run pinch-hit home run from Jay Johnstone—and then take an 8–6 lead the following inning on a Steve Yeager sacrifice fly and a Davey Lopes RBI single—both off of Tommy John, now in the game to pitch a couple of innings of desperate relief for a vaunted Yankee bullpen that suddenly looked very human. Mr. October would make his presence felt in the top of the eighth with his requisite moonshot World Series home run to pull the Yankees to within a run, but closer Steve Howe slammed the door on New York's bid for a ninth-inning rally to secure an 8-7 victory and knot the World Series at two games apiece.

Game Five, unlike the previous afternoon's affair, would be a crisply played pitcher's duel between veteran hurlers Ron Guidry and Jerry Reuss. Reuss would give up an RBI single to Lou Piniella in the top of the second and then shut down the Yankees for the rest of the game. Guidry was nearly flawless until the bottom of the seventh with one out. Mixing his fastball and signature slider, he was pitching a two-hit shutout with nine strikeouts in the game. But then the "Comeback Kids" suddenly came to life, with Pedro Guerrero and Yeager lining back-to-back home runs into the left-field pavilion to give the Dodgers a 2-1 lead. Guidry had gone from pitching the World Series game of his life to now being on the losing side in an instant. "At the Major League level, particularly in the postseason, the margin for error is so narrow that one or two pitches can make all the difference," Reuss explained. "Guidry throws a slider to Guerrero and then tried to throw a fastball by Yeager, they both hit home runs, and that changed the complexion of the game and ultimately the series."

With the Yankees still trailing 2-1 in the bottom of the eighth, Bob Lemon went to his bullpen and brought in Goose Gossage to keep things close. With two outs and Lopes on first, the fireballing Gossage let loose with a high and tight fastball that struck Ron Cey on the left side of his helmet, dropping him on his back, where he lay motionless, arms spread apart. "I thought he was dead at home plate," recalled Rick Monday. After several minutes, Cey was helped off the field and taken into the Dodgers' training room before a trip to the hospital for observation.

Back out to the mound to pitch the ninth, Reuss would continue his mastery of New York, finishing things off with a strikeout of Aurelio Rodríguez to yield a thrilling 2-1 victory and give the Dodgers a 3-2 lead in the World Series. Reuss's reaction after the final strike was one of sheer exuberance—leaping off the ground and throwing his arms up high above his head—as his teammates (and Lasorda, of course) rushed out to the mound to join the celebration. "It was just pure joy," Reuss recalled.

As for the Yankees, matters would go from bad to worse from a public relations standpoint. Early the next morning, Yankees owner George Steinbrenner—who was regularly captured on ABC-TV cameras showing fits of frustration throughout New York's meltdown in LA—was reportedly involved in a fistfight in a Wilshire Hyatt elevator with a couple of Dodgers fans. The next day's newspapers around the country showed photos of Steinbrenner with a heavily bandaged left hand. Some players and media members believed it was more than likely that "The Boss," as he was often called for his brutally tough management style, made up at least the part about battling Dodgers fans in defending the pride of the pinstripes. But it still made for great copy.

Yet, if Steinbrenner's alleged fisticuffs were an attempt to rally his troops in Game Six back at Yankee Stadium, it fell on deaf ears. The Yankees, even with the return of Graig Nettles, were no match for the surging Dodgers and fell behind 8–1 in just the fifth inning before meagerly losing by a final score of 9–2. In the "Year of Fernandomania," the '81 Dodgers proved to be the most resilient postseason team in the modern era, with comebacks in all three rounds of the postseason, and were now crowned as the world champions of baseball.

Steve Garvey saw added significance to this latest Dodgers championship. "The Dodgers moved to LA in '58 and won a few World Series since the move," he noted. "But the '81 world championship was really the first true 'Los Angeles' Dodgers championship because, with the other teams that won titles, they still had Koufax and Drysdale—guys that played in Brooklyn."

Garvey then emphasized the impact Valenzuela had on this championship team. "As for Fernando, he was such an integral part of the on-the-field, off-the-field [dynamic] in terms of a cultural change within the ballpark that had a ripple effect throughout baseball. It was such a multifaceted effect by an individual at a time that arguably changed the contexture of the game—the culture of the game. And from what was an emphasis on Black integration in baseball, he probably started an integration toward the Hispanic culture in the game."

Garvey's eloquent words on Valenzuela were equal to that of his performance in an '81 World Series in which the first baseman led all Dodgers regulars with a .417 batting average yet was mysteriously not one of the three World Series co-MVPs. Those honors would go to Guerrero, Yeager, and Cey. For Guerrero, being a World Series MVP was put into his head even before the series began. "After we beat Montreal to win the pennant," Guerrero recalled, "Lasorda grabbed me and told me, 'Pete, come here! We're going to New York. We're going to be in the World Series. Can you imagine if you become the MVP?!' I looked at him and said, 'Oh! I'm going for it!'" For Cey, aside from what he did at the plate and on the field, his courage to even play in Game Six after the brutal beaning he took from that Gossage fastball clearly played a part in his being named a co-MVP. "The day of Game Six," Monday recalled, "Cey got to the ballpark early and he was still light-headed. But the team had him running early in the day—he's such a *tough* guy. Remember, he was also coming back from that broken wrist he had and came back early for the Montreal series. He was still playing with discomfort from that, too." As for Yeager, despite hitting just .286, two of his hits were home runs, with the second being the biggest hit of the entire series—the dinger off Guidry that put his club ahead to stay in Game Five. Still, when the name "Steve" was bandied about the winning clubhouse as one of the three MVP winners, it was widely assumed by media and some players that "Steve" would be attached to the last name "Garvey." In fact, up at the podium where Bowie Kuhn and ABC commentator Bob Uecker were presenting the MVP award, they initially congratulated Garvey and not Yeager, before being notified of the mistake. Uecker would have to uncomfortably turn to Yeager after Garvey had already expressed his gratitude for being a part of the trio receiving the honor.

But for Garvey and the rest of the Dodgers, this was all about a team that came together to overcome numerous hurdles during both the regular season and the playoffs, making personal distinctions like World Series MVP awards far less relevant than the achievement of winning a championship. "The important thing is to win," Reuss said. "But the *way* you go about doing it says something about the people who were part of the club that does it. It's a special thing to come from behind not just once but three times. And that's what the '81 club did. Coming from behind was our burden to bear, but in each particular case we were able to do it and go on to win the world championship."

Another prime example of the Dodgers' all-for-one, one-for-all mentality was how they handled the hoopla surrounding Valenzuela, which, while well deserved, overshadowed the remarkable achievements by his pitching staffmates. "The others got lost in the shuffle," Monday observed. "Burt [Hooton] was the MVP of the championship series against Montreal. And you look at what Jerry [Reuss] was able to do, it was phenomenal. And Bobby Welch as well. We had guys on the staff that, when they started a ball game, they wanted to finish it. And on that entire rotation, you only had one guy that had an ERA above 3.00. *Can you imagine that today?*" Yet, the staff remained selfless, taking the mania over Fernando in stride. "Every time I think of that," Reuss reflected, "I just look at my World Series ring—that's all the credit I need. That's all that concerns me. You can say the same about Hooton, who had an early winning streak and finished 11-6. I was 10-4. Fernando was 13-7. So Hooton could also be one of those people that you look at their performance and say, *You know, we couldn't have won without him.* You add Bob Welch, who went 9-5, to the mix, and we had four starters that could give you innings and keep you in ball games. So, when you have four guys that can do that, you've got to like your chances."

Monday was another player who put team over personal achievements, even when his home run in Montreal was one of the most iconic moments in the history of the game. "My number-one event wasn't the home run, no, no, no," he said. "My number one would be the final hour of the World Series, when you're the champion, when you don't have another out that you have to get, when you don't have another team that you have to beat. And you're with the guys that got you all the way down the road. Those moments in the locker room afterwards are so special. On the field and in the dugout are fine, but then you go into the locker room and it's a quieter moment that you share with one another. I wear this [World Series] ring every day because it not only reminds me of that feeling of the last out but also the journey to get there and all the people it took to get there. Not just the players but coaches, the manager, the guys in the front office, the secretaries, and everybody else. That's why I wear this every day. Dusty [Baker] says he brings his out and wears it when he needs luck. I wear this because those were my teammates and my buddies, and we accomplished something pretty damn special."

In the weeks following the World Series, Valenzuela would become the first player to be named Rookie of the Year and winner of the Cy

Young Award in the same season. But far more significant than the celebrated hardware was that Fernando had captured the hearts and imaginations of millions of baseball fans—old and new, American and Latin American—including many of those who had shunned the Dodgers for more than two decades as a direct result of the leveling of the Chavez Ravine neighborhoods of Bishop, Palo Verde, and La Loma to make way for Dodger Stadium.

Things around Chavez Ravine would never be the same again.

The Legend Grows 21

While it's probably unfair to compare anybody to Jackie Robinson,
the closest I ever came to being around someone like him was
to be around Fernando the years I covered him—and watched
how people responded to him and the impact he had.

—KEN GURNICK, longtime Dodgers beat writer

What a difference a year made for Fernando.

It was early March 1982 at Dodgertown in Vero Beach, Florida, the
same venue where, just twelve months earlier, Valenzuela had been
doing his best to merely earn a spot on the club's Major League roster. But now, the light-speed evolution of Valenzuela was complete. No
longer a relative unknown out of the bullpen, he was now the defending Cy Young Award winner with a World Series ring. No longer in the
shadows, he was now the most important Latino athlete since Roberto
Clemente. No longer Mexico's most eligible bachelor, he was now mar-
ried to the former Linda Burgos, an elementary school teacher from his
home country.

Despite his sudden fame and fortune, Valenzuela remained close with
his family and didn't lose sight of where he came from. Right after the
World Series ended, he returned to Mexico, where his family tended
to several acres of farmland that, under a government program, paid
the Valenzuelas around two thousand pesos a month (approximately
$100). But the fortunes of the family would soon dramatically change,
as Fernando was in the planning stages of building a lavish home for
his parents that would later be described by some locals as the "Hearst
Castle of Etchohuaquila."

Throughout the off-season, he stayed in shape by doing what he did best—pitching—whether it be playing winter ball for Los Mayos de Navojoa or taking the mound against one of his six brothers in pick-up games.

It was also during this time that he had become a full-fledged darling of Madison Avenue. Valenzuela was endorsing everything from soft drinks to coins to flashlights for a reported minimum of $50,000 a spot—a figure higher than his salary for the entire 1981 baseball season. And his total earnings for endorsements could have been much more had Antonio De Marco not insisted on rejecting offers from companies selling chiles, tamales, guacamole, enchiladas, or *cerveza*, with the agent believing that they may have stereotyped his client as *too Mexican*. "All offers being equal," the shrewd and image-conscious De Marco told *Sports Illustrated*, "[Fernando] will always go for the American name, the American product. Mexican products are different. He'll always get a great share of that action."

However, for all the endorsement money Valenzuela was generating, he knew full well how vastly underpaid he was as a Dodger, and he was going to make it known to the ownership that he was a young man who demanded respect. He knew his meager $42,500 salary in 1981 was a tremendous bargain for the Dodgers not just by his performance but in how he put fans in the seats. Valenzuela starts led both leagues in sellouts, with eleven of his twelve at Dodger Stadium pitched before full-capacity crowds. No Dodgers pitcher had ever done that before—not even Koufax.

Not yet eligible for arbitration, the Dodgers unilaterally renewed Fernando's contract under the provision of baseball's basic labor agreement. The Dodgers brass, headed by team president Peter O'Malley, slow-rolled any serious talks of giving Valenzuela a raise. And when contract talks finally began in earnest, De Marco asked for a cool $1 million on behalf of his client for the 1982 season. When the Dodgers scoffed at that proposal, Valenzuela didn't take it lightly, opting not to report to spring training. "I am only twenty-one," Valenzuela told reporters during a personal holdout that would ultimately last three weeks. "But I am a man to be considered with dignity. [The Dodgers] have decided what the contract says. We have been treated like children."

If anything, Valenzuela's salary request and holdout only earned him more respect from his veteran teammates. "I knew Fernando was of superior intelligence when he asked for a million dollars," Dusty Baker said. "Tommy Lasorda, who loved Fernando, said, 'How can he ask for a million dollars?' I was like, *Fernando can count. He can count when the stands are full. He* was *Fernandomania.*"

Even the Dodgers' "Kiddie Corps," still simply grateful for the opportunity to be in the big leagues, didn't blame Valenzuela for not reporting to camp. "First of all," Tom Niedenfuer said, "Fernando brought more than just a superior win-loss record and ERA to the game of baseball. He had another aspect that he could use as a negotiation tool—Fernandomania—and the average attendance he drew at all the stadiums he pitched in. The other part was that I was just twenty-two, so I was just worried about going down to spring training and having a good spring. That was during the time when no one was going to hold out and miss the season or anything. So no one was too worried that Fernando wouldn't be back."

But with the Dodgers' powerful public relations machine hard at work, Fernando's holdout wasn't doing much for his otherwise pristine image. "The Dodgers, more or less, kind of portrayed him as the villain—or at least his agent as a villain," opined Ken Gurnick, who had just started covering the Dodgers that spring. "Here was this hero that led them to the World Series and won all these awards and everything—and now it became about the money. So that was kind of a sour note to begin my coverage of Fernando."

With two weeks left before the start of the regular season, Valenzuela would end his holdout and settle for $360,000, a figure far less than he deserved, but a salary that the Dodgers' PR machine pumped as the highest ever for a second-year player in baseball history. O'Malley released the driest of statements, which read, "All of us in the Dodger organization appreciate the success Fernando enjoyed in 1981, and we are happy he is rejoining his teammates in preparation for the 1982 season."

But the reality was that Fernando had no choice but to fall in line. Had he not ended his holdout and accepted the deal, O'Malley said the team might suspend him—an unthinkable act. After Valenzuela reported to camp two days later, reporters huddled in a news conference and asked him if he felt his holdout had tarnished his reputation in any way. "It's hard to tell," he said, with Jaime Jarrín interpreting. "The people will have to tell you that, and they will know if I was right in defending my rights."

After the press conference, he jogged around the field with the rest of the team and then proceeded to throw 105 pitches to Pedro Guerrero, Steve Garvey, Ron Cey, and Dusty Baker under the hot Florida sun. Despite it being Fernando's first day of spring training, he was already in midseason form.

*

On the heels of a 1981 season in which Valenzuela's impact was both sudden and profound, 1982 was the beginning of a new chapter in his Dodgers career, which would have two phases—the years through 1986 as the best left-hander in baseball and perennial All-Star and the final four, after a shoulder injury transformed him into a serviceable pitcher at best.

While '82 was slightly muted compared to the ferocity of '81 at the height of Fernandomania, the fervor remained. "There still was a carnival [atmosphere] surrounding him," recalled Gurnick. "When we traveled to different cities, there would be a press conference on the day before he pitched so that he could be left alone on the day that he did pitch. That still happened. The difference was that in '81, he really was new. By '82, having already won the World Series, the Cy Young, and the Rookie of the Year, even if he was no longer new, there was still a clamoring for him because of his success. But that newness—like, *Where did this guy come from?*—had worn off. That part had changed. There was not the fairy tale of some kid coming from the dust fields of Mexico anymore. Everybody knew that story by '82."

Valenzuela shrugged off any hurt feelings induced by his contract dispute to produce another remarkable season; he won nineteen games and finished third in the National League Cy Young voting. And he was still packing in crowds both at home and on the road, with the percentage of Mexicans attending games at similar levels to the year before. It was clear that this new Dodgers fan base was here to stay because of El Toro.

"The socioeconomics of Fernando was a perfect storm," Garvey said. "He comes up, the Hispanic community is looking for a hero and a kind of idol—and the disposable income [of the Mexican community] goes to baseball. And to this day, the Hispanic community and their influence on baseball is a huge part of Dodger Stadium."

There was still a sense that a Fernando start was a sort of escape and a safe haven for Mexican Americans and their struggle living in the

United States. "Because they owned Fernando," Dr. Richard Santillán of the Latino Baseball History Project told *USA Today* in 2021, "they were first-class citizens at the ballpark. Once they left the ballpark, that's a different story."

Valenzuela would finally reap some of the Dodgers' financial windfall for his efforts both on the field and for packing stadiums from coast to coast. In arbitration he would be awarded a $1 million salary for the '83 season—the first Major League player to eclipse seven figures in the process. But for Fernando and the Mexicans who adored him, it wasn't just about the money—it was about what the money meant. "He was really like a beacon of hope, of the possibilities despite the adversities that immigrants faced, and Fernando faced—not being able to speak the language and [being] poor and so forth," continued Santillán. "That's why Fernando resonated."

The '82 season would be a heartbreaker for the Dodgers. The club had battled back from being ten games out of first place on July 28 to holding a three-game lead in the NL West with twelve games to play. But Los Angeles then proceeded to lose eight games in a row (six of them by just one run) before finishing the season one game behind a surprising Atlanta Braves team that had come off a sub-.500 campaign the year before.

It was also the sad ending of the Dodgers' old guard that had enjoyed so much success together over the years. Two mainstays who should have retired in Los Angeles would depart: Garvey for San Diego via free agency and Cey, who would be traded to the Cubs for two prospects—neither of which ever saw the light of day in a Dodgers uniform. Both Garvey and Cey would maintain their All-Star-caliber play for several more years while leading their respective clubs to the postseason in '84.

The Dodgers, meanwhile, were going full throttle with their youth movement—installing Greg Brock at first and '82 Rookie of the Year Steve Sax at second, while moving Guerrero from the outfield to third base. The transition from the veterans to the Kiddie Corps worked well, at least initially, for the Dodgers in '83, as the club reclaimed the NL West title before losing to the Phillies in the NLCS, three games to one. The Dodgers' only victory of the series was a game two masterpiece, pitched by Valenzuela, in which he gave up just one run over eight innings.

With more of the Dodgers veterans from their glorious recent past either on their way out or contributing in limited roles, Valenzuela had now clearly secured his status as the face of the franchise.

*

The Dodgers took a big step back in 1984, finishing in fourth place with just their second losing record over a sixteen-year period. Their offense, so recently the envy of the National League, was now one of the league's weakest. Fernando's three home runs in just seventy-nine at bats were more than what Dodgers second baseman Sax accumulated and was equal to the number that shortstop Dave Anderson hit. Run production was so poor that Valenzuela, despite a sterling 3.03 ERA, posted a losing record of 12–17. Still, in large part due to sellout crowds at most of Fernando's games, the Dodgers had the highest attendance in baseball, with more than three million fans.

With four full seasons as the ace of the Dodgers' pitching staff, the still-reserved Valenzuela was largely credited as being a leader by example for the other young pitchers. "He was such a great teammate," Niedenfuer said. "We had a great pitching staff then, and everyone knew their part. As great as Fernando was, we had four other wonderful pitchers in Reuss, Hooton, Welch, and now [Orel] Hershiser, who came up in '83. But it was Fernando who definitely helped drive all the starting pitchers a little more."

Valenzuela now represented so much more than being a baseball player. He had in fact galvanized the Mexican community both in United States and south of the border and was idolized by millions.

Not long after the 1984 season ended, another icon of the Mexican people of that period, Cesar Chavez, would give his landmark address at the prestigious Commonwealth Club of California in San Francisco in which he prophesied the burgeoning social, economic, and political influence of Latinos across the country. The timing of it perfectly coincided with the emergence of Valenzuela and other Latino sports figures—including two-time Super Bowl–winning coach Tom Flores—in what was deemed by some, if somewhat prematurely, the "Decade of the Hispanic."

"It was one of the first times that Cesar was very introspective, putting himself and his movement in a historical context and looking at the influence that he came to understand that his movement had beyond the fields," said Chavez aide Marc Grossman about the labor leader's 1984 speech. "He talked about this phenomenon which, I think, is very reflective of the phenomenon of Valenzuela because what happened in the fields could be replicated elsewhere. He said that all Hispanics, urban and rural, young and old, are connected to the farmworkers. And he told how they all lived through the field . . . where their parents had and shared that common humiliation. So he asked how they could progress as a people if farmworkers, men and women of color, are condemned to a life without parole; how they could progress as a people if they're denied self-respect; and how their children could become lawyers and doctors and judges while this injustice was permitted to continue.

"Cesar went on to say how farmworkers should acknowledge how they allowed themselves to become victims of a democratic society," Grossman continued. "And that by addressing this historic problem, they gained competence and pride in an entire people's ability to create the future. And he talked about that when the union became visible, and Chicanos started going to college in greater numbers and running for office and asserting their rights across a broad spectrum of issues— that's when he saw that the message had taken effect. He added [that] he didn't really appreciate it at the time, but the coming of the union signaled the start of great changes among Hispanics that are now only beginning to be seen. And he talked about the people he met in every part of the country and said the one thing he heard most often from Hispanics, regardless of age or position, and many non-Hispanics, was that the farmworkers [union] gave them the hope they could succeed and the inspiration to work for change. I think that's the phenomenon that Valenzuela also represented—giving hope to people that they could be something more—that they could succeed. The two men—Chavez and Valenzuela—shared a lot in common in terms of their origin, the faith they gave people, and the example they gave people."

Thus, throughout this era, Chavez and Valenzuela would become tremendous sources of ethnic pride and encouragement for millions of Latinos in every corner of the nation—even as the marginalization of the group, to a large extent, continued.

*

The start of the 1985 season was reminiscent of Fernandomania four years earlier. Valenzuela would be named the National League's "Pitcher of the Month" in April, opening the season with a remarkable string of forty-one and a third innings without allowing an earned run. The scoreless streak to begin a campaign broke a seventy-three-year-old Major League record. The only difference was, like the previous season, that the team was hardly scoring any runs for Valenzuela. In fact, at month's end, despite pitching to a microscopic 0.21 ERA, Fernando had a *losing* record of 2–3.

The frustration would continue three months into the season as Valenzuela admittedly had better control of his screwball and superior command of his repertoire than he had in '81—as his 2.34 ERA would attest—yet sat with an 8–8 record. Aside from Valenzuela, it was the coming-out party for Hershiser, the young right-hander whose star would shine bright that season with a 19–3 record and a 2.03 ERA. Jerry Reuss and Bob Welch would both contribute fourteen wins with ERAs under 3.0. Yet, despite all the company Fernando had on a pitching staff that was loaded, there was no mistaking that he was still the acknowledged ace of the staff and one of baseball's elite stars. The week before, when his record stood at 7–8, he very well may have been the first pitcher to ever grace the cover of *Sports Illustrated* with a losing record.

Yet, for all his stardom in one of the world's major media markets, he remained mysterious and private. Part of that was owed to his intensely protective agent, De Marco, the gatekeeper of Valenzuela's family life, which now included two small boys—Fernando Jr. and Ricardo. It was De Marco who wouldn't allow Fernando's wife and children to be approached or photographed, and the address of their three-bedroom condominium in downtown Los Angeles was off limits to anyone who dared to ask him for it. So tight a bond did De Marco have with the Valenzuela family that he was godfather to Ricardo, and Fernando and Linda were godparents to De Marco's two-year-old granddaughter.

The other primary factor that kept a degree of separation between Fernando and much of the outside world remained his reliance on the use of an interpreter. Unlike numerous superstar athletes from foreign lands who came to the United States and quickly learned and utilized their English to expand their brand, five years into his Major League career Valenzuela was still an outlier in this respect. And while he still exemplified dignity, class, and a sense of humor, the language barrier had an impact on his relationship with an otherwise adoring media. "When [the press] covered him, even on the field, Jaime [Jarrín] was there and did a great job being his translator and a kind of middleman," Gurnick recalled. "But anytime a player, not just Fernando, uses an interpreter, it creates a chasm. The writers feel that you never really know if you're getting the true answer because the club might want to craft a certain message. But after a few years, even though Fernando was still using Jaime during press conferences, just because we were around [Valenzuela] all the time, you developed a relationship with him and knew that he understood certain [English] words."

But Fernando's limited English didn't keep him from doing good work away from the ballpark—especially when it came to giving back to the Latino community. During the summer of '85, he appeared in a Spanish-language version of the "We Are the World" video to help raise awareness of and funds for starving children in Latin America, and he paid numerous visits to elementary schools, primarily in low-income Hispanic areas of Los Angeles, stressing the importance of staying in school. "I'm flattered at having the privilege of being a role model," he told *Sports Illustrated*. "Yes, it's a serious responsibility. But it's a responsibility that I can best live up to by pitching as well as I can and hoping that it's enough of a contribution for us to win."

Valenzuela certainly held up his end of the bargain in that regard—even if the Dodgers were floundering as a team to that point. On July 2, following a three-hit, 3–0 complete game shutout from Fernando, the Dodgers still found themselves stuck in second place, three and a half games out of first place. The club simply lacked firepower from their offense.

But then things started to click. Over the next six weeks, the Dodgers finally started hitting to back up the masterful pitching, going on a 29–9 run to find themselves, on the morning of August 17, in first place with a commanding nine-game lead in the National League West. They would maintain much of that edge when they hosted the Mets in the most highly anticipated Dodgers game in years, played on September 6, a Friday night at Dodger Stadium. The hype of the match-up between the game's two greatest pitchers—Dwight Gooden and Valenzuela—was being pegged as the baseball equivalent of an Ali-Frazier fight. It was the first of a crucial three-game series against a Mets club talented enough to knock Los Angeles back into the pack in their division—and Dodger Stadium was electric all evening long. "I've never had more calls from people trying to get tickets," Niedenfuer recalled. "That was probably one of the toughest tickets to try and get for anybody because Gooden was pitching his greatest year then. And it really lived up to its billing."

Gooden, who would end up going 24-4 with a 1.53 ERA in winning the Cy Young Award that season, struck out ten without yielding a walk over nine shutout innings, while Valenzuela was *even better*—hurling *eleven* shutout innings to a Mets lineup that was the most potent in the National League. Yet, despite Fernando's awe-inspiring performance, he would get a no-decision, as the Mets would win it, 2-0, in thirteen innings.

The Dodgers would split the two remaining games of the Mets series and hold on to clinch the division title three weeks later, setting up an infamous National League Championship Series face-off against the St. Louis Cardinals.

Valenzuela would regularly receive religious relics from fans, and he would need them, given what was about to come in this playoff series. The Dodgers took the first two games of the best-of-seven NLCS in Los Angeles, making it look rather easy. In the first game, Valenzuela outdueled Cardinals ace and twenty-one-game winner John Tudor, 4-1. Then in game two, the Dodgers, behind superb pitching from Hershiser and an offense that pounded the Cardinals' other twenty-one-game winner, Joaquín Andújar, early and often, routed St. Louis, 8-2. With the Dodgers outclassing the Cardinals in every phase of the game, it looked like a near certainty that they were on their way back to the World Series for the first time since '81. Even after the Cardinals won the next two games in St. Louis to tie the series, the Dodgers were set up well with Valenzuela and Hershiser rested and ready to pitch in games five and six.

Game five generally went as planned in the pitching department, as Valenzuela, despite occasional bouts of wildness, yielded just two runs through eight innings—but left with the game tied at 2-2. After the Dodgers went down quietly in the top of the ninth, Niedenfuer was brought in by Lasorda to keep the Cardinals scoreless and force extra innings. The reliever would start the bottom of the ninth by retiring that year's NL MVP, Willie McGee. Up next was Ozzie Smith, widely regarded as the greatest defensive shortstop of all time and winner of thirteen consecutive Gold Glove Awards—but a .262 lifetime hitter with no power. His spectacular glove was the *only* reason he would one day be inducted into the Baseball Hall of Fame. With Smith not a home run threat, Niedenfuer's strategy was to go right after him with fastballs, and initially it worked well, as he quickly jumped ahead 0–2 in the count.

But then the jinx of all jinxes occurred. As Smith dug in prior to the next pitch, NBC posted a graphic noting, "Ozzie Smith has not homered batting lefty in 2,967 career at bats." And then it happened. Two pitches later, Smith did the unfathomable, turning on a Niedenfuer inside fastball and driving it deep down into the right-field corner and into the stands for a game-winning home run. Busch Stadium erupted as Smith raced around the bases with his right arm raised high above his head in exultation before ultimately jumping onto home plate (if he did, in fact, ever actually touch it) as his teammates mobbed him. The Cardinals had swept the Dodgers in St. Louis in shocking fashion.

The only consolation for the Dodgers was that they were going home for the final two games of the series. And in game six, it would be a repeat of the game two pitchers—Hershiser and Andújar. At the outset, the game would pattern itself much like the first meeting between the two pitchers. The Dodgers would jump ahead 4–1 after five innings and appear to be in full control of the game. But the Cardinals rallied in the seventh, first scoring off Hershiser with a two-run single by McGee and then tying the game off Niedenfuer with a run-scoring triple by Smith.

However, the Dodgers would jump back out in front, 5–4, when Mike Marshall hit the first pitch of the bottom of the eighth inning high and deep and just barely out of the reach of a leaping Andy Van Slyke into the right-field bleachers for a home run. The partisan crowd at Dodger Stadium roared—both in celebration and in relief—and the usually reserved Valenzuela was the first to pop out of the home team's dugout to congratulate Marshall.

With no further damage inflicted on the Cardinals, the Dodgers would take that one-run lead into the top of the ninth, needing just three more outs from Niedenfuer to send the series to a seventh game. The frame started out well enough for LA, with the hard-throwing Niedenfuer striking out César Cedeño with a 95-mile-an-hour fastball. But then the speedy McGee singled and—representing the tying run—promptly stole second to move into scoring position. Seemingly unfazed, Niedenfuer jumped ahead of Ozzie Smith, 1–2, but then lost him on three straight pitches out of the strike zone to put Cardinals on first and second and still just one out.

Now the pressure was back on the Dodgers, with tremendous speed on the bases and Smith representing the winning run on first. The threat of a double steal was very real, and the game slowed down to a snail's pace as Niedenfuer's attention was split between McGee bouncing off second and the batter, Tommy Herr, at the plate. After jumping ahead 0–1, Herr hit a grounder to third. Dodgers third baseman Dave Anderson, in for defensive purposes for Bill Madlock, fielded the ball, touched third, and fired across the diamond to Brock at first for what initially appeared to be a game-ending double play. *But no!* Third base umpire John McSherry called it foul—and Herr would stay alive with an 0–2 count. Replays would confirm that McSherry made the right call, but it didn't take away the sting the Dodgers felt in the realization that, had the ball been hit a mere six inches to the right, they would have been victorious.

Niedenfuer would ultimately prevail in retiring Herr on a slow chopper to first for the second out, but the tying and winning runs in McGee and Smith advanced to second and third. That brought up the dangerous Jack Clark, the Cardinals' most prolific run producer, and presented Lasorda with one of the biggest decisions of his long and illustrious managerial career. *With the open base at first, should he have Niedenfuer intentionally walk Clark?* Lasorda paced the Dodgers' dugout like a caged animal—spewing obscenities before muttering, "Should I pitch to that mother-fucking Van Slyke?" to pitching coach Ron Perranoski on the bench. Van Slyke was just 1-for-10 in the series, but, as a left-handed hitter against the right-handed Niedenfuer, he would have an advantage in that regard.

Lasorda opted to have Niedenfuer face the right-hand-hitting Clark. With more than fifty-five thousand fans on their feet and with tension running high in Dodger Stadium, Scioscia visited Niedenfuer on the mound to go over signs—wanting to keep them simple—as there was no room for error. Any cross-up in pitches with McGee on third could prove disastrous. The battery mates were also leery of Smith stealing signs from second base. Now on the same page, Niedenfuer, pitching from the stretch position, delivered his first pitch to Clark—a belt-high fastball. Clark jumped all over it—crushing the pitch into the left-field bleachers for a three-run homer. Left-fielder Guerrero fired his glove into the ground in disgust as the ball soared over his head. Niedenfuer wore a dazed expression. Scioscia knelt in disbelief. Remarkably, St. Louis had taken a 7–5 lead. The crowd, so vocal just a moment before, now sat in stunned silence.

For the second straight game, the Cardinals, a club known all season long for their speed, had used the long ball to hit two of the most dramatic home runs in postseason history.

Van Slyke, whom Lasorda didn't want Niedenfuer to face, would end the inning by hitting a harmless pop-up to Scioscia. The Dodgers skipper's question, posed to Perranoski just minutes earlier, had been answered—his closer should have pitched to Van Slyke instead of Clark. It would be a decision that would haunt Lasorda for decades to come— perhaps even more so than his decision in the 1980 one-game playoff to start Goltz over Valenzuela.

The Dodgers would go down quietly in the bottom of the ninth to conclude the most crushing defeat and postseason series in team history.

*

The aftershocks of the Dodgers' '85 NLCS defeat would reverberate over the next two seasons. The club would have identically poor 73–89 records in 1986 and 1987, finishing in fifth and fourth place, respectively, in the NL West. Despite this, Valenzuela managed to have the best all-around season of his career in 1986.

"Mike Scott won the '86 Cy Young Award, but I feel that Fernando had a better year," said Gurnick. "He was just playing on a lousy team and had to do it all by himself. . . . It was easy to get credit in the good years, but some of his best years were when he had no help. You look at his numbers he put up—the innings, the wins, the strikeouts, and the complete games—pitchers don't do that anymore. And Fernando did them on some bad Dodgers teams. I understand why he's not in the Hall of Fame, but on the other hand, I don't think he's gotten enough credit for being as good as he was for as long as he was."

With the Dodgers now a second-division team and out of the spotlight, Valenzuela's last shining moment on the national stage was his appearance in the 1986 All-Star Game. It was Fernando's sixth straight year as an All-Star—and his last—yet this stint was clearly his most astounding. Valenzuela entered the game in the fourth inning and struck out Don Mattingly, Cal Ripken Jr., and Jesse Barfield in order. Then, in the top of the fifth, he started the frame by fanning Lou Whitaker and Teddy Higuera to make it five straight strikeouts, tying the All-Star Game record originally set by fellow screwballer Carl Hubbell in 1934. He then retired Kirby Puckett on a groundout to short to end the inning. Valenzuela would complete his dominance of the American League by shutting them down again in the sixth to complete his three shutout innings of work—yielding just a single to Wade Boggs on a pop fly to shallow center field. It was simply a masterful performance.

Fernando would finish the '86 campaign with twenty-one wins, the most of his career, and a remarkable twenty complete games—easily the most in baseball and a figure that hasn't been matched in either league since.

Valenzuela again would lead the National League in complete games in 1987, making it the third time he led the Senior Circuit in this category in his seven years in the big leagues. For the first time, however, the workload appeared to be taking its toll. Fernando pitched to the highest ERA of his career, a hair under four runs a game. He also led the league in three dubious statistics—hits allowed, walks allowed, and wild pitches. And for the first time in four seasons, he struck out fewer than two hundred hitters. This begged the question, *Was overuse of Valenzuela's magical arm killing the Dodgers' so-called "golden goose"?*

"When you look at the complete games and the workload," Fred Claire said, "I don't think there's any question that was a factor for Fernando. You look at his twenty complete games in '86. I would bet you there wasn't twenty complete games in the National League last year." (In 2020 there were just eighteen complete games in the National League.)

But while Lasorda was the one responsible for sending Valenzuela out to the mound as much as he did, Fernando was the rare breed of pitcher who always wanted the ball. "In fairness to Tommy, our staff, and everyone involved," Claire said, "Fernando *wanted* to be on that pitcher's mound. I *never* saw a time when Fernando was on the mound and was happy to give Tommy the ball. That wasn't going to happen. Fernando was a warrior. A lot of great heroes from Mexico were in boxing, and this may sound like a strange analogy, but I think Fernando captured that fighting spirit from them. He had the instincts of a fighter."

Reuss believed Lasorda was simply doing what he felt was best for the Dodgers. "If you're a manager of a ball club, you've got to go with the guy that you think is best. So if Lasorda believed that Fernando going deep into every ball game was his best resource, then that's why he did what he did."

It's also difficult to predict how pitching as often as Valenzuela did would affect him. After all, one of his contemporaries, Nolan Ryan, albeit a different kind of pitcher, was still throwing fastballs in the 90s through his twenty-seventh big league season. "When you get a lot of strikeouts like Fernando did," Reuss continued, "you're going to throw a lot of pitches. Now, what kind of effect will that have over your career? Everybody's a little bit different, so it's hard to answer if he was overused or not."

Some would say the workload went with the territory of being an all-time great pitcher during the period in which he pitched. "Fernando was certainly one of the greatest left-handers in Dodger history," Steve Brener said. "There's Koufax and Valenzuela just like there's [right-handers] Don Drysdale and Don Sutton. When there was a big game, Fernando was there to pitch it, and he didn't come out of the game. He gave Tommy and the team every last ounce when he was out there. Today pitchers go five and six innings. Fernando was throwing, on average, 130 to 140 pitches a game. He was an iron man, to say the least. I don't recall any time he was hurt. Every four or five days he was out there. He wanted the ball and he wanted to pitch."

Through Valenzuela's first seven full seasons in the Major Leagues, no pitcher faced more batters (7,413), had more strikeouts (1,448), or allowed more walks (659) than he did. From 1982 through 1987, he pitched no fewer than 251 innings—a staggering figure. His 3.11 ERA over that period was second only to Nolan Ryan's. Valenzuela was the most durably outstanding pitcher in the game.

Unfortunately, that was about to change.

Missing the Party   22

In a year that has been so improbable, the impossible has happened.

—VIN SCULLY on NBC-TV after Kirk Gibson's
game-winning World Series home run

All seemed right in Fernando Valenzuela's world at the start of the 1988 campaign. With a contract that would pay him $2.05 million for the season, he was baseball's highest-paid pitcher. In the hit movie *Bull Durham* released that spring, he got a shout-out from Annie Savoy (Susan Sarandon) when she gives pitching advice to Nuke LaLoosh (Tim Robbins), saying, "Haven't you ever noticed how Fernando Valenzuela doesn't even look when he pitches? He's a Mayan Indian. Or an Aztec. I get them confused." And on April 4 he would receive his sixth Opening Day assignment—one short of the Dodgers record—in a game against the rival Giants. But a 5–1 loss, in which he got through only six innings, would be a harbinger of things to come.

Something was clearly amiss. Valenzuela had lost up to 10 miles per hour off his fastball, and his screwball had consistently been ineffective. Through his first three months of the season—when he registered a record of just 5–8 with a 4.39 ERA—Fernando would repeatedly remark to the press that he didn't feel as if anything was physically wrong but that perhaps, on occasion, he was simply not giving himself enough time to warm up.

But after a July 30 defeat by the Astros in which Valenzuela left the game in the fifth inning after it was determined that he had injured the front part of his left shoulder, El Toro was for the first time in his career put on the disabled list. It would end a remarkable run of 255 consecutive starts over his eight seasons with the Dodgers. Tommy Lasorda had his suspicions all season long. "I always felt that something was wrong," he told reporters after the announcement to put Valenzuela on the disabled list was made. "But [Fernando] would never tell you because he's such a tremendous competitor. It's good to know, though, that we're able to take care of him. The longer he pitches with it, the more injurious it is to his health."

Still, it was debatable as to the role that Lasorda played in protecting his star pitcher, especially after he told reporters that day how he believed Valenzuela may have been injured long before the '88 season. "After he won twenty-one games in 1986," Lasorda said, "I saw him go a little backward in spring training. I think that's when it started. That was the first time, to me, he didn't look like the same Fernando." That revelation was startling, to say the least. After all, if that was something Lasorda had observed in Valenzuela a season and a half earlier, it's mystifying why he wouldn't have had him evaluated.

But while Lasorda has long been criticized for overusing Valenzuela, there were some observers who believed that Fernando largely living and dying with his devastating screwball—the pitch that made him famous—ultimately came at a cost. "I can't swear by it, but I do think that the screwball probably had a lot to do with wearing out Fernando's shoulder," Ken Gurnick said. "But [the screwball] also had a lot to do with his success when it was good. Fernando was never a fireballer, but if he lost a little off the fastball and the speed difference with the screwball wasn't as great, it made the screwball easier for hitters to pick up. So I think the shoulder kind of led to the deterioration of both pitches and just made him easier to hit. Was he overused? Eventually, everybody is done in from overuse. So I kind of reject that word unless you're going to apply it to Koufax and [Bob] Gibson and everybody else. When Fernandomania was going on [in 1981] was it overuse when he was throwing six or seven complete games in a row? Well, if he isn't being overused, then we're not talking about him [all these years later]. Which is it that you want? If you want greatness, are you going to take this guy out in the sixth inning when he hits ninety-five pitches and he's never going to win a Cy Young Award? You can't cherry-pick what you want from Fernando and say he would have been even better if he didn't do this or that. This was the package—Fernando was a workhorse. Tommy used him and Fernando did things that nobody else in his time did. Overused? If he hadn't been overused, he wouldn't have been Fernando."

Still, at least initially after being placed on the disabled list, there was a good deal of optimism that Valenzuela would return to form later that season. Dr. Frank Jobe, who examined Fernando, said that he wouldn't require shoulder surgery. While contending that Fernando had some loose tissue fragments in his shoulder, Jobe said that "there weren't enough to make it a big deal." Instead, he recommended a rehabilitation regimen that included various stretching exercises for his left arm and shoulder. Though the diagnosis was encouraging at that time, Valenzuela was clearly concerned. Ever the competitor, this time was different—he was not going to rush his rehabilitation. "I don't want to go out and pitch anymore if I'm not ready," he told reporters. "I don't help the team, and I don't want to kill my career."

For some observers, Valenzuela going on the disabled list with a shoulder injury was like Superman succumbing to kryptonite. "I still remember Lasorda saying that after 255 starts, Fernando was going to rehab," said Mark Langill, then a beat reporter for the *Pasadena Star News*. "There was just a shock that this great pitching machine had suddenly become unplugged. Before the injury he was so talkative and then suddenly when he got hurt, he was quiet. He still pretty much had that same Fernando mystique and aura. The only thing that had changed now was, *Oh my gosh—he's human!*"

If this was to be the beginning of Valenzuela's descent, how ironic it was that the so-called "Mexican Sandy Koufax" the Dodgers had long searched for was quickly approaching the number of innings pitched by Koufax himself, who was done at a young age.

Fernando would return to the mound eight weeks later to start a September 26 game against the Padres. His catcher that night would be Rick Dempsey, who described Valenzuela's demeanor as more serious than the happy-go-lucky pitcher of the past. "He got mad at me on the bus trip going down to San Diego," Dempsey recalled. "He was mad because some of us were making too much noise. So he was difficult to call pitches with when I was catching him that game. It was just your typical baseball stuff that goes on with a band of brothers. But the thing with Fernando then was, when he got focused, don't mess with him because it irritated him. He was so good at what he did, he just didn't want to goof around, didn't want to laugh, and didn't want to joke. He just wanted to go out there and win. He was a tough, tough guy out on the field. He wanted you to call the right pitch and he would do his job. He was incredible. His body rhythm and the things he was capable of doing with that screwball—and then throw the fastball by you. He had a unique delivery, and he made it work."

But despite pitching as well as could be expected in his first game back—giving up two runs while striking out three—he left after just the third inning. He would be long gone when Mickey Hatcher's RBI single in the eighth would prove to be the game-winning hit in the Dodgers' division-clinching game. While nobody expected Valenzuela to go nine innings, it would have been poetic justice for him to have at least earned the win in this most unlikely of Dodgers titles.

The Padres game would be Fernando's last start of the year. Despite pitching an impressive four innings out of the bullpen to pick up a save in the second-to-last game of the regular season, he was left off the post-season roster. It was determined by Dodgers brass that, after being out for two months, Valenzuela simply didn't have the stamina to start and that he took too long to get loose to pitch in relief. It was a gut-wrenching decision for all involved. Thus, Fernando would play the unfamiliar role of spectator as the Dodgers faced daunting odds against baseball's two powerhouse teams—the Mets in the NLCS and then the Oakland A's in the World Series. Without him, the Dodgers were perilously ill-equipped. Or so it seemed.

What the Dodgers did have in their arsenal was Orel Hershiser, who was nothing short of extraordinary throughout the regular season, notching a 23-8 record and 2.26 ERA—numbers great enough for the Cy Young Award. If that wasn't impressive enough, he was now peaking as October approached. Hershiser closed out August with three complete game victories while surrendering just four earned runs. But he was just getting started. In the month of September, he would pitch five consecutive shutouts and would have had a sixth had he received any run support; he left that game against the Padres after hurling ten shutout frames in what would eventually be a 2-1 San Diego victory in sixteen innings. Far more significant was that he had now pitched fifty-nine straight scoreless innings, breaking Don Drysdale's twenty-year-old record of fifty-eight. "At least [the record] stays in the family," Drysdale would tell the *Los Angeles Times* after the game.

To complement Hershiser, the Dodgers had a ruggedly intense slugger in Kirk Gibson, whose grit and leadership meant every bit as much as his statistics, which earned him National League MVP honors. "Kirk was a great example of how hard you have to play the game," Dempsey said. "He did crazy things, like scoring from second base on a passed ball one time in Dodger Stadium. And all that did was give everybody so much energy."

But what nobody saw coming was a group of reserve players who were nicknamed, appropriately enough for Hollywood, the Stuntmen. And no player personified their gritty, grinding, team-effort spirit more than Dempsey himself. The backup catcher would hit .400 in a limited role against the Mets' vaunted pitching staff in the NLCS and reflected glowingly on the '88 Dodgers, a club that exceeded everyone's wildest expectations. "We were a very low-ranked, low-rated ball club at that time because we had a lot of older guys," said Dempsey. But the Stuntmen included "players like Mickey Hatcher, Franklin Stubbs, Danny Heep, myself, and names nobody knew anything about. But we knew how to play, and we developed something that I'd never seen in all my years in baseball—a camaraderie that was so complementary. We were two teams within one. They called us the Stuntmen—all the backup guys at spring training that got to play the second halves of ball games when the starters like Steve Sax, Mike Marshall, and Kirk Gibson pulled themselves out of games. We'd come in and start scoring runs. And we kept coming from behind, so they called us the Stuntmen. And we took it seriously. We had so much fun and knew what our roles were going to be—not everyday players, but guys that would come in when the club needed us the most."

The NLCS was predicted by many to be a mere stepping-stone for the New York Mets on their way to the World Series. They had dominated their head-to-head matchups against the Dodgers during the regular season, winning ten out of the eleven games and outscoring them 49–18. But the Dodgers had a plan—especially when playing in New York. "We had a team meeting at Dodger Stadium about the series against the Mets," Dempsey recalled. "I listened to the scouting report and then got up and said, 'Listen, we all know how good they really are, and we've got to slow their momentum down. But one thing we *really* have to do is to take the Shea Stadium crowd out of the game, because that crowd gives them an intensity that's hard to beat. So every time they start to get really loud, just call time out. Let the crowd burn out so that our pitchers can think about what they need to accomplish and putting the ball where they need to put it."

Through the first four games of the series, the Mets had maintained their mode of play from the regular season. New York held a two-games-to-one lead and led 4–2 in the ninth inning of game four at Shea Stadium with Dwight Gooden dealing. The Mets were three outs away from taking a dominating 3–1 lead in the series when the Dodgers' John Shelby led off the inning with a walk. That brought up Mike Scioscia, a contact hitter, who had hit just thirty-five home runs in eight and a half big league seasons. But Scioscia would do the unthinkable, hitting the biggest home run of his life by ripping a Gooden fastball over the right-field fence to tie the game at 4–4. The intimidating Shea Stadium crowd was now in a state of shock. But not everyone in the ballpark was amazed by Scioscia's dinger. "Mike hitting that home run was no surprise to me," Dempsey said. "He just happened to be the person in that slot where it was time to produce—and he did! But those kinds of things happened to us that year on a regular basis, so we got to the point where we almost expected it. That team focused on accomplishing certain things better than any team I ever played on—and I played on some great ball clubs."

The game would remain tied until the top of the twelfth, when Gibson homered over the right-center field fence off Mets reliever Roger McDowell to give the Dodgers a 5–4 lead. But the Mets battled back, loading the bases in the bottom of the inning with just one out and their two best hitters—Darryl Strawberry and Kevin McReynolds—due up. After Dodgers reliever and longtime Mets closer Jesse Orosco retired Strawberry on a pop-up to second base, Lasorda went to his bullpen and brought in Hershiser to face one batter, with the game—and, really, the series—on the line. The strategy worked, as Hershiser got McReynolds to hit a weak fly ball to Shelby in center field to end the game and tie the series at two games apiece.

For as great a victory as it was for the Dodgers, it was a devastating defeat for the Mets. And when the Mets would lose the NLCS in Los

Angeles three nights later behind a Hershiser 6-0 shutout in game seven, history would look back at that fourth game as the end of the Mets' halcyon days of the mid-1980s.

As for the Dodgers, they were now one giant leap closer to pulling off a miracle. But they faced another tremendous hurdle in what was truly a perfect ball club: the Oakland A's. This A's team was historically good. They had won 104 regular season games, easily winning the AL West by 13 games. Then they swept the Boston Red Sox in 4 straight games in the ALCS. The team featured the "Bash Brothers," sluggers Jose Canseco and Mark McGwire, the most fearsome one-two punch since the days of the "M&M Boys," Roger Maris and Mickey Mantle, nearly three decades earlier. Their starting rotation was led by ace Dave Stewart, now in the second of four straight 20-win seasons. And out of the bullpen was future Hall of Famer Dennis Eckersley, as great a reliever during this period as there ever was in Major League history.

"We were the worst-ranked team on paper in World Series history playing the best-ranked team on paper in World Series history," Dempsey said without exaggeration. If things weren't ominous enough for the Dodgers, Gibson, their best everyday player, was likely out for the World Series with injuries to his left hamstring and right knee, sustained in the NLCS. "'Gibby' played hard all the time," Dempsey said. "When he got hurt in the Mets series, we were all wondering whether or not he was going to be able to play. We figured he was, but then he said to us, 'Listen, I'd be hurting the ball club trying to go after a fly ball, so I have to sit this one out.' But the one thing he could do was swing the bat, and we were just hoping that he'd get his chance.'"

As it turned out, in one of the most epic moments in baseball history, Gibson's opportunity would come—sooner than anyone anticipated. It was Game One and the Dodgers were losing 4-3 in the bottom of the ninth. LA was down to its final out, with Eckersley pitching like a man against boys—first retiring Scioscia on a harmless pop-up to short and then striking out Jeff Hamilton. But then the Dodgers were given a glimmer of hope when pinch hitter Mike Davis drew a walk, putting the tying run on base. This would bring up pitcher Alejandro Peña's spot in the order, a natural opportunity for Gibson to pinch-hit—if he was able to.

Unbeknown to anyone other than Lasorda, hitting coach Ben Hines, batboy/assistant equipment manager Mitch Poole, and Gibson himself, the physically impaired slugger who could barely walk much less run had been taking swings in the batting cage for the last two innings. Gibson, who didn't even come out along the third base line for the pregame introductions, had wanted to see if he would be able to pinch-hit should an opportunity in a key moment present itself.

"It was kind of a routine night for me as far as picking up towels and everything in the training room," recalled Poole. "We could hear Vin Scully on the air talking about how we were going to be without the services of Kirk Gibson. Late in the game, Gibby was being worked on [by the trainer] but then got up really quick, looked around, saw me, and said, 'Mitch, go get my uniform.' I dropped the towels and went and got his uniform. As he's putting it on, he goes to me, 'Can you get some balls ready for me?' We had this little area for [hitting] tees. So I got the tee ready as Hines walks by and Kirk goes, 'Hey, Ben, can you help me out here?' This is between the seventh and eighth innings, and Hines says, 'Ah, no. Why don't you get Mitch to help you out?' and goes to the bench. So Gibby goes to me, 'All right, let's get down to business.' After a while, he goes, 'I need to be able to see the ball moving, so I need you to toss the ball because it's not going to come to me just sitting there [on the tee].' So he's there swinging and he's hurting—you could hear it. He was grunting and moaning, but halfway through that he just goes, 'Mitch, I need you to go down there [to the dugout] and tell Tommy that I can hit.'

"So I ran down there, and I'm yelling from the entrance to the dugout," Poole continued. "Tommy's all the way at the other end, but he wouldn't even listen to me. I saw him turn his head, but he still wasn't listening. So then I *screamed* at him, and all the players are looking at me like, *What the heck?* So finally he comes over and goes to me, 'What is it? Can't you see that we're trying to win a game here?' I go, 'Tommy, Gibby just told me that if you've got a spot for him, he can hit.' Tommy's eyes popped out of his head, then he ran up the ramp, and Gibson told him what he could do. So Tommy goes running back downstairs, and Gibby and I continue to toss. Then we stopped, and Gibby went down to the bench. I don't think [the coaches] wanted him down there at that time because they didn't want him to be seen by [the A's]. I went down there, too. But because I wasn't in my normal uniform—instead, in a T-shirt and a pair of cutoff jeans—I couldn't go to the bench. But I did stand in the photo-well area, so from chest-high I could see everything out on the field."

What Poole, like the nearly fifty-six thousand fans at Dodger Stadium and millions more watching on television, would see was Kirk Gibson determinedly walking up the dugout steps to the on-deck circle, where he began taking practice swings as the ballpark erupted in anticipation—prompting Scully to say in a dramatic tone, "And look who's coming up." The crowd rose to its feet. It was remarkable theater. Now in the batter's box facing the great Eckersley, Gibson took two mighty cuts, fouling both outside fastballs straight back and looking very uncomfortable in the process. With two bad legs, he couldn't push off his left leg, and with his right swollen knee he couldn't land on it. With the weight shift of his swing hampered, he was using all arms to try to drive the ball. But Gibson continued to battle, working the count to 3–2 after Davis stole second base, to dramatically improve the situation for the Dodgers. Now, a single would likely tie the game. But Gibson had far greater aspirations in mind if he got a pitch he could handle. He also had a sense of what pitch was coming next—thanks to a report from Mel Didier, the Dodgers scout who had convinced the club to acquire Gibson in free agency that year. "Gibby didn't have much in the tank," Dempsey recalled. "But Mel gave us the scouting report that Eckersley always threw the backdoor slider in 3–2 counts to left-handed hitters. Eckersley couldn't read that Gibby could not get around on a fastball; he just didn't have the bat speed to do it. But a slider comes in a lot slower."

Eckersley would hang the next offering—the breaking ball Gibson was looking for—over the heart of the plate, and Kirk made him pay, swinging his muscular arms forward and lifting a high fly ball into the right-center field bleachers for a game-winning two-run homer to send the crowd and the Dodgers into a frenzy. As Gibson hobbled around the bases—the ecstasy overriding his pain—his teammates gathered around home plate, giving him a hero's welcome when he eventually arrived. It was just such a Hollywood ending. You could almost hear the music from the final act of the movie *The Natural*. Kirk Gibson had become Roy Hobbs.

For the young batboy, Gibson's clout fulfilled a premonition he had had during the at bat. "After Gibby took a couple of swings off Eckersley— even with him struggling up there—something came over me," Poole recalled more than three decades later. "It was like I saw the flight of the ball going into the right-field stands. I'm like, *God, that would be awesome.* And it was just a few pitches later that he hit it with the same freaking flight of the ball, and into the same location in the stands, as I had envisioned. I got chills then and I'm getting them right now. It was supernatural. You could almost think that God grabbed that ball in midair and just dropped it out there, because Gibby had no business doing that in his condition."

Although it was just the first game of the World Series, it was an extremely uplifting victory for the underdog Dodgers and a devastating blow to the mighty A's. A somewhat shell-shocked Eckersley, to his credit, said all the right things after the game. "I get a chance to bounce back," said the reliever, who had forty-five saves that regular season and four more in the playoffs. "It's not like they won the seventh game. We've still got a lot of baseball left. It's easy for a player to handle success. The toughest part of this game is failure. You really find out about a person when they fail, and I'll be back. [Gibson's home run] was the lowest moment of my career, but I've got a chance to redeem myself."

But the Dodgers, to their credit, wouldn't allow that to happen—thus taking Eckersley out of save situations for the rest of the series—and winning the World Series in five games. Some outstanding Dodgers pitching, which limited the A's to just a .177 batting average and eleven total runs, as well as some clutch hitting by a decimated LA lineup, stymied Oakland. Hershiser, with dominant performances in Games Two and Five, would be named World Series MVP—just as he was the MVP of the NLCS—to climax a two-month run of pitching excellence unmatched in baseball history.

The '88 Dodgers had pulled off the unlikeliest of world championships. Not even the '69 Mets, long considered the ultimate underdog when they went from lovable losers the first seven years of their existence to a World Series championship over the heavily favored Orioles, could match this Hollywood team that won with castoffs and pixie dust after most of their prominent players went down with injuries.

Meanwhile, Fernando may have earned his second World Series ring, but he had missed all the fun.

Leaving LA in Style   23

Valenzuela's mystique never wore off all those years after Fernandomania.
—RUSS ORTIZ, Los Angeles–born former Major League pitcher

One of the beauties of baseball is how, on any given day, something extraordinary and unprecedented can occur. One of those rare days occurred on June 29, 1990. It began in the East, when A's ace Dave Stewart pitched a 5–0 no-hitter over the Toronto Blue Jays at SkyDome. These were back in the days when a no-hitter occurred about as often as a total eclipse of the sun. But because it was Stewart, the former Dodger and teammate of Valenzuela's who had pitched it, there was a pregame buzz in the Los Angeles clubhouse. News of the extraordinary achievement spread like wildfire between the media and the players.

About thirty minutes before Valenzuela was to take the mound at Dodger Stadium, he reportedly wondered aloud if there might be a second no-hitter thrown that night—perhaps even by him. After all, even at this point in Valenzuela's career he was still capable of pitching a gem. If it were to occur, it would be the first time in the modern baseball era that two no-hitters would be pitched on the same day.

"I think Fernando could have said it," Mark Langill mused. "But I think that he could have said it tongue-in-cheek and as just something to say. It was definitely not like Joe Namath by the pool [guaranteeing the Jets' Super Bowl III victory] announcing what's going to happen, you know? It may have just been a throwaway comment as far as, *Hey, I'll get one, too,* because it wasn't like him [to boast]."

Both Stewart and Valenzuela had been struggling coming into their games that day, with the A's pitcher dropping his last three decisions and Fernando two of his last three. But Fernando, now a twenty-nine-year-old veteran with a lot of mileage on that left arm of his, had reinvented himself into an effective pitcher who was getting by more on guile than on the nastiness of his repertoire from earlier in his career. "Fernando was very fortunate that he was not a pure power pitcher," Tom Nieden-fuer said. "He always relied on being able to pinpoint his control and have four or five different pitches. So the adjustment for him when he did start to lose some arm speed off his fastball wasn't as difficult as with many other pitchers."

As for Valenzuela's screwball, it was as menacing as ever. "It never changed," said Mookie Wilson, who came up the same year as Fernando and battled him for years as a New York Met. "The screwball was his 'out pitch.' Fernando still had that great screwball throughout his entire Dodger career."

On this warm early summer night at Dodger Stadium, Valenzuela took the mound against the Cardinals while hoping to bounce back from a dreadful performance just five nights before—a 10–6 drubbing at the hands of the Reds—which saw Fernando give up eight earned runs in five and a third innings.

Clearly, this game was *very* different, as only one Cardinal reached base (on an error by left fielder Kirk Gibson) off Valenzuela through six innings of play. Yet, despite the zeros El Toro was putting up on the scoreboard, the Cardinals were often going deep into counts with several hard-hit balls that were belted to the deepest parts of the outfield. In a strange way, nobody seemed to have a sense that history was in the making. "He did not have *anything* exceptional that night," said Nied-enfuer, who was now a member of the opposing Cardinals. "But he still had his will to compete, which brought him over the edge. This game reminded me a little bit of Game Three of the '81 World Series when he threw a gazillion pitches. You knew that will of his was still there. You knew anything was a possibility."

"I remember looking up at the scoreboard in the sixth inning," recalled Langill, who covered the game that night. "You saw that Fernando was pitching a no-hitter, but it wasn't like the night that Ramón Martínez struck out all those Braves [in his 1995 no-hitter] and there was an electricity in the stadium. In this one, there wasn't *any* electricity until the seventh inning, because that year Fernando had been so inconsistent. It wasn't like he started off with six strikeouts and looking like Koufax or anything like that. He seemed kind of all over the place in the strike zone. It was like, *Hey, it's the sixth inning and the Cardinals have no hits*, but you don't really consider him working on a no-hitter. It was more like, *Well, we'll see—there's still a long way to go*."

But by the seventh inning, fans were catching on, and a crescendo of cheering became louder with every out Valenzuela registered. One of those fans at Dodger Stadium was a sixteen-year-old American Legion pitcher named Russ Ortiz, who would one day grow up to pitch in some pretty big Major League games himself. "My friends and I were sitting in the nosebleed seats in the right-field bleachers," Ortiz recalled. "Watching it from afar, some of the balls hit off Fernando looked like they were going to be home runs—it was hard to judge. But I also saw that he was keeping hitters off balance. He was a pitcher who still had good stuff. He had the appearance of a man that had control of the game. By the seventh inning, we're like, *Oh, shoot—he hasn't given up any hits!* So now the baseball superstition comes into play—*Let's not talk about it!* Some of my American Legion teammates left early because, realistically, they figured the no-hitter probably wasn't going to happen and didn't want to deal with the traffic. But my brother and I stayed, thinking it would be super cool to be able to see one live."

In Valenzuela's remarkable career to that point, he had thrown seven two-hitters and no one-hitters. As he entered the seventh inning, he was in rarefied air, even for himself. After retiring Willie McGee to start the inning, he issued back-to-back walks to his good friend Pedro Guerrero and Todd Zeile, with the dangerous Terry Pendleton coming to the plate. With a 3-0 Dodgers lead, one swing of the bat could not only end the no-hit bid but also tie the game. Pendleton would make a bid to do just that, hammering a ball to deep left field but falling just short of the wall for the second out of the inning. Valenzuela would then retire the next hitter, José Oquendo, on a sharp grounder to third to end the threat and keep the no-no alive.

In the Dodgers' half of the seventh, Fernando would help himself at the plate, singling and later scoring on a two-run single by Gibson to give LA a commanding 5-0 lead. Now with the game itself appearing to be secure, the only drama left was the possibility of nearly forty thousand fans witnessing baseball immortality. "In the eighth inning," Ortiz said, "everybody in the stadium was anxious and hanging on every pitch—just pins and needles. The excitement and anticipation were off the charts. *Every* pitch mattered now."

Valenzuela would go deep into counts against the first two hitters—Rex Hudler and Ozzie Smith—increasing the tension level before retiring them both. Craig Wilson would then end the inning with yet another deep Cardinals drive—this one near the left-center field fence. Fernando was now just three outs away from baseball nirvana.

After the Dodgers picked up an insurance run with a Juan Samuel solo home run in the bottom of the eighth, Valenzuela walked back out to the mound to start the ninth with the crowd standing as one. After striking out Vince Coleman looking for the first out, he walked McGee on four straight pitches. That brought up Guerrero, who knew Valenzuela's pitching tendencies better than perhaps any opposing hitter in baseball, making him a serious threat to break up the no-hitter. "Fernando was tough," Guerrero said. "Even though I knew him so well, he was *really* tough. I remember facing him in the Caribbean Series in Mexico one time. I went as a replacement player for the Dominican baseball team that he pitched against. After facing him, I thought, *Damn, that screwball he's got, he's one of the best pitchers I've ever seen!*"

Now they were going head to head once again, though with much more on the line. Valenzuela quickly got ahead of Guerrero 0–2 and was now just one strike away from achieving a feat he could never reach during his halcyon days. But Guerrero made a strong bid to ruin Fernando's night, smashing a hard ground ball with authority up the middle. "As soon as I hit it," Guerrero recalled, "I thought it was going to be a hit because I hit it so hard." But the ball tipped off Valenzuela's glove, misdirecting it to the right and directly over second base—precisely where Samuel was positioned. Samuel fielded it, touched second, and fired to first for a game-ending double play that secured a no-hitter for Valenzuela. "It was funny," Guerrero said, "because I ran so hard to first base and just heard the sound of the first baseman's glove and I said, 'Oh my God!' I really thought I was going to get the hit to end the no-hitter. But I wouldn't have felt good if I did break it up."

Up in the Dodgers' broadcast booth, Vin Scully spun his magic once again with the perfect call, exclaiming to his audience, 'Fernando Valenzuela has pitched a no-hitter at 10:17 in the evening of June the

29th, 1990. If you have a sombrero, *throw it* to the sky!' Then, in a classic old-school broadcasting way, he didn't utter another word until well after Fernando had left the field and made his way into the dugout. Scully let the roar of the crowd paint the picture of the momentous occasion.

As for the man of the hour, Valenzuela's reaction was muted when compared to most mound celebrations after a no-hitter. After Scioscia hugged him with such force that Fernando was moved backward a couple of steps, El Toro shook his teammates' hands, gave a few casual high-fives, and then walked briskly toward the dugout, bypassing reporters and giving a quick tip of his cap to the fans.

"I was standing next to him after he pitched his no-hitter," Langill recalled. "There was excitement, but it wasn't like he broke character and suddenly was hugging everyone and yelling, *Oh my God! This is great!* It was a big smile, but it was still very applied and analytical. I think the smile was a little bigger, the eyes twinkled a little more because of the moment, but he was still Fernando."

The total time that had elapsed between the last out and when he took his first step off the field was just forty-nine seconds. It was a vintage Valenzuela move—never wanting to draw too much attention to himself. "That was Fernando," Fred Claire said. "You never saw him jumping up and down or throwing himself into the arms of the catcher. He was the ultimate professional. It was near the end of his Dodger career, and it may have surprised everyone in the ballpark, but in my mind, it didn't surprise Fernando. Even though Fernando was not the pitcher he had been, there was always the possibility of an outstanding game simply because of who he was as a pitcher. When you look at the grace of some of the greats, a proper analogy [to Valenzuela's no-hitter] was when Babe Ruth hit three home runs in a game in the last week of his career. Or when you look at some of the all-time great fighters who were capable of a great moment regardless of their age or stage of their career. This was Fernando's moment."

As for the young Ortiz, he was ecstatic that he stayed until the end to watch his hero reach the highest of heights. "It was the greatest thing ever!" he said. "We were riding high on the way home while reminiscing about what we just saw. Not just because it was a no-hitter but because it was *Fernando* who did it. He was just so loved by so many people."

The no-hitter would prove to be the last magical night for Valenzuela at Dodger Stadium.

*

After finishing the 1990 season with an even 13-13 record and an ERA of 4.59—the highest of his career and worst among National League pitchers with more than thirty starts—Fernando entered the following spring training in unfamiliar territory as a long shot to make a stacked Dodgers starting rotation. Even before spring training began, there was talk the Dodgers would trade or even release their iconic pitcher. But Valenzuela, ever the fighter, started March 1991 pitching his best spring training ball of his career.

The pinnacle of that success occurred when the Dodgers traveled to Monterrey, Mexico, for a game against the Milwaukee Brewers. Valenzuela started that contest in front of nearly thirty thousand of his compatriots in a festive atmosphere. But while some viewed Fernando's return to Mexico as a joyous occasion, others almost cringed at the timing of it. "There was an awkwardness when they had that exhibition game in Mexico," Langill recalled. "It just seemed like the Dodgers brought him back in '91 because of that game."

Still, for five innings, Fernando single-handedly overpowered the Brewers by giving up only two hits while facing just sixteen hitters—one over the minimum—while also slugging an RBI single in a 6-1 Dodgers victory. It may have been only an exhibition game, but his thrilling performance gave goose bumps to those who witnessed it. "We knew Fernando's importance to his country before we came down here, but to see it, to feel it, to hear it . . . it was an extraordinary moment," Peter O'Malley told the *Los Angeles Times*'s Bill Plaschke. "This is one of the most exciting experiences I've had since I've been with the ballclub."

Even Claire, who later that month would have to decide Valenzuela's fate with the team, was impressed, telling Plaschke from his seat behind home plate, "It's not just great to see him pitch like this in his country, but it's great to see him pitch like this period."

As for Valenzuela, who was uncharacteristically anxious prior to this critical start because he had something to prove, was elated with his play on several levels. "I think today was a little more important to me than a usual game," he told reporters while icing his arm in the training room. "It was important for me to come back here and show the people what is going on—show the people that my arm is fine. There were people today who came a long way from Sonora. They shouted to me, 'We still remember you!' Today was so nice. The way I played[,] I think the people enjoyed it a little bit. I think they now believe a little bit."

Alas, the rest of spring training would be far less kind to Valenzuela, as he ended the spring with a 1-2 mark and a 7.88 ERA. The writing was on the wall. Despite the occasional glimpses of greatness—like his no-hitter the previous season—Valenzuela simply wasn't the same dominating pitcher he was prior to 1987. All those innings in the first seven years of his career had taken its toll. Claire, who twice signed Fernando as a free agent, first in 1989 and again in 1990, would now be faced with an extremely difficult decision on whether to keep not just an all-time Dodgers great but an icon to millions.

"I remember vividly in the spring of '91 not wanting to release Fernando from the Dodgers without giving him the opportunity to show that he could continue to help us," Claire said with emotion three decades later. "So, to have released him before the '91 season would have been to say, in my own mind, that I didn't think Fernando could do it anymore. But I wanted to give him the opportunity. Now, Fernando may not have seen it that way. And that's his viewpoint. But I didn't want him to have a feeling that I didn't believe in him, because I did believe in him. But in the spring of '91, it became obvious to me that he wasn't going to be able to help us. And I've never run away from the fact there was a monetary part of this because I had to make the decision when I did because, after a certain date [April 2], we would have owed him that year's salary [$2.55 million]. So I also had an obligation to the Dodgers to handle the fiduciary responsibilities as best as I could."

Still, for Claire and the rest of the Dodgers brass, it was a difficult time. "I'll never forget meeting in Tommy's office with Fernando," Claire said, referring to the day of Valenzuela's release. "I thought about [how] this kind of bookends to that first Fernando start in 1981, when I sat with Tommy, and now here I was again in Tommy's office with him and Ron Perranoski letting Fernando know that we were going to release him and sharing our great appreciation for all that he had done for us. When I told Fernando of my decision, he said, 'Thank you very much,' and left the office. That story really hasn't been reported, but the facts are the facts.

Fernando's agent [and attorney] Dick Moss filed a grievance with the players' association—and all this can be verified. We had a meeting in Los Angeles, and I explained to [MLBPA executive director] Don Fehr's assistant the pitchers that we had in 1991 and that I gave Fernando the chance [to make the club], but it was clear that he wasn't going to be able to be a part of the starting staff. And I think in a quote, Fernando acknowledged that and knew that he wasn't going to be of any help in the bullpen. So, after explaining my reasoning, Fehr's assistant said, after Fernando may have left the room, 'We have no case here.'"

As far as where this ranked on the scale of his toughest baseball-related decisions he ever had to make, Claire is pragmatic about it. "I've had to make a lot of them, so I don't rank them," he said. "In one sense, I have to factor in the fact that I felt, in my own mind and heart, that I had done everything I could to keep Fernando with the Dodgers. So it was simply a decision. They're never easy—*never*. Anytime I ever released a player, I never once told them they couldn't play. I told many players to not let what I'm doing here impact their belief in their ability to play."

While Dodgers fans and the Latino community the world over had heavy hearts over Valenzuela's release, Claire didn't recall any backlash over it, adding, "I could be wrong, but I think the fans understood that it's hard to let a great player go, but that Fernando had a great, great run with us. And they knew from my quotes that I felt he was one of the all-time great Dodgers with a great heart and great ability."

Dusty Baker, who said he considered Valenzuela "one of the top five players, top five teammates" he ever had, believed fan reaction to Fernando's release was more negative than Claire knew of or perhaps acknowledged. "You have to understand that Fred was a PR guy [before becoming general manager]," Baker said, alluding to Claire's experience in providing a positive image for the Dodgers organization. "The [Dodgers] pitched the shit out of Fernando for a six-year period. They *really* rode him—then let him go."

For the first time since the now thirty-year-old Valenzuela was a teenager, he found himself in no-man's land—a pitcher without a team. Valenzuela should have eventually retired as a Los Angeles Dodger instead of leaving the club unceremoniously through release. *Hadn't the Dodgers always projected a family atmosphere for its players and fans?* But this was the cold business side of baseball at work, the same side that also watched other Dodgers greats of Valenzuela's era, like Sutton, Garvey, Lopes, Cey, and Baker, finish their careers elsewhere. "I've been talking to you guys about this for some time," a proud, yet heartbroken Fernando told reporters that day. "I'll be somewhere, I don't know where." So the man who broke the glass ceiling for Mexican players and dramatically altered the Dodgers' fan base at Chavez Ravine in becoming an idol, folk hero, and inspiration to millions in the Latino community would now have to attempt to jump-start his career elsewhere.

Unthinkably, Fernando Valenzuela was now a former Dodger.

The Long Road Back to Glory   24

My career is not over. I still believe in myself. I can still play.
—FERNANDO VALENZUELA, after being released by the Dodgers in 1991

It would be nearly five long, challenging years before Valenzuela would recapture a semblance of his former greatness on the mound, which spoke more about the measure of this man, his perseverance, and his love of the game than even his supreme talent. By this point, Fernando was a wealthy man, never needing to work another day in his life. Yet, he pressed on to resurrect his baseball career.

Two months after being released by the Dodgers, he signed with the California Angels, at the time an uplifting turn of events for his legion of fans in Southern California. More than eighty thousand of them turned out for the two games he would pitch for the Angels in a nod to the drawing power he still possessed in the region. But after getting roughed up in those starts, he was again let go and wouldn't throw another big league pitch that season.

In 1992 Valenzuela hit rock bottom, signing with the Detroit Tigers, only to be sold to the Jalisco Charros of the Mexican League before he even threw a pitch for the big league club. The Mexican League is often the last chance for former Major Leaguers hoping to hang on in the game. Everything about the league, from playing conditions to accommodations to the equipment, is well below big league standards—hardly a place for a pitcher who for years had captured the imagination of baseball fans the world over.

Initially, things went from bad to worse for Valenzuela. He started the season with lopsided losses in his first three games with the Charros, and after five games his record sat at 0-5. But Valenzuela improved tremendously as the season wore on, and his legendary screwball was working effectively again. He finished strong, throwing a two-hitter in his final game, to compile a season-ending record of 10–9 with a modest 3.86 ERA. "You wait and see," Valenzuela's greatest advocate, Mike Brito, told *Los Angeles Times* writer Michael J. Goodman after that last game. "Fernando's going to come back. He's going to make it in the big leagues. People are going to say Mike Brito was right."

Brito's words would indeed prove prophetic. Baltimore Orioles assistant general manager Frank Robinson was intrigued by a positive scouting report of Fernando based on his performance for Mexico during that winter's Caribbean Series and recommended the club give him a shot at making their rotation. With an assist from his persistent agent, Dick Moss, to get a deal done, Valenzuela was signed to a Minor League free agent contract with the Orioles and received an invitation to their 1993 spring training camp as a nonroster player. Fernando made the club as they headed north to start the season and was a serviceable starter for a team in desperate need of pitching. He finished the year with an 8–10 record but threw 178⅔ innings, proving his workhorse durability once again. For his performance, he earned a $400,000 incentive bonus—nearly double his salary. Yet, despite his efforts, the Orioles didn't bring him back for the 1994 season, and he returned to Jalisco—posting far better results there than in the past. His 10–3 record with a 2.67 ERA and eight complete games caught the interest of the Phillies, where he made his return to the big leagues that summer.

Like a movie right out of Hollywood, just ten days after signing with Philadelphia on the afternoon of July 3, he was back on the mound at Dodger Stadium in a triumphant return. The sellout crowd of 54,167 was in a state of utter confusion. The Dodgers were a first-place club, in the thick of a pennant race, and had another fan favorite, Orel Hershiser, pitching for the home team that day—marking the first time a pair of Dodgers Cy Young Award winners opposed one another in a game. Yet, with Fernando on the other side, the crowd was often torn between for whom and for what to cheer—a precarious position to say the least. When Valenzuela struck out Dodgers slugger Mike Piazza to end the first inning, they cheered wildly. When Fernando came up to bat in the top of the third inning, the crowd gave him a standing ovation and then roared when he proceeded to rip a single up the middle off Hershiser—

the first hit Orel had allowed that game. It was like old times, with the crowd chanting, "*México, México!*" throughout the game.

"It was nice that they remember," Valenzuela said afterward. Hershiser took it in stride, telling reporters after the game, "I was glad they were cheering him. That's what you want the home crowd to do when they see a returning champion."

Valenzuela, who admittedly battled nervousness and excitement early in the game, kept the Dodgers off balance mostly with a cut fastball. He pitched well, giving up just two runs on six hits before being lifted for a pinch hitter in the seventh inning. The Dodgers winning the game 3–1 was secondary to what it meant for Dodgers and Fernando fans that day. "I thought it was beautiful," Tommy Lasorda said. "The fans appreciated all that he did for them."

Fernando continued to pitch well when called upon by the Phillies, but a baseball strike derailed the rest of the season the following month. It was a cruel development for Valenzuela, who had worked so hard to restore his career and had appeared on the cusp of fulfilling that goal.

*

Valenzuela was on the move again the following spring, signing yet another contract with a new team—this time the San Diego Padres—just three weeks prior to a strike-shortened 1995 season. For Fernando, signing with the Padres represented his best opportunity since his Dodgers days—a match made in heaven. Not only was San Diego near the Mexican border, but the Padres were a very young team with promise and had just hired a bright rookie manager named Bruce Bochy. Valenzuela also had an ally in the front office. "Our president, Larry Lucchino, had a history with Fernando from Baltimore," Bochy recalled. "So he knew Fernando and said, 'Listen, I just want you all to take a look at him.' Larry really believed in him, so the driving force was Lucchino."

Fernando, now a big league elder statesman at age thirty-four, was an instant hit with some of his young, starstruck teammates, who looked up to him as one of their childhood heroes. Pitcher Tim Worrell, who grew up in Los Angeles, was just thirteen years old at the outset of Fernandomania. "The Dodgers were my team," Worrell recalled. "I had most of their pictures up on my wall—and Fernando was one of them. Now, all of a sudden, I'm his *teammate!* At the beginning, I still felt like a thirteen-year-old around him. It was like I wanted to get his autograph and just go, *Wow! Hey! This is awesome!* Then, once that kind of wears off, you see him as a veteran pitcher who's done it for a long time and you're just trying to pick up everything you can from him."

Another Padres pitcher, Scott Sanders, who also grew up in California, was just as thrilled. "I grew up watching Fernando," he said. "The Dodgers were my second-favorite team after the Padres, but I always followed Fernando's career—especially his rookie season, when he won all those games and did amazing things. When he signed with us, it was toward the end of his career, but I was still so excited to meet him from day one—he had a great vibe."

And for Padres catcher Brian Johnson, who grew up in Oakland, the Padres locker room was like a fantasy camp for him. "Talk about favorites," he said. "Fernando was one of my favorite teammates of all time. And Rickey Henderson [acquired by the Padres in 1996] was like a god to me. So to my left in the locker room was Ricky and to my right was Fernando. When I met each of them for the first time, I was like, *Man, I really hope they're a good guy.* And they both were. But I remembered Fernandomania like it was yesterday. It was really fun to be with him. It may have been the twilight of his career, but he was still a competitor. I could see where that success came from earlier, where he had a little more of his fastball and command of his stuff. But he still had his screwball—his pride and joy."

Despite the awe that Fernando inspired in some of his younger teammates, he just wanted to be one of the guys and remained humble. "The players loved being around him," Bochy recalled. "He was a prankster there with them. He loved the camaraderie. He loved being in the clubhouse. That's who Fernando was and was all about. You could tell that's when he was happiest. He probably didn't have to pitch again—he made enough money—but this guy just loved baseball. He loved his teammates and had fun with them. But they saw him compete, not just on the mound but at the plate. He'd give you a good at bat, too. This guy was a true competitor."

"He had a big jovial laugh and a big smile that took up his whole face," added Johnson. "He loved having a good time. Where his personality really came out was during batting practice. He *loved* to hit. And he felt like he was the best hitter on the planet! It was fun for him, and you got him talking smack to the other guys and other guys talking smack to him. It was great to see."

As far as the loner that Valenzuela was early in his career, to some on the club that part of him still existed to a degree. "The language barrier was still there," Johnson said. "He's a lot like Rickey Henderson in a lot of ways. Both are smart, savvy guys but not a whole lot of education behind them. I don't want to say there's an inferiority complex, but maybe there's a little bit of that—especially with the language barrier on top of it [in Fernando's case]. They both can be very quiet, but it's also because they are astute observers. They could be a little reclusive and guarded at times, too, and not wanting to share a whole lot. With Fernando, there were many different sides of his personality."

Sanders, quite possibly Valenzuela's closest friend on the team, saw a different side of him. "Fernando was definitely *not* a loner," he said. "When I tell you that we spent a lot of time together, we spent *a lot* of time together. Number one, he's a prankster, he loves cracking jokes. He loves pulling pranks on people. He's just a fun, happy-go-lucky person who just likes to really enjoy life. We'd hang out if we got treatment in the trainer's room or play cards in the break room. We watched TV together in the lounge. We ran together every day, played catch together every day. After every game, we would go sit in the sauna and talk. So, no, he definitely was not a loner. And, obviously, when the games came, he was all business."

By spending as much time with Valenzuela as he did, Sanders was stunned by his athleticism. "I played with some really good players like Ken Griffey Jr., A-Rod, Sammy Sosa, and Tony Gwynn," Sanders said. "But I tell people all the time that Fernando is one of the best athletes that I ever played with. People look at me like, *Are you crazy?* But when we played together in '95, I was eight years younger than he was. We would go out and play, and people always looked at Fernando and his big barrel chest and used to think he was out of shape. I'm like, *Guys, you don't get it, man. When I run, this dude is right there with me, step to step.*"

For those in Valenzuela's inner circle, like Sanders, he was also a teacher and mentor. "Fernando's one of my favorite teammates ever," he said. "He was a really big rock for me in the beginning of my career that I always look back on. He was a blessing for people like his team-mates. At the time, we had a bunch of young starting pitchers on our team, and he was one of the veterans that we didn't trade away. Just his presence alone in the clubhouse was huge. He was always there to help a young guy when needed—whether they were struggling on the mound, struggling at home, or struggling with anything in life. Sometimes there were jokes, and sometimes we'd talk about my outing and what I did well or did badly. He was always saying to keep a level head—never too high, never too low. With him, you couldn't really tell if he went out and pitched nine innings or pitched just one inning—he was such a competitor. That's what we needed as a young club in San Diego in '95 and '96 because of the veteran pitchers like Andy Benes and Bruce Hurst we had traded away."

The Padres also knew that Valenzuela would help them at the gate. Prior to his arrival, San Diego had a fire sale of sorts, trading some big names as part of a youth movement. "We were the Las Vegas Stars," said Worrell, likening the big league club to their Triple-A affiliate. "They just relocated us to San Diego. Well, maybe I should say we were the Las Vegas Stars with Tony Gwynn." The club knew that Fernando, still an icon in the Latino community, would bring in thousands of extra fans for each of his starts. "We were really struggling for attendance," recalled Sanders. "Obviously, as soon as Fernando signed with us, it generated this humongous buzz down in San Diego—which is so close to Mexico. Any time Fernando took the mound, right away, you always had more fans. It was always a better and livelier atmosphere when he pitched."

As anticipated, residents of Mexico would cross the border to see Valenzuela pitch. "I remember there being some issues and problems with parking [around Jack Murphy Stadium] when he pitched," Bochy said. "We had plenty of parking, but sometimes they would park on the roads and there would be too many cars. It was kind of like a soccer game because that was really popular, too. When Fernando pitched, it was definitely a different crowd. They were louder and, of course, chanting for him, so it was pretty obvious to all of us there was an influx coming from Mexico. Some of the games were like Mardi Gras, but with mariachi bands. It was cool to see how far they would come to see their hero. It was really amazing. And I think Larry [Lucchino] saw that part of it, too. Because, let's face it, we're in the entertainment business as well as in it to win, and he knew that Fernando would bring both. And he did. And it was good for the players to see because he was so humble. He took time out for the fans. But I think they saw who this guy was and what he was about and how many people he impacted. So, it was enlightening for all of us."

As the Padres' fortunes improved on the field, the fervor over Fernando increased as well. "You started to see more [Mexican] flags, you could see more sombreros," Sanders said. "There was a buzz, an excitement in the crowd when he pitched. And a lot of it was coming from Tijuana and all the different places in San Diego with Hispanic communities that would come out and really support Fernando. I think Fernando finally felt back home in San Diego. It wasn't LA, but it was close enough. I think for the first time in probably four or five years, he felt like, *Okay, I've got a fan base that loves me. I've got an organization that loves me.* And he just really settled in."

The more Valenzuela pitched in San Diego, the better he got. He was feeding off the crowd and the results were encouraging. "Fernando gets all the credit," Bochy said. "I think he knew we believed in him—hopefully he did. But it wasn't a case where we tweaked him or changed anything. His sense of determination helped, but I think pitching in San Diego and the crowds that he drew there was a motivator for him. What I admired about him as much as anything was his passion for the game. And that word *passion* gets thrown around, but this guy would be the first one out there to shag and take batting practice. He just loved being on the field and playing baseball."

Valenzuela had also developed a new pitch in San Diego—a cutter. "His screwball always went away from righties and into lefties," Sanders explained. "Well, at the end of the day, when you're around for as many years as he was, you face guys over and over again, and they know what to look for. Now, suddenly, he came up with this cutter and he started to control the inside [of the plate] to a righty and the outside to a lefty. Now he commanded both sides of the plate against all hitters."

Valenzuela would finish the '95 season with an 8-3 record, his first winning season since 1986. The Padres greatly improved from an awful 47-70 record in 1994 to a far more respectable 70-74 mark and third-place finish in 1995. It was a team on the rise in great part due to Valenzuela's quiet leadership and revival on the field. But even the wildest of optimists couldn't have predicted what would come for Fernando and the Padres the following season.

*

If the '96 season was to be Fernando's last hurrah, he certainly made the most of it. The surprising Padres battled the defending NL West champion Dodgers neck and neck all summer long and found themselves in a tie for first place on the afternoon of August 16, when San Diego would begin a historic three-game series with the Mets in Monterrey, Mexico—the first-ever regular-season Major League games outside of the United States and Canada.

Valenzuela's resurgence and reinvention of himself were fully complete by that point; he was sporting a 9-7 record with a 3.87 ERA when he returned to his home country as a conquering hero. "He was healthy again," Bochy noted. "He built some strength back in his shoulder and was back to the way he was because he knew how to pitch. He had the weapons, he had a tremendous changeup, and now he had the cutter that he went with a little bit more. And he kept hitters honest by pitching inside. He just became a little bit more of a complete pitcher, and a little smarter."

Fernando also developed a trust factor with his catcher. "It's hard to reinvent yourself and come to grips with not being able to do all the things you used to be able to do," Brian Johnson said. "It takes some time to figure it out. What I did was introduce him to taking advantage of those early innings to create space instead of trying to strike everybody out. I think that was a kind of oasis for him—something new he hadn't really tried before because he [had] relied on that fantastic screwball . . . so much over the years. Now he was using his fastball to push people off the plate. When he was ahead 0-1, 0-2, or 1-2, we would use a four-seam fastball and throw it into the guy's body—by his kneecap—to push the hitter back. All we wanted to do was move his feet. We didn't want to hit him. But that's how we created space. You have to be able to improve your margin of error so that if you throw a bad pitch, it's a pop-up, or it's off the end of the bat—it's not a home run. That's why Fernando was *really good* in '96."

On several levels, the pageantry of the Monterrey series would represent Valenzuela's finest moments in baseball—and he knew it even before the Padres landed in Mexico. "Fernando and I sat on the plane together as we usually did," Sanders recalled. "It was the first time that I could sense that he was excited about [a series]. For the first time, I could feel like he had some pressure on him. Not that he was nervous or scared, but I could tell that this game he was going to pitch was going to mean more to him than pitching back in San Diego—or even in LA."

Valenzuela was scheduled to pitch the opening game of the series in what would prove to be an electrifying, carnival-like atmosphere due to his presence. In fact, Worrell, who was slated to start the second game of the series, felt like the invisible man next to Fernando. "Just to have Major League Baseball down there was huge," he said. "But add to that having Fernando pitch the first ever [regular-season] MLB game down there made it crazy. Fernando and I had to go to a press conference the day before the series, and nobody really wanted to talk to me. I remember walking in there with Fernando [and] thinking, *This is pretty cool—but I'm probably not going to get a question all day. Why am I even here? But that's all right. I'll just sit there.* But it was cool—and I did get some questions my way. Fernando handled himself like a pro."

The Padres players and coaches knew that Valenzuela was beloved by Mexicans, but they didn't realize the full extent of that adoration until this series south of the border. Even the bus ride from their hotel to Estadio Monterrey, escorted by a police motorcade, left an impression. "People were following our bus down the road," Sanders recalled. "Fernando's fans were everywhere. I was sitting next to him and I could see it in his face how determined he was—like, *It's game time.* It's how I imagined what he must have been like in '81, '82, and '83. Later, when we went out to play catch, the place was jam-packed. It wasn't a humongous stadium, but people were on the streets trying to get in."

"The Monterrey games gave us a deep appreciation of just how much this guy was loved and how iconic he was down there," Bochy added. "Some of the things I saw, I was like, *Are you kidding me?* I mean, this guy was like our Babe Ruth—that's what he was like to his country. We had a sense of it, but until you see it firsthand—how big and popular this guy was to them—you wouldn't believe it. There were fans hanging on the walls trying to get in that ballpark the first night. And while I'm sure a lot of them wanted to see a Major League game, they were there to see their guy—to see Fernando. In my entire life, I never saw anybody that got that kind of attention, ovation, infatuation. That's how big he was. And the fact he was so humble made it even cooler—he just took it in stride. But it was pretty cool to be a part of it because none of us had seen anything like that in all our years in baseball."

For their part, the Padres rallied around their man, pouring it on against the Mets to build a stunning 15-0 lead after six innings. "We kicked the crap out of them," recalled Sanders. "It was one of my favorite games I've ever been a part of." Added Johnson, "We were all so excited for him. We all knew what was going on and really wanted to play well for him, have him really look good."

Meanwhile, Fernando was spectacular, mowing down the Mets inning after inning to the chants of "*Tor-o! Tor-o! Tor-o!*" from the partisan crowd in a flashback to the old Fernandomania days. "I would hate to attempt to put into words what he meant to Mexico," Worrell said. "Doing what he did in that game was such a big deal. My understanding of Latino baseball is that it's usually a festive atmosphere. But having Fernando there put it over the top all the more."

The atmosphere was festive not only for the fans but for the Padres as well. "When he took center stage and did so well, it was really fun for us as a team," Johnson said. "We really enjoyed watching and supporting him in that game and throughout the series."

Valenzuela was removed from the blowout during the seventh inning. After his departure, however, the Mets would make things interesting, scoring seven runs in the ninth, before falling short to the Padres, 15-10. The game, and the series, would prove to be a tremendous success. Leonard Coleman, who was president of the National League at the time, called it "a significant step in the international growth of baseball." And there was little doubt that, without Fernando Valenzuela, it never would have occurred.

*

With Valenzuela's victory in the Monterrey game against the Mets in the books, the Padres found themselves alone in first place by a full game over the Dodgers. But despite playing at a torrid pace the rest of the way, behind standout performances from MVP Ken Caminiti (40 HRS, 130 RBIS), Steve Finley (30 HRS, 95 RBIS), the incomparable Gwynn (.353 batting average), and closer Trevor Hoffman (42 saves, 2.25

ERA), the Dodgers kept pace with them. For many of the young Padres, Valenzuela kept them loose during the pressure-packed final stretch of the season. "Seeing Fernando's demeanor had a calming influence on us," Worrell said. "You're watching a guy out there that has obviously been through [pennant races] before. He showed us how we needed to act—there was no panic in him. As a younger player, everything seems to be the end of the world when it's not. But Fernando didn't get caught up in anything too much. And his sense of humor really helped. The guy spoke really good English by this time, and he would still pull the '*no hablo*' thing and I would be like, 'Fernando, you're full of crap!' He would just laugh at me."

"The guys loved being around him," Bochy said. "They were watching a guy that was a little older, probably didn't have the same stuff, but they saw a competitor that competed as well as any pitcher I've ever had. This is a guy that went down to the Mexican League and worked his way back. He was all about winning and didn't care how he got there. If he gave up six runs and we would score seven, he was good with that. I talked with my pitchers about him. I once said to them after a game he pitched in Colorado, 'You see this guy? He didn't get frustrated with the bloopers falling in or a cheap home run. He just kept going and going and ended up winning the game at the end of the day.' Nothing fazed him."

When the Padres slipped a game behind the Dodgers on September 7, Valenzuela stopped their two-game losing streak with a masterful performance over the Cardinals the next day, notching his thirteenth victory of the season to get them back on track. San Diego would win six of their next seven games to move a game and a half in front of the Dodgers. The determined Valenzuela was practically willing the upstart Padres to a National League West title. "If you just looked at his eyes and his demeanor," Johnson said, "there was no need to see the speed of his pitches on the radar gun. It was fun to be able to see that gleam in his eyes and his aggressiveness. It was like being a part of history to catch for the great Fernando Valenzuela and to help him get through a game and really see him at his best. It was like I could envision what he was like during his prime by the way he carried himself and by the heart and soul that he put into every pitch. For a young Major League player, it was monumental for me."

The Dodgers would move two games in front of the Padres as the two clubs began a season-ending three-game series in Los Angeles. Remarkably, San Diego would sweep the trio of games to capture the division title in what was clearly a satisfying moment for Valenzuela five and a half years after his sudden release by the Dodgers. Los Angeles would settle for a wild-card berth. For Fernando, in a season in which he would win thirteen games—the same number of victories he had in his rookie Cy Young Award season for the world champion Dodgers of 1981—a return to the postseason made for an ideal and appropriate bookend to his iconic career.

However, the ultimate, perfect ending of another world championship would not transpire, as the Padres would get swept by the Cardinals in the NL Division Series, 3–0, ending their Cinderella-esque season. Valenzuela didn't start any games in the series, a decision that Bochy rues to this day. "One of my regrets is that I probably should have started Fernando in one of those games because of his poise, his composure, and his experience," Bochy said. "With the year he had, that was probably the one time I looked back and questioned myself."

Valenzuela had given San Diego everything he had left in the tank in '96 and would retire the following season after splitting the '97 campaign with the Padres and Cardinals. But in a career in which he won 173 Major League regular-season games and pitched in nearly three thousand innings, his impressive statistics told only a small part of the story of one of the most inspirational figures in sports history.

Legacy   25

A life is not important except in the impact it has on other lives.

—JACKIE ROBINSON

More than forty years have passed since Fernandomania began in earnest on that bright shiny Opening Day at Dodger Stadium in 1981. In the years since, nobody has transformed baseball's landscape more than Valenzuela, whose presence was as sport-altering as Babe Ruth and Jackie Robinson were in their day. So, when considering the immense, revolutionary impact Valenzuela had on the game, the Mexican people, and the global Latino community at large, his legacy as an inspirational and transcendental figure is secure. Thus, it's incomprehensible how Valenzuela, now a man in his sixties, would still not be honored with one or both of the game's two highest tributes for excellence. His iconic number 34 officially still remains in circulation with the Dodgers, and there is no plaque in his honor hanging in the hallowed corridors of the National Baseball Hall of Fame in Cooperstown.

Of the two prestigious distinctions, the Dodgers' slight of not retiring Valenzuela's number is one of the great omissions in baseball today. And ironically, the Dodgers organization seemingly doesn't disagree. Proof of this is the fact that no Dodger has worn Valenzuela's 34 since he was released by the team in 1991. "He's irreplaceable," Dodgers president and part-owner Stan Kasten told MLB.com in 2021. "When you think of our particular history, which we are so proud of and talk about every day, you can't talk about it without mentioning Fernando's impact. We have Jackie Robinson, and we know his status in popular culture. We then had Sandy Koufax, who became an icon for Eastern Europeans trying to assimilate into America right at that time. And then the next wave was Fernando, who captured the attention of the entire Hispanic world."

So why hasn't Valenzuela's number been retired?

The Dodgers have a long-standing tradition of retiring the numbers of only those players who played most of their careers with the club and were later inducted into the Hall of Fame. However, an exception was made for non–Hall of Famer Jim Gilliam, the beloved former player and first base coach who died just before the start of the 1978 World Series. This deviation from the club's standard protocol in such matters would seem to have set a precedent and make the case for retiring Valenzuela's number a no-brainer. "They absolutely should make the 'Gilliam exception' for Fernando," said Lyle Spencer. "Whether or not he belongs in the Hall of Fame, his number should be retired. They made an exception for Gilliam, so there's precedent. That's the crucial thing. I loved Gilliam—he and I were close, and I was devastated when he died—but [his number was retired], I believe, because he was an O'Malley favorite. So if you made that exception [for Gilliam], why can't you make an exception for a guy that did arguably as much for your fan base as anyone—except Jackie?"

The staunchest guardian and protector of Valenzuela's number 34 has been longtime team clubhouse and equipment manager Mitch Poole, who for years oversaw giving out uniform numbers to new players. Poole's employment with the Dodgers dates back to when Fernando pitched for the club. "We're all family down there in the clubhouse," Poole said. "I felt close to Fernando when he played, but I grew even closer afterward. So I never wanted to give that number out."

Poole admits there were some close calls, particularly in recent years, in keeping Valenzuela's 34 off the market. "Bryce Harper, I would think, would have been a possibility [had he signed here]," Poole said of the slugger who wore that number with the Washington Nationals. "But look, Bryce is wearing [number] 3 now on the Phillies, so it didn't seem like it was too [revered] a number for him. But there have been many guys, like Manny Ramírez, that asked me for 34. With Manny, he asked me for that number because of Big Papi [David Ortiz]. But I told him I didn't want to give it out and I didn't. So we went through a lot of different numbers that he was looking to pick out. We made jerseys with like three or four different numbers for him, just because he kept on changing his mind all the time. And finally, he was going to be 66, but it ended up being 99 which worked out great for him.

"There was also one of our Minor League coordinators, Jerry Weinstein, who actually wore 34 here [at Dodger Stadium] during some early workouts. And I'm like, *Man, that's sacrilegious to me right there*. I don't know where he got the jersey from. We didn't put it on his back. I think that maybe somebody in the Minor Leagues did it for him or that it was a number that he wore in the Minor Leagues. But usually [keeping numbers out of circulation] transcends over that, too. Minor Leaguers don't wear guys' numbers that you don't want them to wear up here."

While Poole understands that ultimately it's up to the Dodgers' front office to decide if 34 could be given to another player, he doesn't steer away from making his strong feelings on the matter known. "In my own heart, I feel like that's a number that, at least for the Mexican community, [shouldn't be used]. Many of them have come to me and said they were very thankful for the fact that nobody did use it. And since no player has worn it since Fernando, I'm kind of happy with that. It's been my call, but the Dodgers could have overridden me many times, but they chose not to."

Poole would later become the visiting clubhouse manager, with Alex Torres assuming the duties of the home clubhouse, shifting the decisions about team members' numbers to Torres. Not surprisingly, the humble Valenzuela doesn't publicly make a federal case over his number; he told Mike DiGiovanna of the *Los Angeles Times* in 2021, "If anybody wants to wear it, it's fine by me. If somebody asks for it, no problem. I know it's going to happen sooner or later, but who knows?"

Steve Garvey, another Dodgers icon who had his number (6) out of circulation for two decades, though it still isn't retired (in 2022 it was being used by Trea Turner), is another advocate of having the number 34 retired. "Nobody has worn his number and I don't think anyone should," he stated. "They should have retired it a long time ago." As for Garvey, should the Dodgers one day retire his number 6, he would be just the thirteenth player in Major League history to have his number retired by two different teams (the Padres being the other). The twelve existing players with retired numbers are *all* in the Hall of Fame.

As for Valenzuela, if his number was ever going to be retired, many believed there was never a more appropriate time to do so than during the 2021 season, when the fortieth anniversary of Fernandomania was being celebrated by the Dodgers and recognized regularly by the press. But it never came to be. "I think the Dodgers really erred in not honoring Fernando by retiring his number," said Jay Jaffe, author of *The Cooperstown Casebook*. "It's a no-brainer. Restricting jersey retirement to Hall of Famers seems to me just a very petty way to go. Why withhold that kind of honor and that kind of love while he's still here to enjoy it? I wish the Dodgers would do it for Fernando because I think that's the capstone of what he's meant to the organization."

While the Dodgers did honor Valenzuela—along with Don Newcombe and Garvey—in 2019 in its inaugural "Legends of Dodger Baseball" class to recognize his impact and achievements on and off the field, the permanent plaque that honors him at Dodger Stadium is still no substitute for retiring his number. The club is not doing itself any favors by adhering to its unwritten "Hall of Famers only" rule in the case of Valenzuela.

"While it's unfair to compare anybody to Jackie Robinson," said sportswriter Ken Gurnick, "Fernando had an impact on the Dodgers and Los Angeles and baseball that sets him apart from all other players—above and beyond. No one should ever wear his number again, as a sign of respect for what he meant and continues to mean to the Dodgers and the community. I think the organization should take the next step [and make it official]. There won't ever be another Fernando, just like there won't ever be another Koufax or another Jackie Robinson. It's not like you're setting a precedent that now is going to open the floodgates. That's not going to happen."

Even Fred Claire, who worked in the Dodgers' front office for three decades and understood the team's stance on retiring numbers, has expressed his belief that the time is right to finally retire 34. "I can recall when we made the decision to retire [Jim Gilliam's] number," he said. "And it's probably the appropriate time to [retire Fernando's]. I would be in favor of that. Jim was a dear friend and in so many ways embodied the Dodgers. I can remember the great Vinny [Scully's] description of Jim with one word: 'ballplayer.' I remember the emotion of Jim's loss at a relatively young age [forty-nine]. It's the same reason why I would say Fernando's number should be retired—because it seems like the right thing to do. And I've always thought, in life, if you try to think of the right thing to do, you usually end up on the right side of the equation."

But despite all the support for retiring Valenzuela's number, there is still hesitation from both the current and former ownership. In a *Los Angeles Times* "Dodger Dugout" piece in which readers sent in questions to Peter O'Malley, the former Dodgers owner gave a definitive answer to the question of retiring Valenzuela's number. "On my watch, we established the policy to retire the numbers of our players who had been elected to the Baseball Hall of Fame," he said. "The Dodgers have been fortunate to have many extraordinary players, but I think the policy is sound." After waxing poetically about the lone exception of Gilliam, O'Malley added, "Fernando's impact on the organization, the city and all of baseball was historic and monumental. Fernando-mania was one of the most enjoyable times for me. He has always been a significant representative of the Dodger organization and I am sure he'll be recognized most appropriately. [The year] 2021 is the 40th anniversary of Fernando-mania and he deserves all the tributes that the organization and fans are putting together."

Except retiring number 34.

If there is anything in baseball that is truly a "feel thing," it's the act of retiring a number. It's more indicative of what a player means to a club, a city, and its fan base—and, in Valenzuela's case, an entire culture—than mere statistics or other criteria. Time will tell if the Dodgers eventually grasp this concept.

*

Induction into the National Baseball Hall of Fame is a far more precarious business than having one's number retired. In addition to historically great player stats, the Hall of Fame asks voters to consider such attributes as integrity, sportsmanship, character, team contributions, and general impact on the game. It's at least the perceived absence of some of those attributes that have kept some of the greats of the game, like Pete Rose, Barry Bonds, and Roger Clemens, out of Cooperstown.

There are currently two paths that may lead a former player into the Hall of Fame. The first is through the Baseball Writers' Association of America (BBWAA), which votes annually from a ballot of players who had at least ten years in the Major Leagues and have been out of the game for more than five years. A player named on at least 75 percent of the ballots receives the honor of induction. A player can stay on the ballot a maximum of ten years (it was fifteen years for players from Valenzuela's era) and remain eligible if they continue to receive votes on at least 5 percent of the ballots.

However, players who fail to get elected through the BBWAA voting process can still get enshrined in the Hall of Fame a second way—through a panel formerly known as the Veterans Committee. That committee, which previously considered all retired players in baseball history, has now been divided up to address two separate time frames. One is the Classic Baseball Era subcommittee, which addresses the period prior to 1980 and includes the Negro Leagues and pre–Negro League stars. The other is the Contemporary Baseball Era subcommittee, which addresses 1980 to the present, which is the period of Valenzuela's career. Players in their respective era who gain at least twelve of sixteen votes make it into the Hall of Fame.

While there have been controversial selections from the BBWAA, the Veterans Committee votes have been far more vulnerable to criticism. Its nod for a lifetime .260 hitter, Bill Mazeroski, and the Today's Game subcommittee (an earlier subcommittee since replaced by the Contemporary Baseball Era one) selection of Harold Baines, who never finished higher than ninth in the MVP voting in any of his twenty-one seasons, were particularly baffling, as both were solid yet unspectacular players. And on the other side of the voting equation is someone like Steve Garvey, who checked all the boxes in being Hall of Fame worthy but is still on the outside looking in. Garvey was the preeminent National League first baseman for more than a decade during the 1970s and 1980s. His credentials as a complete ballplayer are simply staggering. In the period from 1974 to 1985, he was a ten-time All-Star; set a National League record for consecutive games played (1,207); won an NL MVP (1974) and four Gold Glove Awards; collected more than 200 hits in four different seasons; and was one of the greatest postseason performers of all time, batting .338 in 222 at bats while winning two NLCS MVP awards (1978, 1984) and a World Series trophy (1981). Yet, in the conventional writers' vote, he topped out at 42.6 percent. Only time will tell if the Classic or Contemporary Baseball Era subcommittees decide to right a wrong by electing him in the future.

"I've been on the ballot every time I could possibly be . . . from the five years after I retired, so I've got that going for me," Garvey said. "The dynamics have changed in terms of voting in that [with the subcommittees] you've got sixteen voters—four or five Hall of Famers, some front office people, two sabermetrics [experts], and the press. I get the sabermetrics and the press every time. God willing, it will happen, and then we'll have a fun time. But it doesn't diminish [what I accomplished]. I don't lose sleep over it. I have a body of work that nobody else has if you look in terms of Gold Gloves, consecutive games, postseason and All-Star Games. I had the most hits between '74 and '84 of anybody in baseball. If you look at the top ten, eight of them I think are Hall of Famers. But even beyond statistics, I think you have to look at individuals whose careers had the greatest and most positive effect on the game. In my case, I stood up for women in the press and was probably more outspoken than anybody about the need to allow them to get into the clubhouse so they could do their job and so forth. I set up the very first counseling company for athletes and was a significant member of the [MLB] Players Association when we needed to establish the union."

Garvey's absence from the Hall of Fame leaves him and his contemporaries scratching their heads. But the thought process of both the BBWAA and the Veterans Committee members remains in the eyes, minds, and hearts of their voters—no matter how suspect they may be at times. All of which bring us to Valenzuela—another Dodger with a mix of greatness both statistically and in how he impacted baseball and society.

First, a look at Fernando's numbers. Author Jay Jaffe, for one, has doubted that Valenzuela's statistics are quite Hall of Fame worthy. "Unfortunately, I can't make a really strong case for Fernando," he said. "I wish I could because he's so dear to my heart. There are those who have as many wins as him, 173, which is not a lot, that are in the Hall of Fame. But, for me, from the advanced statistics standpoint, it's very tough. He's got a comparatively short career with less than three thousand innings. Even though he pitched parts of seventeen seasons, he's got the injuries, he missed a full season, had very few innings at the end of his career, with some years that are almost washes. He had that concentrated workload in the '80s. And then, other than that nice rebound in 1996, not a lot that's particularly valuable for a Hall of Fame case and really kind of closer to a league average pitcher in the end in terms of adjusted ERA+ [i.e., adjusted earned run average—a score of 100 being the league average]. I wish I could make a case for him because I think what he did for baseball was bigger than some of the guys who are in the Hall of Fame."

A common debate over Valenzuela's statistical worthiness for the Hall of Fame is how his six dominant seasons (1981–86) matched the same number of years of Koufax's supremacy. But the comparison doesn't quite add up for Jaffe, who also happens to be a lifelong Dodgers fan. "I think it's a very superficial argument," he said. "The degree to which Sandy Koufax was better than his peers during that six-year run is unparalleled. And, yes, it's propped up by the degree to which run scoring across the game was down—especially in Dodger Stadium. Koufax had like a 1.00 ERA at home during that second half of his career. With Fernando, just sticking to ERA+, he had 135 as a rookie, then 122 in '82, and goes down to 96 in 1983—still an All-Star but with an ERA worse than the league average. Then he jumps back up to 116 in '84, which is fine, but he was 12–17 that year. That's not going to get you a lot of recognition, though it certainly wasn't his fault, as run support was scarce. Then he goes back up to 141 in 1985, which was maybe his best year all around. And then he wins 21 games and has a 110 ERA+ the next year and was in the Cy Young Award race. But Sandy Koufax was blowing the doors off the Cy Young races in his last four years [winning three of them]. To line them up in a head-to-head comparison, Koufax was much better than Fernando, relatively speaking, against their leagues."

However, if Valenzuela fell short on career statistics, even as his career ERA was equal to that of Hall of Famer Tom Glavine, he overwhelmed with both his team contributions and a societal impact that puts him in rarefied air with just a handful of players in baseball history. "He should be in the Hall of Fame—without question," Nomar Garciaparra stated. "I think there's a misconception sometimes of what the Hall of Fame is about. It's not always just what players do on the field. Their impact can be so much greater than that. That's why the Hall of Fame is there. It's honoring those who have impacted the game and not just honoring those who played at the highest levels. I know what Fernando meant to me and my family being Mexican and playing for the Dodgers. It's immeasurable."

With the 2019 induction of Marvin Miller, there now appears to be more value placed on those individuals who impacted the game than there was in the past. So, while Valenzuela peaked at just 6.2 percent of the vote from the BBWAA in 2003, there is hope he will receive far more support when the Contemporary Baseball Era subcommittee convenes in the future.

"I was hoping he would have gotten more overall Hall of Fame votes [from the BBWAA]," said José Mota. "For someone that captured and captivated the attention and earned the respect of the entire league, he deserved more [consideration]. Look at the innings pitched, the strikeouts, the hits allowed. But there's so much more. You have to talk about morals, what he represented, how he behaved—no scandals, no controversies—he just went out and did his job. And who had a better story? He opened doors for more Mexican players to be seen in a different light. It used to be [teams] would buy Mexican players in September to call them up and see what they could do. Now they want these Mexican players in their systems and developed. Now you hear, 'It looks like he could be the next Fernando.' How many times do you hear that? It's like what they used to say about who could be the next Koufax. If Fernando Valenzuela went into the Hall of Fame today, I don't think you would hear any complaints about it."

Lyle Spencer, a Hall of Fame voter for many years, lobbied for Valenzuela. "My feeling was different from . . . most of my colleagues," he said. "I thought a very important part of the consideration process was the impact you made on the game—whether it was positive or negative. Did you lift the game or hurt the game? So, I was an outspoken champion not just for Fernando but also for guys like Maury Wills and Tommy John—guys who impacted the game for a particular reason. Wills revolutionized the game [with the stolen base] and opened doors for Lou Brock, Tim Raines, and Rickey Henderson. The game was pretty staid to that point. Tommy John, quite obviously, stood out because of the surgery, but he was also a 288-game winner and was successful in all three major markets. But with Fernando, he's the most underrated, undervalued, and underappreciated of them all. His impact is unprecedented in my opinion in terms of what he did for the sport, elevating it and expanding boundaries. You have to go back to the pre-Fernando days to understand how it was before he came along. I started covering the Dodgers in the early '70s, and I can't recall seeing a lot of Latinos at games back then—maybe 5 percent at that time. There were some lingering bad feelings over the whole Chavez Ravine relocation and the profound impact of what it did to people who lived there in that community. But then Fernando comes along, and Latinos started coming out because they identified with him. My guess is that a high percentage of these new fans were young fans and they remained Dodger fans for life. It was powerful and sustained itself to the point that around half the crowds at Dodger Stadium today are Latino. How many guys in the Hall of Fame had as much enduring impact on that game than him?"

In fact, Valenzuela not only brought a legion of new fans into Dodger Stadium but turned supporters of rival teams like the Padres and Giants—as well as the Angels—into Dodgers fans. "Growing up, I lived a short drive from Anaheim [Angels] Stadium," recalled baseball writer José de Jesus Ortiz. "But we never went, whereas we were at Dodger Stadium all the time. Fernando just gave us a sense of pride that, *wow*, there's a Mexican American star who looks like us who we could cheer on. I still remember sitting in the left-field bleachers while Fernando was throwing a bullpen session. After he was done, I extended my hand, and he shook it. It was one of the coolest moments. It took me a long time to realize that the bleacher seats weren't the best seats in the stadium."

Taking it a bit further, Valenzuela's impact transcended baseball, with a reach far beyond the United States, Canada, and Mexico. "He inspired so many kids throughout Latin America that might have had doubts about themselves," Mota said. "What people noticed was this humble kid that didn't look like a baseball specimen, so they believed if he could succeed, they could too. In Mexico, if they have enough talent, they'll be given a chance now because of Fernando. The same holds true not just in my country, the Dominican Republic, where there are a zillion great baseball players, but also in other places, like Colombia, Nicaragua, Venezuela, and Puerto Rico. Fernando was not Mexican for us—he was just a Latino guy. He had a plethora of countries that identified with him and considered him as one of [their own]."

Some believe Valenzuela was the biggest Latino ambassador to ever play the game. "I've made this argument," said Jesus Ortiz. "Roberto Clemente is 'The Great One,' but culturally, Fernando Valenzuela has been more significant in terms of bringing a fan base that didn't exist in baseball."

Others feel Valenzuela was one of the greatest role models the game has ever seen. "He was a person many of us could relate to," Mexican-born union leader Teresa Romero said. "He was the best at his profession and never lost that humbleness. Many people become very famous, and they change. They want more money, they become more arrogant, and I never perceived that about Fernando. His legacy was being the best but remaining the same person he was when he started. He was able to ultimately inspire a lot of young people to accomplish more than they could ever have believed they could accomplish. I want to emphasize that, in our community, sometimes we don't have very public role models. I think Fernando was a role model for young people then and for generations to come—even in Mexico. My nieces and their children there know who Fernando is, despite being too young to have seen him play. They are proud and take ownership of that, like one of us accomplished what he did. By working hard, he succeeded, and that's inspiring to them. He was able to influence the lives of many people in a positive way. I wish we had more public figures like him that young people could look up to."

If Valenzuela does not get voted into the Hall of Fame, despite his iconic cultural status and his years as a dominant pitcher, he could and should receive the Buck O'Neil Award, an honor given by the Hall of Fame once every three years to "an individual whose extraordinary efforts enhanced baseball's positive impact on society, broadened the game's appeal, and whose character, integrity, and dignity are comparable to the qualities exhibited by O'Neil." By its very definition, the award was practically created for Valenzuela. "It's not a plaque in Cooperstown," Jaffe said, "but it is for long and meritorious service to the game in ways that maybe aren't as easy to quantify or to pigeonhole. I think Fernando would probably be somebody who should be recognized in that context."

Until that time may come, Valenzuela will continue to enjoy his member status in the Mexican Baseball Hall of Fame, Caribbean Baseball Hall of Fame, and the California Sports Hall of Fame. And he can take pride in knowing how, as a Mexican trailblazer, he built a legacy that lives on and thrives both on the diamond with compatriots and Dodgers standout pitchers Julio Urías and Victor González and in the stands with as many 34 jerseys worn by fans as ever before. Valenzuela's legend has forever been cemented in baseball history as the phenomenon that made baseball an obsession with Mexican and Latino communities around the world, while giving a level of redemption to a Dodgers organization and its complicated history in Chavez Ravine.

ACKNOWLEDGMENTS

In writing this book on Fernando Valenzuela, a truly transformative Dodger, my nearly three decades as a baseball author have come full circle. My very first book, *Out at Home*, released in 1995, was a collaboration with Dodgers outfielder Glenn Burke, a trailblazer in his own way. Those were very different times. Amazon, Facebook, and Twitter didn't exist yet, and, because of the most damaging baseball strike in the history of the game, the first edition was self-published after our publisher backed out of the deal. For those reasons, and with Glenn dying of AIDS, promoting and selling the book became an extremely challenging ordeal. I decided the best use of the little money I had to promote the book was to run an advertisement in *Baseball Weekly*. The ad had a small photo of the cover, some flashy blurbs, the price, and a small space for buyers to write their mailing information to get sent a copy. It was archaic by today's standards, but it served its purpose back then.

Within a week, I started receiving envelopes with enclosed checks sent to a post office box I had rented. Two of those envelopes had the iconic "Los Angeles Dodgers" script lettering as the return address. One of them was from then-Dodgers general manager Fred Claire, and the other was from the team's broadcasting and publications assistant, Mark Langill. I immediately mailed each a copy of the book, and we forged a mutual respect. All these years later, the two of them provided tremendous input into and assistance for my Fernando Valenzuela project.

In Claire, there may not be a greater gentleman in the game, and his kindness toward me will never be forgotten. As for Langill, I enjoy talking baseball history with him more than I do with anyone else. He has now long been the Dodgers' team historian, and his knowledge of the club—and baseball in general—is simply remarkable. Both men exemplify the class of the Dodgers organization.

For those of you who are familiar with any of my other books, you know that I have no greater friend and supporter of my work than Dodgers broadcaster Tim Neverett. It's a relationship that began way back in 1984, when we were in our first year at Emerson College and began playing baseball there, which we did for four years. We were also broadcasting partners, covering Emerson basketball games together. As seniors, we were assigned press credentials to Fenway Park to work on a reporter package together. It took me thirteen takes to get my stand-up portion of the package just right. Tim did his flawlessly on the first one. I think I realized then that he would become a renowned broadcaster and I would become a writer. As usual, Tim introduced me to everyone he could at Dodger Stadium so that they could give their own personal insight into Valenzuela. The project never would have taken off like it did without his assistance.

While on the theme of Dodgers broadcasters, I want to add that I had the tremendously good fortune to interview the legendary Jaime Jarrín. It's likely that no one understands Valenzuela better than this Ford C. Frick Award recipient. I wish him well in his retirement after a tremendous run as the Dodgers' Spanish-language broadcaster, a role he took up in 1959. One of Jarrín's broadcast booth colleagues who is also a close confidant of Fernando, Pepe Yñiguez, was also extremely gracious with his time and had great enthusiasm for this project. And longtime Angels and current Dodgers broadcaster José Mota provided me with wonderful stories and insight into Valenzuela from their forty-year friendship.

Continuing with the media, prolific sportswriter Lyle Spencer not only covered the Dodgers during Fernandomania but had a special bond with him and most of his teammates. Lyle's perspective on that period and the Dodgers players was invaluable. Spencer would introduce me to longtime Dodgers beat writer Ken Gurnick, who was a tremendous help in providing insight into Valenzuela's postmania years. And many thanks go out to José de Jesus Ortiz, the first Latino to serve as president of the Baseball Writers' Association of America, for providing me with a feel for what Fernando meant to the Latino community.

In my attempt to convey the struggles, hopes, and fears of the Mexican immigrant in the United States, I couldn't have found two better sources than Marc Grossman and Teresa Romero to interview for this book.

Grossman served as Cesar Chavez's press secretary, speechwriter, and personal aide for nearly a quarter century. Romero is the first Latina and first immigrant woman to become president of a national union—the same United Farm Workers labor union that Chavez once led—in the United States. Their intellect was matched only by their graciousness and sincerity.

After the Dodgers moved from Brooklyn to Los Angeles, their first home game was played at the LA Memorial Coliseum. Carl Erskine was the starting pitcher that day for the Dodgers. To speak with the ninety-four-year-old Erskine by telephone about the joyous reception the city of Los Angeles gave the Dodgers in those early days of West Coast baseball was nothing short of a religious experience for me. Talk about living history—that was it!

Naturally, I interviewed as many of Fernando's teammates from different parts of his career as possible. It was a privilege to speak with Dodgers greats from the 1981 World Series championship club who lived and witnessed the apex of Fernandomania.

Rick Monday took a precious hour of his time before he was to broadcast a game at Dodger Stadium and provided me with wonderful insight into and anecdotes about not just Valenzuela but those supremely talented and colorful Dodgers teams, as well as his own dramatic home run that put LA in the '81 World Series.

Steve Garvey was one of my idols growing up. As a kid, I patterned my batting stance after his and greatly admired the way he played the game. In my mind, he truly belongs in the Hall of Fame. To spend several hours with him—first by telephone and then in person—was a special thrill for me. His transparency, candor, and storytelling made for fulfilling and enjoyable conversations.

Jerry Reuss displayed great character and modesty in our interview. Reuss had a spectacular 1981 season and postseason and was one of the best pitchers in the game during the height of Fernandomania. It would be understandable if, after four decades, he had grown at least a little bit tired of his own magnificent '81 season being overshadowed by all the attention given Valenzuela. But it was just the opposite. Reuss understands the significance of what Fernando represented, and his answers to my questions were all class—just like the man himself.

Dusty Baker is one of my all-time favorite people in baseball. I first met him in 1995 by the batting cage at Shea Stadium, when he managed the San Francisco Giants, and I presented him with a copy of *Out at Home*. I knew the bond he had with Glenn Burke from their Dodgers days, as he took on the role of big brother to him. He invited me into the visiting manager's office to talk about Burke, who had just passed away, for a few priceless moments. We've stayed in touch ever since. I knew it would be vital to interview Baker for this book, though I realized it wasn't going to be easy. As the manager of the Astros, Dusty's schedule was hectic during the regular season, so our talk would be delayed nearly six months—following the World Series—before finally happening. As he was with Burke, Dusty was a true mentor to Fernando, and our discussion about him was as delightful as I knew it would be. It was well worth the wait.

Pedro Guerrero was one of the co-MVPs of the '81 World Series and one of Fernando's best friends on the team. Although Pedro had a massive stroke in recent years and his English is limited, he could not have been warmer or tried harder to give me some of his personal memories of El Toro.

Like Fernando, Tom Niedenfuer, who would go on to become the Dodgers' closer, was a rookie in 1981. He provided insight into how Valenzuela's performance and coolness under pressure lifted him and the other younger players on the team up and got them to believe anything was possible.

Near the end of Valenzuela's tenure in Los Angeles, the Dodgers were a team that would shock the baseball world and win an unlikely World Series championship in 1988. Two of the so-called "Stuntmen" from that club were Rick Dempsey and Danny Heep—both of whom helped paint the picture of that miracle team for me with their words.

Several dark years after Fernando's release from Los Angeles and after his sustained effort to work his way back into a regular starting role, he landed on his feet in San Diego, helping a young Padres team to a division title in the twilight of his career. I was most fortunate to have the opportunity to interview legendary manager Bruce Bochy, along with players from that club whom Valenzuela had influenced— Scott Sanders, Brian Johnson, and Tim Worrell. All four of them were extremely accommodating and enthusiastic about this project.

To gain perspective from the other side—Valenzuela's opponents—I interviewed rivals from the New York Mets, including manager Davey Johnson and outfielder Mookie Wilson; from the Houston Astros, closer Joe Sambito; from the Montreal Expos, Hall of Fame outfielder Andre Dawson, reliever Jeff Reardon, and the ever-colorful southpaw Bill Lee; and from the Cincinnati Reds, Bruce Berenyi.

In one of the most enjoyable aspects of this book project, I interviewed a couple of Latino players who grew up revering Valenzuela: the great shortstop Nomar Garciaparra and pitcher Russ Ortiz.

Longtime Dodgers director of publicity Steve Brener not only helped me get in touch with some of the Dodgers I interviewed for this book but also provided me with his own take on Fernandomania. Brener was simply an indispensable resource.

Legendary Dodgers scout Mike Brito, who signed Valenzuela to his first big league contract and was as close to him as anyone for more than forty years, provided a valuable look into Fernando's earliest days in baseball and some of the hidden aspects of his psyche.

Others to thank for their thoughts and experiences with Valenzuela include the keeper of Fernando's number 34, longtime Dodgers clubhouse man Mitch Poole; baseball author and historian Jay Jaffe; longtime Mets PR and media relations VP Jay Horwitz and former Mets outfielder and television analyst Art Shamsky; veteran broadcaster and Yankees public address announcer Paul Olden; Hollywood voice actor David Bronow; and Vermont secretary of agriculture Anson Tebbetts, a longtime broadcast news figure.

Others who were not interviewed but helped with this project included promoter Marc Nehamen; Robert Diamond of the Elias Sports Bureau; Juan Dorado, the Dodgers' director of player relations and publicity; and my dear friend, the noted author and renowned environmentalist Tom Kostigen.

I also want to thank my longtime literary agent Robert Wilson, a trusted friend and confidant who always delivers in providing spot-on advice throughout my various book projects.

My utmost gratitude goes to the University of Nebraska Press for believing in this project and understanding its importance not just in baseball but in our society. As such, I would like to acknowledge senior acquisitions editor Rob Taylor and associate acquisitions editor Courtney Ochsner, as well as the rest of their team, which includes senior project editor Sara Springsteen, assistant project editor Kayla Moslander, publicist Anna Weir, publicity manager Rosemary Sekora, and Ann Baker, manager of editorial, design, and production. The copyeditor was Maureen Bemko.

Thank you to my double-play partner in life, Habiba Boumlik; our pride-and-joy children, Alex and Sabrina; and my biggest fan—my mother JoAnn Cadmus—for all their love and support.

And finally, various publications and websites aided me greatly in my research on Fernando Valenzuela and the plight of the Mexican immigrant in the United States. The remarkable website BaseballResearch.com gave detailed information on every game Valenzuela ever pitched. YouTube allowed me to watch many of the biggest games of his career, giving me a better feel of so many of them. Other sources included the Elias Sports Bureau, *Los Angeles Times*, *Los Angeles Herald Examiner*, *New York Times*, *Washington Post*, USA *Today*, *Sports Illustrated*, the *Fernandomania @ 40* documentary series, the Associated Press, *Pacific Historical Review*, MLB.com, LasMayores.com, and *The Sporting News*.

The following books were also used and referenced in this project:

They Bled Blue: Fernandomania, Strike-Season Mayhem, and the Weirdest Championship Baseball Had Ever Seen, by Jason Turbow, Houghton Mifflin Harcourt

Stealing Home: Los Angeles, the Dodgers, and the Lives Caught in Between, by Eric Nusbaum, Public Affairs/Hachette Book Group

Fernando!, by Mike Littwin, Bantam Books

The Cooperstown Casebook, by Jay Jaffe, Thomas Dunne Books

1958 Los Angeles Dodgers Year Book

Game of My Life—Dodgers, by Mark Langill, Sports Publishing

Other works by Erik Sherman

Two Sides of Glory: The 1986 Boston Red Sox in Their Own Words

After the Miracle: The Lasting Brotherhood of the '69 Mets
(with Art Shamsky)

Davey Johnson: My Wild Ride in Baseball and Beyond
(with Davey Johnson)

Kings of Queens: Life Beyond Baseball with the '86 Mets

Out at Home: The Glenn Burke Story (with Glenn Burke)

Mookie: Life, Baseball, and the '86 Mets (with Mookie Wilson)

A Pirate for Life (with Steve Blass)